Putting
Dell
on the
Map

Putting
Dell
on the
Map

A History of the
Dell Paperbacks

William H. Lyles

Contributions to the Study of Popular Culture, Number 5

Greenwood Press
Westport, Connecticut • London, England

Library of Congress Cataloging in Publication Data

Lyles, William H.
  Putting Dell on the map.

  (Contributions to the study of popular culture,
ISSN 0198-9871 ; no. 5)
  Bibliography: p.
  Includes index.
    1. Paperbacks—Publishing—United States—History.
2. Dell Publishing Company—History. 3. Popular
literature—Publishing—United States—History.
I. Title. II. Series
Z479.L94 1983   070.5'09775'97   83-1641
ISBN 0-313-23667-4 (lib. bdg.)

Library of Congress Catalog Card Number: 83-1641
ISBN: 0-313-23667-4
ISSN: 0198-9871

First published in 1983

Greenwood Press
A division of Congressional Information Service, Inc.
88 Post Road West
Westport, Connecticut 06881

Printed in the United States of America

10 9 8 7 6 5 4 3 2 1

To Pat.
"I see (as in a map)
the end of all."

Contents

Illustrations   ix
Preface and Acknowledgments   xi
Persons this *BOOK* is about———   xv
What this *BOOK* is about———   xix
Introduction   xxi
A Note on Dell's Numbering System   xxiii

1. Dell Paperbacks, 1942-1951   3

2. Dell Paperbacks, 1952-1962   18

3. Dell's Changing Contents   28

4. The Dell Series: An Overview   38
    Reprint Series   38
    Dell 10^c Series   38
    Dell First Editions   39
    Laurel Editions   42
    Other Series   43

5. Dell Paperbacks, 1962-1982   45

6. Artwork: The Front Covers   56
    1942-1951   56
    1952-1962   74
    Authors' Reactions and Accuracy of the Covers   79

7. Artwork: The Back Covers   83
    Maps of Large Geographical Areas   86
    Maps of Smaller Geographical Areas   89

Maps or Diagrams of Smaller Areas   94
Diagrams or Floor Plans   103
Miscellaneous Designs   108
Other Features   109
Authors' Reactions   110
Postscript   117

8. Other Dell Features   119
Logo   119
Front-Cover Blurbs   120
Character Lists   124
Lists of Key Items (tantalizer-pages)   127
Title-Pages   129
Chapter Titles   130
Other Features   130

Notes   133
Bibliography and References   141
Index   147

Illustrations

Map by Piet Schreuders   frontispiece

1.   Helen Meyer, "the doyenne of Dell."   10

2.   Employees of Western Printing & Lithographing
   edge-staining Dell paperbacks.   10

3.   Artists at Western's Creative Department, January, 1943.   .63

4.   *Dreadful Hollow* (#125, 1946), cover by
   George A. Frederiksen.   63

5.   *She Ate Her Cake* (#186, 1947), cover by Gerald Gregg.   63

6.   *The Crooking Finger* (#104, 1946), cover by Gerald Gregg.   64

7.   *Half Angel* (#118, 1946), cover by Gerald Gregg.   64

8.   *Wiped Out* (#165, 1947), cover by Gerald Gregg.   64

9.   *Appointment with Death* (#105, 1946), cover by
   Gerald Gregg.   64

10.   *Jokes, Gags and Wisecracks* (#152, 1947), cover by
    Gerald Gregg.   65

11.   *Cold Steal* (#142, 1946), cover by Gerald Gregg.   65

12.   *Bad for Business* (#299, 1949), cover by Gerald Gregg.   65

13.   *Now, Voyager* (#99, 1945), cover by Gerald Gregg.   65

14.   *Ill Met by Moonlight* (#6, 1942-1943), cover by
    Gerald Gregg.   66

15.   *Skyline Riders* (#250, 1948), original cover painting
    by Earl Sherwan.   66

16.   *The Bat* (#652, 1953), cover by Walter Brooks.   66

17.   *Blood on Biscayne Bay* (#D342, 1960), cover by
    Robert McGinnis.   66

18.   Robert Stanley and his wife and model, Rhoda.   67

19a-b.   *Fools Die on Friday* (#542, 1951; #1542, 1953), both
         covers by Robert Stanley.   67

20a.   *Quiet Horror* (#D325, 1959), rejected cover by Seymour
         Chwast; published cover by Push-Pin Studios.   68

20b-c.   Replacement back cover and front cover for *Quiet Horror*.   68

21.   Dell back-cover maps.
         a. *House of Darkness* (#237, 1948).   97
         b. *Beyond the Dark* (#93, 1945).   97
         c. *The Continental Op* (#129, 1946).   97
         d. *Scotland Yard: The Department of Queer Complaints*
            (#65, 1944).   97

22.   Dell back-cover maps.
         a. *Ladies in Hades* (#415, 1950).   98
         b. *With This Ring* (#83, 1945).   98
         c. *Suspense Stories* (#92, 1945).   98
         d. *Holiday Homicide* (#22, 1943).   98

23.   Dell back-cover maps.
         a. *Sailor, Take Warning!* (#155, 1947).   99
         b. *See You at the Morgue* (#7, 1943).   99
         c. *The Dead Can Tell* (#17, 1943).   99
         d. *Dance of Death* (#33, 1944).   99

24.   Dell back covers.
         a. *Rim of the Pit* (#173, 1947).   100
         b. *Backwoods Woman* (#557, 1951).   100
         c. *Week-End Marriage* (#73, 1945).   100
         d. *What a Body!* (#483, 1951).   100

25.   Dell back-cover maps.
         a. *The Corpse in the Corner Saloon* (#464, 1950).   101
         b. *The Crimson Feather* (#207, 1947).   101
         c. *Q as in Quicksand* (#301, 1949).   101
         d. *What Rhymes with Murder?* (#631, 1952).   101

26.   *Chinese Red* (#260, 1948), back-cover map.   102

27a-g.   Dell keyhole logos and decorated endpaper design.   121

28a-b.   Dell's title-pages.   122

29a-b.   Dell advertisements, 1940's.   123

Preface and Acknowledgments

Seven years ago, in 1976, I began to collect and to study the Dell paperbacks, particularly the "mapbacks." At that time, few people took early paperbacks seriously, so it was easy to buy them for ridiculously low prices, 2/25¢, for example, prices that allowed me to amass a collection of Dells in three years. Throughout those years, I managed to involve many people in my study; somehow I became the unofficial historian of the Dell books, although I am not sure how it happened.

In 1981, I had a closely typed 1,000-page manuscript. At the suggestion of my editor, Marilyn Brownstein, I split the manuscript into two parts. One part became *Dell Paperbacks, 1942 to Mid-1962: A Catalog-Index* (Westport, Conn.: Greenwood Press, 1983), which provides a catalog listing of all Dell paperbacks produced up to the middle of 1962. It also contains an index of all Dell authors; an index of anonymous titles; subject index; cover artist index; map index; list of motion-picture, television, and play tie-ins; list of Dell's special series; and a list of advance blurbs on Dell First Editions. This reference volume can be used separately from the present work, although I hope interested readers find that the two are useful partners.

The present book, the second half of my original manuscript, is a historical treatment of the Dell paperbacks referenced in the other volume. But it is not a history of either Dell Publishing or of Western Publishing, the company which produced the books. Both Dell and Western are concerned with products other than the paperbacks, which are the only concern here. And it is not an official history; I have relied on the memories of past and present employees of both Dell and Western, as well as on printed sources and the books themselves, but the conclusions I reach are my own. If any omissions or errors are brought to my attention, I will make the necessary corrections in any future edition.

I thank Dell Publishing Company for permission to reproduce covers, and Western Publishing Company for permission to use material from *The Westerner*.

And I thank the following people for their help:

Former and present Dell employees: E. Bayne, Cathy L. Collins, George T. Delacorte, Jr., Jean Duffy, Isabel Geffner, Peter Guzzardi, Bruce Hall, Mae-ling Hom, A. Hughes, James R. McLaughlin, Emily Matamorose, Helen Meyer, Beatrice O'Shaugnessey, Charles Saxon, W. A. Swanberg, Carl Tobey, and Julia M. Wallace.

Former and present Western employees: Edwin Bachorz, Allan Barnard, J. J. Barta, Stephen Becker, Walter Brooks, Knox Burger, Rocky Cashio, Craig Chase, Jack Crowe, Arlene Donovan, Donald I. Fine, George A. Frederiksen, Gerald (and Nell) Gregg, James E. Gunn, Ben Hallam, James E. Hawkins, Joy Joslyn, Robert Kissner, Dick LaVoie, Edmund Marine, Mark M. Morse, Dorothy Nelson, the late Lou Nielsen, Edward Parone, Gerald Poplawski, Robby Robinson, Bernard Salbreiter, Jeff Sass, Albert Stoffel, Frank E. Taylor, and Don Ward.

Authors, editors, and artists: Robert Abbett, the late Martha Albrand, Delano Ames, James Bama, C. L. Barber, S. Omar Barker, Harry Bennett, O. G. Benson, Lurton Blassingame, Ray Bradbury, Zenith Brown (Leslie Ford), Erskine Caldwell, John Canaday, Frances Cavanah, Victor Chapin, David Cort, Malcolm Cowley, William R. Cox, George Harmon Coxe, Dan Cushman, the late Frederic Dannay (Ellery Queen), Dorothy Salisbury Davis, L. Sprague de Camp, Actea Duncan, Mignon G. Eberhart, William Donohue Ellis, Ralph Ellison, George and Kay Evans, Jack Finney, James M. Fox, Dana Fradon, Michael Gilbert, Irwin Glusker, Eaton K. Goldthwaite, C. W. Grafton, David H. Greene, Albert Guerard, Donald Hamilton, Mitchell Hooks, Geoffrey Household, Dorothy B. Hughes, Hilda Hulme, Jack Iams, Robert Jonas, Victor Kalin, Hilda Krech, Alice Elinor Lambert, the late Richard Lockridge, Patricia McGerr, Robert E. McGinnis, James McKimmey, Marya Mannes, Louis Marchetti, Jerry Marcus, David Markson, Sara Elizabeth Mason, Harold Q. Masur, Kenneth Millar, the late Nicholas Monsarrat, Henning Nelms (Hake Talbot), Lenore Glen Offord, Wayne D. Overholser, Zelda Popkin, Richard Powell, Walt Reed, Mary Renault, Audrey and William Roos, Earl and Marguerite Sherwan, Robert Stanley, Aaron Marc Stein, Theodore Sturgeon, William Teason, Robert Terrall, Lawrence Treat, Louis Trimble, Rita Vandivert, Jean Francis Webb, Anna Mary Wells, Jan Westcott, Richard Wilbur, and Paul Winterton.

Others: Mrs. Robert Bezucha, Charlie Bishop, Thomas L. Bonn, Steve Buck, Lance Casebeer, Ann Cook, Nina Crane, Billy C. Lee, Madeleine Morrissey (of Dana Perfumes), Mary Ann Rea (of Cherokee Productions), Sandy Sandulo, Jack Schaffner, Piet Schreuders, Louise

Smith, Emily Toth, Jo Ann Vicarel, Ian Wedegartner, and Donna Whiteman (of The American Heritage Publishing Co.).

I especially thank those individuals who allowed me to quote from our interviews and correspondence. I could never have completed my research without such generous help. After finishing this book, I sincerely believe that there exist no better people than authors and artists and others involved in the creative process of making and publishing books. Contact with these individuals made me eager to finish both this book and its companion volume. And I extend very special thanks to Gerald Gregg, Don Ward, Walter Brooks, and J. J. Barta. Marilyn Brownstein, of Greenwood Press, is truly responsible for helping make this book a reality. And Patricia Ryan Lyles made it possible in too many ways to mention.

Persons this *BOOK* is about—

EDWIN BACHORZ,
supervisor, composing room, at Western Printing & Lithographing (WP&L), Racine, Wisconsin; handled typesetting of Dell paperbacks, 1942-1950's. Retired.

ALLAN BARNARD,
edited Dell books, 1948-1963 (WP&L, Racine & New York City); specialized in popular fiction, bought reprint rights to *Peyton Place*. Later, a vice-president, Bantam Books; now retired.

J. J. BARTA,
ordered type for the Dell books, 1940's (WP&L, Racine), had galleys proofread and prepared the books. Formerly assistant director, Rights & Royalties Dept., Western Publishing; now retired.

STEPHEN BECKER,
copy-writer on Dell Books, 1955-1956 (WP&L, NYC). Now a novelist.

RUTH BELEW,
a Chicago artist, drew most of the Dell back-cover maps, 1942-1951. Current whereabouts unknown.

WALTER BROOKS,
art director, Dell Books, 1952-1960 (WP&L, NYC); revised the look of the paperbacks. Now a free-lance artist.

KNOX BURGER,
editor, Dell First Editions, 1952-1960 (WP&L, NYC). Now a literary agent, NYC.

GEORGE T. DELACORTE, JR.,
founder of Dell Publishing Company. Retired.

GEORGE A. FREDERIKSEN,
assistant art director (WP&L, Racine), worked on Dell Books, 1942-1951.
Retired.

GERALD GREGG,
artist who airbrushed most of the early Dell covers, 1942-1951 (WP&L,
Racine). Retired.

JAMES E. GUNN,
apprentice editor, Dell Books, 1951-1952 (WP&L, Racine). Now a
science-fiction writer and teacher at the University of Kansas.

JAMES E. HAWKINS,
editor, Dell Books, 1945-1955 (WP&L, Racine & Poughkeepsie), orga-
nized Production Editorial Dept. in 1955. Retired.

RALPH MacNICHOL,
compositor (WP&L, Racine), excised anti-religious references in Dell
Books (although not authorized to do so). Deceased.

HELEN MEYER,
"the doyenne of Dell," began as secretary, later president, chairman,
Dell. Now at Doubleday.

LOU NIELSEN,
worked on Dell Books, 1944-1951 (WP&L, Racine), edited humor books,
assisted Lloyd E. Smith. Died, 1979.

BERNARD SALBREITER,
lettering expert, Dell Books, 1942-1951 (WP&L, Racine). Retired.

EARL SHERWAN,
free-lance artist who did early Dell covers, 1940's. Now a sculptor.

LLOYD E. SMITH,
early "one-man publisher" of Dell Books, 1942-1951 (WP&L, Racine).
Died, 1971.

ROBERT STANLEY,
free-lance artist, painted many Dell covers, 1940's & 1950's. Now lives in
Florida.

OTTO STORCH,
art director, Dell Publishing, 1940's; may have designed the Dell "eye-
in-keyhole" logo. Deceased.

WILLIAM STROHMER,
art director, Dell Books, 1942-1952 (WP&L, Racine). Died, 1980.

THEODORE STURGEON,
free-lancer, read and abridged Dell Books, 1950's. Now a science-fiction writer.

W. A. SWANBERG,
edited Dell detective magazines, 1930's & 1940's. Now a well-known writer.

FRANK E. TAYLOR,
executive editor, Dell Books, 1952-1960 (WP&L, NYC), revised entire scope of the books. Now has his own line of books.

FERNANDO TEXIDOR,
art director, Dell Publishing Company, 1940's-1960's. Now believed to be living in Spain.

EDWARD H. WADEWITZ,
founder of Western Printing & Lithographing, later Western Publishing. Deceased.

MORT WALKER,
worked on Dell humor magazines, 1940's. Now a cartoonist.

DON WARD,
editor, Dell Books, 1945-1955 (WP&L, Racine & NYC), specialized in western fiction, ghost-edited "celebrity" anthologies, edited *Zane Grey's Western Magazine*. Currently free-lances and teaches.

and many others:

ROBERT ABBETT (artist), LAUREL BARNARD (Allan Barnard's daughter; Laurel Editions named after her), WILLIAM BELL (early partner of Wadewitz), DON BLACK (editor, Dell Baseball Annuals), WILLIAM F. CALLAHAN, JR. (sales manager, Dell), JEANETTE CISSMAN (Walter Brooks' associate), ROSS CLAIBORNE (editor-in-chief, Laurel Editions, 1960's), ANNE DI STEFANO (office manager, WP&L, NYC, 1950's), FRÉDÉRIC DITIS (editor, Dell Visual Books), ARLENE DONOVAN (Knox Burger's associate), CLIFFORD DOWDEY (editor, Dell pulps, 1930's), PEGGY DUNLEAVY (copy-writer, WP&L, NYC, 1950's), ROLF ERICKSON (art director, Dell, 1961), JOHN FERRONE (editor, Dell Books, 1950's) DONALD I. FINE (managing editor, Dell First Editions, 1952-1960), RICHARD FISHER (managing editor, Laurel Editions, 1950's), YOLANDE FORTIER (Allan Barnard's secretary), DON FREY (prepared map descriptions), JOHN GELLER (sold West Side Printing Company to Wadewitz), BYRON GERE (did artwork on Dell books, 1940's), DAVID H. GREENE (editor, Sunrise Semester Library), BEN HALLAM (artist, WP&L, Racine, 1940's), BRETT HALLIDAY (prolific Dell mystery writer), VIRGINIA HAWKINS (copy-editor, Dell Books, 1955-1960), RUBY HINDS (her legs were a favorite with Western artists), GALEN HOLSHUE (circulation manager, Dell), MITCHELL HOOKS (artist), MARC JAFFE (editor, WP&L, NYC, 1950's), VICTOR KALIN (artist), MILDRED KAPILOW (assistant to Pete Margolies), ROBERT KISSNER (touched up Dell maps), PAUL KUHN (reader & copy-writer, Dell First Editions), JOAN LAMM (designed typography), ART LAWSON (editor, Dell pulps), JUNE LOCKE (daughter of William Strohmer; model for Dell cover), JOHN SCOTT MABON (editor-in-chief, Dell Books, 1951, WP&L, NYC), PETE MARGOLIES (editor, Dell Books, 1950's), EDMUND MARINE (art director, Dell Books, 1952), BARBARA MARKOWITZ (Frank Taylor's secretary), WALTER B. J. MITCHELL, JR. (book sales promotion manager, Dell), MARK M. MORSE (manager, Newsstand Division, WP&L), CARL NELSON (compositor), EDWARD PARONE (editor, Dell Books, 1950's), ELMER PATZKE (compositor), GERALD POPLAWSKI (touched up Dell maps), GLEN ROBINSON (edited western fiction, 1950's), ROBBY ROBINSON (salesman, WP&L), CHARLES SAXON (editor, Dell humor magazines), DORI SCHMIDT (Paul Kuhn's assistant), ROBERT SCUDELLARI (production design manager, Dell, 1960's), ELIZABETH SHARPE (editor, Dell, 1920's), R. A. SPENCER (joined Western, 1907), CARL TOBEY (president, later chairman, Dell), WILLIAM R. WADEWITZ (early Western staff), RICHARD WILBUR (editor, Laurel Poetry series), RICHARD L. WILLIAMS (editor, Dell magazines), STELLA WILLIAMS (proofreader), BETTY REN WRIGHT (proofreader, later editor, Whitman Books), BILL YATES (editor, humor books), FLOYD ZULLI (began Sunrise Semester TV series)

and some sparrows.

What this *BOOK* is about—

• • • 2,168 DELL PAPERBACKS and 577 BACK-COVER MAPS . . . The west side of the ROOT RIVER in Racine, Wisconsin . . . Lurid PULP MAGAZINES of the 1930's . . . An EYE in a KEY-HOLE . . . A "FOOL-PROOF" scheme to shuffle retailers' returns of magazines . . . Drastic ABRIDGMENTS of paper-backs . . . A "CLOSET INTELLECTUAL" working for a giant printing firm . . . The significance of an EDGE STAIN . . . Dell advice to 14-YEAR-OLD GIRLS . . . A cover painting of a DASHIELL HAMMETT STORY, commissioned but never used . . . A possible connection between DELL and TOOTSIE ROLLS.

Wouldn't You Like to Know—

- How and why a giant printing concern and a major publishing company "were in bed together"?
- What is misleading about the famous Dell blurb, "Complete with Map on Back Cover"?
- Why Mort Walker quit Dell?
- Why Dell published so little science-fiction?
- How *Peyton Place* "put Dell on the map"?
- Why Pocket Books sued Dell over a photograph?
- What Dell author thought the Nile ran from east to west?
- Who painted the early airbrushed covers?
- Why an earthy, mustached gypsy woman is clean-shaven on a Dell cover?

- What artist used Shere Hite (*The Hite Report*) as a model for his paperback covers?
- Why Mary Renault wants readers to incinerate Dell editions of her books?
- Why Jack Iams likes his?
- Who drew the Dell maps?
- Which are the most accurate "mapbacks"?

Introduction

Book collectors have traditionally focused on authors or genres rather than on publishers. Yet that is changing, as Jean Peters remarks in a recent article surveying "Publishers' Imprints."[1] Collectors and historians are beginning to realize the values of amassing a collection of a single publisher. One can, for example, simply enjoy the rich variety of such a collection, or delight in the changing design of the books, or wish to preserve in microcosm a piece of history. Until recently, few individuals, and fewer libraries—even those acquiring private press collections—sought collections of paperback companies. One reason was the inherently ephemeral nature of paperbacks, another the enormous bulk of material needed for a complete collection. Yet that too is changing; Thomas L. Bonn has recently commented in his survey of paperbacks that "The acquisition of vintage paperback books is the fastest-growing area of book collecting in the United States."[2]

One of the most collectible runs of paperbacks is the subject of this book: the 2,168 Dell paperbacks (plus reissues) produced between 1942 and May, 1962. In June, 1962, an IBM-numbering system replaced the series numbers formerly used. And since the break between Dell Publishing and Western Printing & Lithographing had occurred shortly before, with resulting staff changes, the date of mid-1962 thus serves as a convenient breaking point for this survey, although books produced beyond that date are mentioned. In general, the Dell books produced after 1962 become less identifiable as series and resemble the output of other mass market companies.

In a study of book production, S. H. Steinberg writes of "the psychology of book-buyers who like to associate a series with its outward appearance as well as its price."[3] And Alfred A. Knopf once commented (about his Borzoi Books of the 1920's) that "A great many readers buy Borzoi Books for their format alone—even when they are not interested in the contents, and that can be said of very few other American books."[4]

They could be speaking of the Dell paperbacks. Authors Margaret Atwood and Stephen King mention them specifically, and affectionately. King, in his collection of essays, *Danse Macabre*, recalls "the forties Dell paperbacks with love."[5] And Atwood includes in her novel *Bodily Harm* a character reading these "museum pieces, Dell Mysteries from the forties, with the eye-and-keyhole logo on the cover, the map of the crime scene on the back, and the cast of characters on the first page."[6]

The Dell "museum pieces," in fact, were part of an exhibit in 1981 at the Gemeentemuseum, in The Hague, the Netherlands—an exhibit arranged by Piet Schreuders. There was even a possibility the exhibit might be picked up by the Smithsonian Institution. Earlier, in 1976, a collection of the Dell paperbacks had been acquired by the Library of Congress, in Washington, D.C. The books are housed—where else?—in the Rare Book Room.

A Note on Dell's Numbering System

Prior to mid-1962, all but a few Dell paperbacks appeared in one of three separate imprints: Dell reprints, Dell First Editions, or Laurel Editions.

Dell reprints contained eight series. The 25¢ series, Dell's only paperback line until 1951, used consecutive numbers from 1-1020. The 10¢ series, in 1951, also used consecutive numbers, 1-36. Later series adopted a letter prefix to denote the price of their books: "D" (35¢), "F" (50¢), "R" (40¢), "S" (60¢), "X" (75¢), and "Y" (95¢).

Dell First Editions, in 1953, began with a mixed price series, numbering 1-109. Unprefixed numbers indicated a 25¢ price. Numbers with letter prefixes indicated a higher price: "D" (35¢), "F" and "FE" (50¢). Later Dell First Edition series used letter prefixes: "A" (25¢), "B" (35¢), "C" (50¢), "K" (40¢), "M" (60¢), and "LB" (35¢).

Laurel Editions, in 1956, used letter prefixes: "LB" (35¢), "LC" (50¢), "LS" (60¢), "LX" (75¢), "LY" (95¢), and "H" ($2.95).

Miscellaneous series included two unnumbered novels (25¢) derived from comic books, two digest-sized "Told-in-Pictures" novels (25¢), four Visual Books (95¢), and six Special Student Editions (10-15¢).

In this history of Dell paperbacks, series numbers appear as parenthetical references; numbers are given only for those paperbacks produced from 1942 to mid-1962. Dates are usually not given. For more information, see William H. Lyles, *Dell Paperbacks, 1942 to Mid-1962: A Catalog-Index* (Westport, Conn.: Greenwood Press, 1983).

In June, 1962, Dell adopted a 4-digit IBM-numbering system; in 1977, the number increased to five digits, later becoming integrated into the books' ISBN numbers. Unlike the series numbers, these computer numbers were not consecutive; a computer assigned a number based on a projection of where the numbered book would fall in an overall alphabetization of all Dell books. Thus, #4332, *The Jungle Books*

(December, 1964), chronologically precedes #1945, *The Dirty Dozen* (May, 1967). Since these IBM-numbered books are not the focus of the present history, and since no book exists which catalogs or indexes the IBM numbers, the present work makes no attempt to provide IBM numbers for titles.

Putting
Dell
on the
Map

1

Dell Paperbacks,
1942-1951

Pocket Books began the modern paperback revolution in 1938 with
stylish covers, a kangaroo logo, and a variety of titles. A year later, the
British Penguins opened an American branch, with substantial titles but
dull covers; after becoming the New American Library in 1948, the
American company used livelier covers but titles of mixed quality. In
1942 Avon began, first with crude covers, gradually replaced by wild
"comic" art—all advertising both genre and general fiction. Popular
Library (1942?) initially used airbrushed covers for mysteries, romances,
and westerns, then sleazy, backwoods covers for its shift into general
fiction. Dell achieved more variety than any of its early competitors. It
did so, at first, with an instantly identifiable format of vibrant airbrushed
covers for its predominantly genre fiction, varying "eye-in-keyhole"
logos, maps on the back covers, lists of the books' characters, and
"tantalizer-pages." The design was merchandising genius; it successfully
attracted buyers, it sold books. The first title was Philip Ketchum's *Death
in the Library* (without a map).

These Dell paperbacks were the joint product of Dell Publishing
Company (New York) and Western Printing & Lithographing (Racine,
Wisconsin). The relationship is not easy to explain, not even for those
who worked at both firms; but in effect, the staff members of Western
who were concerned with the Dell account bought titles for reprinting,
edited the books, provided artwork for the covers, then typeset and
printed the books, which they sold to Dell under an exclusive contract,
renewed yearly. Dell approved both titles and artwork and arranged
merchandising of the books to retailers. Western was always much more
than printers of the books, but Dell was also much more than a
merchandiser.

The books were the idea of Dell, specifically of George T. Delacorte,
Jr., Dell's founder. Delacorte, born in New York City in 1894, had been
working in 1920 for another company but had mistakenly bought much

more paper than the company needed; fired and "paid off" with $10,000, he founded his own company in 1920 at 71 West 23 Street. He had what he calls an "original idea," to use numbers rather than dates on magazine issues, a practice which would prevent buyers from purchasing only what they believed to be current issues. He had as well a "fool-proof scheme" to shuffle retailer returns from one geographical area to another. The ideas netted him $65,000-75,000 the first year, but gradually customers and retailers caught on. By then, Delacorte had made Dell a financial success.[1]

In Dell's early days Elizabeth Sharpe was the editor; Helen Meyer entered the firm in 1924 as a secretary, when Dell had only seven other employees. Meyer, from Select Publications, rose gradually in Dell, eventually becoming its chairman in 1978. A 1976 newspaperman called her "a sweet little grey-haired grandmother of 68 who has been regarded for years as one of the toughest and shrewdest executives in New York."[2] One former Dell employee simply terms her "the doyenne of Dell."[3] (See illustration 1.) Meyer and Delacorte aimed the Dell magazines at the lower middle class audiences rather than at the upper middle class readers of McCall's and Ladies Home Journal. (Ironically, the first dated Dell publication, Virginia Sidney Hale's A Book of Etiquette [1923], seems to appeal to a distinctly upper class audience.) Dell's first magazine was Ballyhoo, a crude humor periodical that was wrapped with cellophane and bore the caption, "Read a Fresh Magazine."[4] Dell also published romantic flings such as I Confess and Cupid's Diary and various pulps such as Five Novels Monthly and All Detective. Most were a bit lurid, but so was Henry Luce's infant Life magazine. These early Dell magazines were edited by Cliff Dowdey, who Frank Gruber remembers "became Clifford Dowdey, the distinguished author of Civil War novels" after he left.[5] Art Lawson replaced Dowdey.

W. A. Swanberg, one of Dell's early editors, recalls the days:

I graduated from college in 1931 right into the great depression, could not find steady work in Minnesota, came to NY and was on the ragged edge when I landed with Dell at $120 a month to start, I think it was. By the time I left I was making $16,000, an enormous salary I thought at the time.

I was glad to go, although I had to squeak along on something less than that for a while as a free-lance writer, and it took me some time to build enough financial backlog to go into the risky field of book-writing. Dell's so-called "sensational" magazines now look prim indeed. But I had edited such pulp mags as All Western and Federal Agent, and a weak imitation of Life mag known as Foto. A dozen years of this was enough.

Still, it was good editorial training, and on the writing side it gave one a sense of narrative. If you didn't have that, you didn't qualify. And it was interesting to work under George T. Delacorte, a brilliant and generous man. He wanted badly to rise into "prestige" publishing, and didn't succeed in doing so until I had left the company. He was particularly kind to me and my wife when I left to join the Office of War Information during WW2, and I had a friendly correspondence with him for years.[6]

Cartoonist Mort Walker worked for several Dell humor magazines, and remembers that Delacorte started him at $50 a week. But Helen Meyer knocked the salary down to $45, "so I would 'have something to work up to.'" Walker recalls his first view of Dell's New York offices: "Instead of a glamorous office with secretaries [and] a staff . . . I had a bare office all by myself amid shipping boxes filled with returned editions and layers of dust clogging my antiquated typewriter." Both Walker and his boss, Charles Saxon, eventually left Dell, because, in Walker's words, "the sham and deceit we were forced to practice every day for the sake of the fans [articles they ghost-wrote as celebrities] revolted him [Saxon]."[7]

Despite such complaints, Dell's success was spectacular. In the 1940's Dell issued 160 million magazine copies per year; earlier, in 1936, Dell had entered the comic field in partnership with Western Printing & Lithographing. Western had the rights to Disney characters; Dell had a name and, through the American News Co., a distribution system. Under the Dell imprint appeared the successful "Four Color" comics and many special issues of comics featuring Disney and Warner Bros. characters. Delacorte considered initiating a paperback line in the 1930's, after he viewed the European paperbacks of Tauchnitz, Albatross, and Penguin. He discussed the idea with Allen Lane (of Penguin) and with publishers Richard Simon and Max Schuster, nearly reaching an agreement with the latter two in 1938, when Simon bowed out. Delacorte wanted to sell the books for 15¢; Simon favored 25¢ or 50¢. Simon and Schuster eventually entered into partnership with Robert De Graff to produce Pocket Books. Delacorte, encouraged by the American News Co. (which had lost most of Pocket Books' business by 1941), joined with Western to begin the Dell imprint in early 1942, possibly even in very late 1941.

The company with which Dell began its long association—Western Printing & Lithographing—began in 1905 as the West Side Printing Company, so named because it was located on the west side of the Root River in Racine, Wisconsin.[8] Edward H. Wadewitz, an employee, bought out the interest from its owner, John Geller, in 1907. Wadewitz formed a partnership with William Bell, who departed a few months after R. A. Spencer joined the firm. Although the firm made little profit in the first year, it hired other employees, including William R. Wadewitz. In 1909 the company was incorporated at $25,000 as Western Printing & Lithographing. In 1914 the firm began producing books for Hamming-Whitman, and when that company defaulted on its bills, Western took the merchandise, a move which inaugurated their successful line of Whitman books.

Western slowly expanded its facilities at Racine and added plants at Poughkeepsie, New York (in 1934), and elsewhere for editing, producing artwork, binding, and printing—becoming the full production concern that E. H. Wadewitz had visualized. And Western has continued to be one of the nation's largest printers, doing work for commercial outfits such as Maytag as well as producing its own lines of books and comics.

In 1940 Western produced a short-lived series of paperbacks called Bantam Publications, with a publishing address of Western's Los Angeles branch. A collection of mysteries, romances, and popular fiction and non-fiction, the books were designed for sale in vending machines, but the paper shortage of World War II ended the series; 29-33 titles were produced, perhaps seven with pictorial covers. Because of their limited distribution, these "L. A. Bantams" are today the scarcest of paperbacks—not to be confused with Bantam Books (of New York), which began in 1946, and to whom Western released the use of the name "Bantam."[9]

Western's paperback relationship with Dell began largely because Dell needed paper, which Western had in 1942, and because Western by this time needed printing work, which Dell could supply in the form of its new paperback line. So Dell Books was born, created by Delacorte of Dell and Lloyd E. Smith of Western. Frank E. Taylor (later executive editor of Dell Books) believes few people really understood this relationship between Dell and Western. Perhaps helpful is the remark by Knox Burger (editor of Dell First Editions) that "Western and Dell were in bed together."[10] The potential problem in this relationship was that there had to be mutually satisfying results: in this case, double profit for double overhead, or at least considerable profit. And there was. A more important problem concerned increasing competition between the two firms about the exercising of creative control, a problem that eventually helped lead to the split between the companies in late 1960.

The Dell paperbacks produced prior to 1945 were primarily the work of Lloyd E. Smith, officially editor-in-chief of the books but really a one-man publisher within Western. According to most accounts, Smith designed and envisioned the series, originating the back-cover maps, character lists, and other distinctive features, even suggesting the airbrushed covers. Born in Waltham, Massachusetts, in 1902, Smith graduated from Trinity College in Hartford, Connecticut, in 1923, then spent two years free-lance writing until joining Haldeman-Julius Publications in Girard, Kansas, as assistant editor of the Little Blue Books for two years. Later, he spent a year as an English instructor at Trinity College. In 1934, he joined Western, where he became an editor in the Whitman division, adding on duties as editor of the Dell Books until that line became too time-consuming. Smith, a collector of books, a well-liked and intelligent man according to those who knew him, was, in

Knox Burger's words, "a closet intellectual working for a giant printing firm."[11] Smith died in 1971, while carrying an armload of books.

Lou Nielsen, who joined Smith in the Dell operation in April, 1944, remembered it as follows:

Mr. Smith read reviews of books as they were published, and then obtained copies of those which might be good for the Dell series. He read the books, obtained the right to reprint by paying an advance on royalty to the hardcover publisher. He had a style which was followed in all the books handled in Racine. Small caps on the first clause of each opening chapter, as an example. In those days the only competitor was Pocket Books and Penguin.

He then estimated the number of pages [that] would be needed to reprint the book. The number of pages had to be either 160, 192, 224, 256, and so on. Also if the reprint would have each chapter starting on a new page or run on at the end of the preceding chapter. I finally worked out a system which worked quite well in determining the page length and all the other angles. However, in those days the books were set on a Linotype and some operators might set a tight line—others a loose line. These just added to the problem. When all the type had been set, galley proofs were supplied. These were proof-read—mistakes noted, and sent to the composing room for needed corrections. A new set of proofs, when checked, enabled the work of marking the proofs for pages. This done, the composing room tied the type for each page separately, and the type and proofs [were] sent to our plant in Poughkeepsie, N.Y., where the books were printed.

Cover art was done by many artists. Some in this area [Racine], some done through our New York offices.

As the line of titles published each month grew in number, more staff was added for proof-reading—mostly women from the [Racine] school system. An experienced editor [James E. Hawkins] took over the task of editing and decided on type, number of pages, etc. With the changes in 1961 . . . the staff working on Dell Books diminished through marriages, opportunity in other of our publishing activities such as Whitman books, etc.

In the meantime I spent more time working with foreign publishers interested in our line of comics, books, etc. Until Dell took over I also checked to be certain our licensors were properly paid for the use of their material.[12]

(Two of the proofreaders were Betty Ren Wright, later editor of Whitman Books, and Stella Williams.)

J. J. Barta, the next to join the operation, recalls that

The main credit for [the humor books] has to go to Lou (Louis L.) Nielsen. . . . I remember helping Lou on these books, but they were really his "babies." We culled the old magazines of those days (Post, Collier's, etc.) for the best cartoons. Lou then selected the ones we planned to put into the Dell books and he worked up the jokes and did the paraphrasing necessary. In any case, he spent a lot of time and effort on these special Dell books. . . .

As time moved on, our department was in a transitional stage, but I don't really know how aware of this any of us were at the time. We were moving from a "creative and editorial" department to a department that acquired rights and paid out royalties. I mean we not only acquired rights for the Dell books, but we also acquired various rights for use by Western's Whitman and Golden Press divisions or subsidiaries. . . . When the management decision was made to transfer all of the typesetting to the control of our Poughkeepsie plant, a number of us found that we were in much different positions!

For example, Lou Nielsen was a top-notch accountant, and because of this capability he became Lloyd Smith's "financial Friday," meaning he had to handle all of the payment records and took on the responsibility of the payouts to writers, artists, agents, and other parties. On almost the same day, two lawyers hired by Lloyd Smith to handle the drafting of contracts and agreements decided to quit, and I volunteered to do this work for Lloyd. He accepted, and since that particular time I have been involved in drafting various contracts and agreements for Western. . . .

. . . on the Dell paperbacks or pocket editions, I order[ed] setting of type, had the galleys proofread, and also paged and prepared these books up to the printing stage for a number of years. As I recall, the back cover maps were either the brainchild of Lloyd E. Smith or someone suggested the idea to Lloyd, who was the head of our Editorial Department as it was called in the old days. Later it was changed to the Rights and Royalties Department. The Dell books were always reviewed and prepared for the setting of type by various of our Western "copy editors," meaning that the original trade editions were examined for typos or misspellings, and, also in this process of "editing," the copy was prepared for linotype setting. The copy editors as well as other "selected" department personnel would make notes of and put down details concerning the layouts or construction of the houses, buildings, or structures in which the murders occurred, and this information was conveyed by Lloyd, I believe, to [Ruth Belew]. I think this woman then originated the artwork for the maps that appeared on the back covers. Artwork was prepared in black and white, and Western's Art Department added the color.[13]

Most of the work at this time was concentrated in the Mound Avenue offices of Western. Artwork was prepared at the new wing on Liberty Street, where Western acquired and then remodeled what had once been the Signal Shirt Company. The next person associated with the Dell operation was Don Ward, who joined Western in 1945. Ward specialized in western novels and began Dell's *Zane Grey's Western Magazine*. He attempted to introduce science-fiction titles into the Dell line, but Lloyd Smith disliked the genre, preferring to concentrate on mysteries, westerns, and romances. Those sold; Smith doubted that science-fiction would. Nevertheless, Ward managed to slip in two books by the respectable H. G. Wells as well as an original science-fiction anthology "edited" by Orson Welles. (The anthology was actually compiled by Ward, who also put together many of the other original Dell anthologies, including many of those with Alfred Hitchcock's byline.)[14]

James E. Hawkins came next to the editorial staff. Hawkins, who had worked at the *Saturday Review of Literature*, became the line's copy-editor from 1945 to 1955, in that time adhering in general to the *Chicago Manual of Style* and doing copy-editing and copy-fitting—i.e., abridging texts to fit page requirements. Hawkins remembers that previously the books often came out a few pages too long, a situation which called for abridgment; coming out too short was fine, since advertisements could then be inserted in the blank pages. He also remembers having a free hand in rewriting and updating the books; for example, he omitted all anti-Semitic remarks in Agatha Christie's books, following the "Let's not make waves" policy of both Dell and Western. In his freedom to use his own judgment on editorial matters, Hawkins often corrected errors of fact from hard-cover editions—inconsistent names, for example. And he checked the back-cover maps for accuracy.[15]

Allan Barnard joined the staff in 1948. Barnard, later a vice-president at Bantam Books, had then and still has what those who know him describe as "a very good nose for popular fiction"; he discovered and bought for $11,000 the paperback rights to Grace Metalious' *Peyton Place*, for a while the best-selling book after the Bible. Barnard lived in Wisconsin and did free-lance abridgments for Lloyd Smith before officially joining Western. Part of his job involved scouting around second-hand bookshops for likely-looking books to reprint. In those halcyon days, Barnard remembers, you could sell most anything: "You smelled something out and bought it."[16] One of his ideas was the reprinting in 1952 of Clem Yore's *Age of Consent* (#622), a racy novel that the Library of Congress once included in its "Delta" collection (for pornographic material). The book sold 98 percent of the copies printed, somewhat less when Dell reissued it in 1965 in a comparatively tame edition.

Barnard edited two books himself, *Cleopatra's Nights* (#414, for Dell) and *The Harlot Killer* (for Dodd, Mead; reprinted by Dell, #797). The first was a modest seller, the second very popular. Barnard's acute judgment may be surmised by a glance at a few of the books he unsuccessfully tried to purchase for the Dell series: Mickey Spillane's mysteries (vetoed by Western because of opposition to the nature of Spillane's work), Jack Kerouac's *On the Road*, J. D. Salinger's books, and Harold Robbins' popular fiction. Collectors can only imagine the appearance of "mapback" editions of Mickey Spillane, who was reprinted instead by New American Library.

The last to join the Racine staff was James E. Gunn, an apprentice editor who worked for less than a year, suggesting possible covers and blurbs and editing (without credit) the humor anthology, *Funny Side Up* (#607). He also worked on Robert Heinlein's *Universe* (#36 in the Dell 10¢ series), contributing the cover idea and the anonymous introduction.[17]

1. Helen Meyer, "the doyenne of Dell," in 1981, posing with two Dell paperback covers. Photo by Piet Schreuders.

2. Employees of Western Printing & Lithographing edge-staining copies of Dell paperback #4, Ellery Queen's *The American Gun Mystery*. From *Western at War* (1943).

This, in addition to a few free-lancers, was the editorial staff in Racine that created the Dell books from 1942 to late 1951.

Some of those books featured drastic abridgments, performed to fit the Dell books to page requirements. The front-cover blurb, "Complete with Map on Back Cover," suggests that the books are textually complete; but they rarely were in the 1940's. The lack of a comma after "complete" creates the deception: it makes the prepositional phrase grammatically restrictive. Don Ward remembers that the phrasing was intentional. The blurb became "With Crime Map [or Map] on Back Cover" in 1947; in 1949 the blurb was dropped altogether.

In August, 1953, the Federal Trade Commission complained about Dell and other paperback publishers' method of handling abridged books. In 1957, the FTC charged Dell with "failing to disclose on covers and title pages when the paperbacks it publishes are abridged versions or reprints under new titles."[18] The notices of abridgments or title changes, the FTC charged, were "not conspicuous enough to be noticeable to average purchasers." Specifically, the FTC maintained that the word "Abridged" was inconspicuous in the lower-right hand corner of the front cover (as it is, for example, on H. H. Knibbs, *The Ridin' Kid from Powder River*, #399, 1950) and that original titles of altered books were often in small, inconspicuous type, in parentheses (as it is on William Ard, *Deadly Beloved*, #991, 1958). "In some instances," the complaint continued, "Dell has failed to reveal in any manner that its books have been previously published."

The Dell abridgments were originally Lloyd Smith's idea; in some cases they do not seem a bad idea; for example, Edison Marshall's *Benjamin Blake* (#431, 1950) seems tediously long to this reader. But readers have a right to the author's original. Rex Stout's *Too Many Cooks* (#45, 1944) omits the important "Recipes" from the final pages of the book; the reissue (#540, 1951) restores them. And Earl Derr Biggers' *Keeper of the Keys* (#47, 1944) is badly abridged, so that the last line of page 5 has dangling modifiers resulting from the rewritten version. The most annoyed author I contacted was Mary Renault, who was unaware the contract with her hard-cover publisher allowed her paperback reprints to be so abridged. But it did; Curtis Brown Limited informed me that Morrow, Renault's American publisher, in subletting to Dell, did not require her consent.[19] Renault feels strongly that "an author should have cut everything cuttable before sending in the ms." and that "not to have unauthorised alterations in the work is, I think, one of an author's basic rights."[20]

Until 1952, advances for authors varied from $500 up, usually not more than $1,000. Royalties were either 1¢ per copy on all copies printed (*not* on copies sold), or 1¢ per copy on the first 150,000 copies printed and 1½¢ per copy thereafter. Such paperback royalties were standard in the

1940's; this was the paperback field in its infancy. Lloyd Smith had a policy of quick payment; Don Ward recalls occasionally sending out checks to authors the same day he received an acceptable manuscript.[21] Generally, authors appreciated the policy. One author, requesting anonymity, commented, however, "All I can recall about those Dell mystery sales was that the pay was miniscule. Things have improved a bit."

J. J. Barta remembers the policy of paying on copies printed:

Most of the early reprint pocket edition agreements of Western with trade publishers or authors called for royalty payments on a printings basis. In those days Western generally paid royalties on the Golden/Whitman products based on production or printing, so it wasn't unusual for us to pay the Dell book royalties on that same basis. Of course, as time went on, the Dell book line expanded enormously and we commenced payment on the basis of sales like other paperback or pocket edition publishers because of the enormous amounts of money involved. I can't say whether or not Dell is responsible for this change. It could have been just a normal development of business, but if it was discussed with Dell from a standpoint of lower costs and pricing of the books, then Dell would obviously have favored the change.[22]

Prior to 1952, Lloyd Smith negotiated or supervised negotiation of most of the Dell book contracts through hard-cover publishers, agents, and authors. Barta aided Smith; as the Special Editorial Division became the Rights and Royalty Division, Barta remembers that clearing rights to the Dell Book collections of cartoons were the most difficult and time-consuming to conclude.[23]

The cost of producing these 25¢ books (the only true line produced under the Dell imprint until 1951) was from 7¢ to 9¢ per book; Western sold the book to Dell for 16¢, Dell to retailers through the American News Co. for 19¢.[24]

Type for the books was set entirely at the Racine plant, under the supervision of Edwin Bachorz. Bachorz remembers that the format of the books' front matter was largely decided upon by the composing-room staff, although type faces had usually been specified beforehand. Two or three galleys of each book were run off on special proof presses in Racine; revisions were made on the galleys, then submitted to the editorial department, who often proofread four times on the first proofs. Afterward, page proofs were run off, then stored for six to eight years in "The Morgue." After final approval by the editorial department, type was shipped to the Poughkeepsie ("Pokip") plant—four or five layers of type per box, each box weighing about 200 pounds.[25]

Typesetting was usually Baskerville, Caldonia, or Granjon, the last giving the greatest yield. Composing-room staff adopted an in-house style, one never formally printed up, but understood. Yet one compositor, Ralph MacNichol, used his own style as well; offended by what he thought were anti-religious references in some books, he practiced his own version of bowdlerization. Anticipating the Moral Majority, he removed, for example, "Christ," "Jesus," and all but one "goddamn" from Cleve F. Adams' hard-boiled mystery, *The Crooking Finger* (#104, 1946).[26] Although the Wadewitz brothers, heads of Western, did disapprove of strong language in general, MacNichol's policy was his own. When James E. Hawkins and Edwin Bachorz discovered the actions of "Mac," they quickly put other compositors to work—Elmer Patzke and Carl Nelson. To Mac they gave inoffensive books.

Trucks left Racine daily for Poughkeepsie, stopping midway in Ohio to exchange loads with trucks coming from Poughkeepsie. All printing of Dell books from 1942 to 1955 was at Poughkeepsie. Printing runs were decided by Dell, including the number of copies slated for Canadian distribution or to be printed in Canada. In general, the earliest mysteries and other books produced until the end of World War II had from 120,000 to 200,000 copies. (In comparison, first printings of Pocket Books averaged 300,000; Bantam, 300,000; Penguin, 200,000; Avon, 100,000.)[27] The 4-digit reprints (e.g., #1174, reprint of #174) usually had 50,000 copies, less for Canadian copies. Until 1949, sheet-fed metal presses were used; then a Babcock Press was installed—a high-speed rotary press which used rubber plates, plates still stored at Poughkeepsie (as of 1982). Most printing was letterpress.

The movement of the Dell books from receipt at Poughkeepsie to shipment is illustrated in the accompanying diagrams, taken from the December, 1950, issue of Western's house organ, *The Westerner*, complete with their figure numbers, as follows:

Figure 6 shows the general layout of the Poughkeepsie plant, part of which is two stories high. The central location of loading and unloading facilities for ten freight cars provides the shortest possible hauls to work areas. Six truck bays are also so located as to keep handling to a minimum. Since rail movements account for 76% of incoming material the position of the sidings is a key feature in this arrangement.

Figure 7 shows the flow of material for Dell Comics and Dell Books, which account for a major share of the tonnage. The handling of roll stocks for these products is a straight line from unloading through the storage area into the Rotary Pressroom. In many cases, rolls can be laid down directly from the cars, without actually entering storage. One-third of the comic tonnage is delivered from the press-room to the Comic Bindery by conveyor. The rest of the comic sections and all of the Dell book sections are handled on standardized skids. The fact that these skids are of uniform size provides the maximum utilization of floor space and the minimum spoilage.

Covers for comics and Dell books follow a route similar to the one shown in Figure 8 for Simon and Schuster books, except that after the cutters, they are

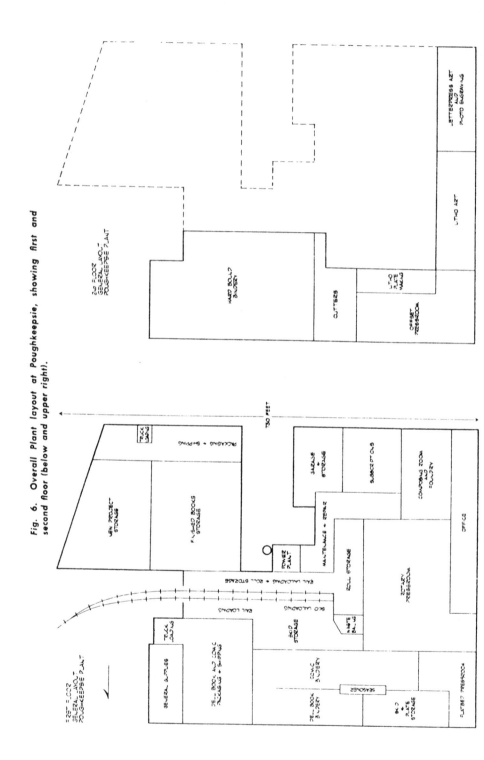

Fig. 6. Overall Plant layout at Poughkeepsie, showing first and second floor (below and upper right).

14

Fig. 8. This flow chart shows the processing of S & S and other hard bound books.

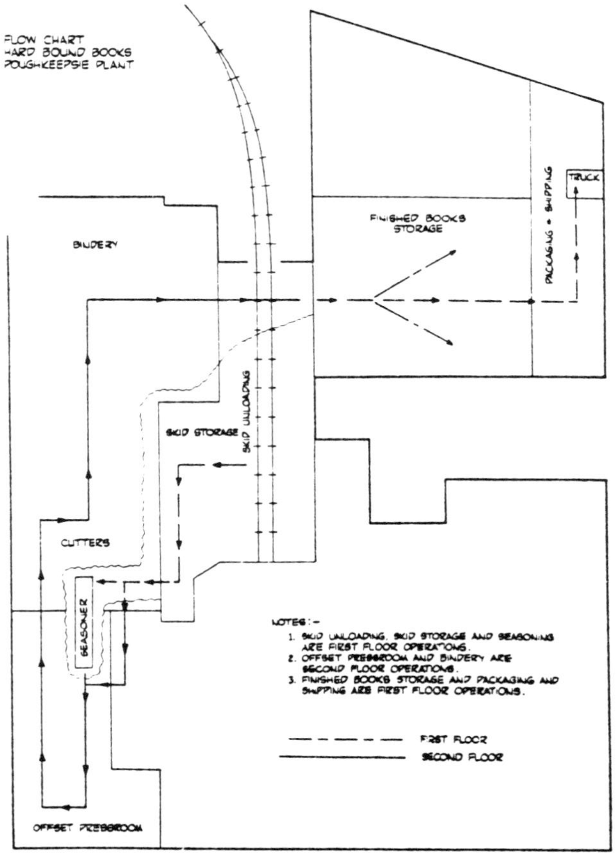

Fig. 7. This chart shows straight-line flow of material for comics and Dell Books (below).

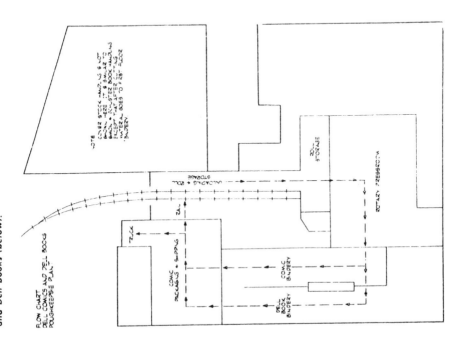

15

brought downstairs to join the inside sections in the comic and Dell book bindery.

From the bindery both comics and Dell books move directly into a packaging area. Comics are wrapped in kraft paper, tied, and put into mailbags or on skids. Dell books are cartoned. From here they both move a short distance either into mailcars or trucks for shipment. About 1,000,000 comic books and 150,000 Dell books follow this path *every day!* The inside sections of these books constitute most of the tonnage and are handled entirely on the first floor.[28]

(See also illustration 2.)

From 1943 to 1957, Dell books were distributed to retailers through the giant American News Co., which, founded in 1846, virtually controlled American distribution of all printed material until 1904. The ANC existed side by side with independent jobbers, which other retailers used as well as they did ANC. Dell had been using the ANC for distribution of its magazines and comics and so had a ready system when it entered the paperback field, much as the Hearst Company had when it began Avon and The Pines Corporation when it began Popular Library. Those few paperback houses without such a system—Red Arrow, Bart House, Lion, Graphic—lasted only a short time.[29]

Dell had branch offices in Canada for both printing and distribution. The Canadian schedule was usually about three months behind the American one; it took that long to ship the plates to the Ronalds Co., Ltd., in Toronto, where the Canadian editions were printed in the 1940's. Distribution there was through independent wholesalers and through large chain stores such as F. W. Woolworth Co. The books originally sold for 39¢, then in 1945 for 25¢—when Dell's New York office assumed control of Dell Books in Canada, under the supervision of Galen Holshue.[30] J. J. Barta explains the Canadian system:

On Canadian or export sales a different royalty rate (or even a different contract) usually applied, which is why the number of copies printed for Canada or shipped to Canada were separately entered on the [royalty] cards. Dell was always responsible for the Canadian figures. In the early days, they may have given us the information somewhat informally after they shipped the copies to Canada, or if we shipped the copies for them, then they gave us the quantities by some method of communication. Later on, I expect the procedures were probably altered for the convenience of both Dell and Western by incorporating into the printing schedules the quantities printed for Canadian distribution. These figures would always have been the figures given to us and approved by Dell.[31]

Circulation and sales of the Dell paperbacks increased rapidly. In 1945, Delacorte estimated that he covered about 40 percent of the existing bookstore outlets; he was also selling the books through department stores, chain stores, and drug stores. In May, 1945, Dell had 25 men in the field handling book and magazine distribution and was rapidly training 100 additional men just to handle the Dell books.

Delacorte estimates that between 7 and 11 million copies of Dell books were sold between 1943 and 1945. Despite the postwar slump in sales in 1946, a situation that improved by 1948, Dell seems to have done well in those years, so that for 1948 Dell could boast it was close to a 60 percent increase in sales for the period from September 1 to December 31. In 1949, 25 million Dell books were sold (compared to sales of 50 million Pocket Books, 30 million for Bantam, 30 million for New American Library, 15 million for Avon, 14 million for Popular Library).[32] Such statistics are difficult to realize correctly, since publishers in this highly competitive field are reluctant to release sales figures. Dell's sales were stimulated by special racks, for which Dell had spent half a million dollars by 1950.[33]

2

Dell Paperbacks,
1952-1962

In late 1951, editorial and artistic control of the Dell books shifted from Racine to New York City, where the Western staff concerned with the Dell books moved. At least some of them moved. Lloyd Smith remained at Racine; he was replaced, briefly, by John Scott Mabon, who resigned after experiencing problems of conscience regarding the sometimes-sensational nature of paperback books.[1] Smith then shuttled between Racine and New York for a short while until Frank Taylor became executive editor of Dell Books in 1952. Walter Brooks took on the duties of art director. And the Dell offices were not far away, exercising more control over the books. Details of that shift and later staff changes (from Western's point of view) appear in the following article, reprinted from the March, 1957, issue of *The Westerner*:

Here is a new Western office location—415 Madison Avenue, New York. It occupies the entire seventh floor of a handsome, modern building in the heart of New York's publishers' row. It's the last word in modern design—automatic elevators, year-round central air conditioning, built-in fluorescent lighting, wall-to-wall windows, attractive furnishings. Fancy? No—functional, and a necessity as Western's staff grows with Western business.

This office is the metropolitan home of Western's Newsstand Division, and is New York headquarters for Commercial Sales and the Whitman Publishing Company. These Western operations, once scattered in four different offices, are now under one roof, with room for further expansion.

Most of the floor is taken up by the Newsstand Division and its creative departments—the editorial and art departments of Dell Books, Dell First Editions, Laurel Editions, Dell Comics and K. K. Comics. The people who work here have helped write the record of growth and success that made the new office necessary and possible. Their story is a typical Western story; it's about people working together, and companies working together, to make something worthwhile.

Western's editors and artists in the Dell Book Division . . . select, edit and design three lines of pocket-sized books for the Dell Publishing Company. *Dell Books* are inexpensive, paper-bound reprints of books previously published in regular hard-cover editions; Western's Dell Book editors have the job of selecting and editing the best and most salable fiction and non-fiction from a flood of books published every day. *Dell First Editions* is the imprint for all the original books specifically written for and published by Dell, and First Editions editors select, edit and revise original fiction manuscripts for this line. Special anthologies and original non-fiction edited by Western's Dell Book staff have, up to now, also been published as First Editions; this year sees the appearance of a third line created for books of this kind, *Laurel Editions*. The books in all three lines are designed as to type, covers and illustrations by a common Art Department, and they are produced by Western at the Pokip plant.

It's the Dell Publishing Company that publishes, promotes and distributes these books. Since the first Dell Book came out in 1943, Western has combined its expert command of book production and design with Dell's vitality and long experience in magazine publishing and newsstand distribution; together they formed a natural team for the production and marketing of pocket-sized books, and a highly successful one.

On the Dell side of the picture, this success has been personally guided by George T. Delacorte, Jr., founder and President of the Dell Publishing Company; major contributions to the growth of the Dell Book lines have been made by Helen Meyer, Executive Vice-President; by Paul Lilly, Vice-President in Charge of Circulation; by William F. Callahan, Jr., Assistant Vice-President in Charge of Sales (Books); by Dell Art Director, Fernando Texidor [;] and, more recently, by Book Sales Promotion Manager, Walter B. J. Mitchell, Jr. These Dell people and others have worked with Western editors and art personnel to help make the Dell line what it is today.

To the end of 1956, Western has produced and Dell published a total of 1,021 Dell Books, and 131 Dell First Editions. Dell Books and Dell First Editions now publish about 120 books a year. Nineteen fifty-six was Dell's biggest book year, with Western's presses turning out 3,300,000 more than ever before. Dell now stands second in the pocket-sized book field (up from fifth in the last five years). And it is still growing.

Here are five current reasons why. Françoise Sagan's *Bonjour Tristesse* [#D166] has 1,600,000 copies in print in the Dell edition, and is still moving fast. William March's *The Bad Seed* [#847 and #F180] has sold 750,000 so far. The Dell edition of Tolstoy's *War and Peace* [#F53] is the fastest-selling paperback in any line as of January 1, 1957, with 600,000 copies already in print. Lucy Herndon Crockett's *The Magnificent Bastards* [#D145 and #F95] (or, if you go to the movies, *The Proud and Profane*) is up to 668,000 copies. The Gesell Institute's *Child Behavior* [#D180, #LC120, and #LS107] is just off to a 500,000 copy start. Nineteen fifty-seven will break new records, with such bestsellers (to mention only three) as [Ross Lockridge, Jr.'s] *Raintree County* [#F58], [Grace Metalious'] *Peyton Place* [#F61] and Françoise Sagan's *A Certain Smile* [#D206].

Western's book staff is proud of this record. Mark Morse heads the operation as Manager of the Newsstand Division, which, of course, includes comics as well as books. As far as the books are concerned, Mark has overall supervision of the work of the editorial and art departments, and is their liaison with Dell Publishing and with Pokip; Anne Di Stefano, office manager, assists him in keeping a complicated system running smoothly.

Executive Editor of Dell Books is Frank E. Taylor. Frank is a product of

Malone, New York, of Hamilton College, and of the University of Minnesota graduate school. He was an editor at Reynal and Hitchcock and at Random House as well as a Hollywood producer, before coming to Western on June 1, 1952. Frank's job is to make final choices of the Dell Book reprints from the hard-cover books that swamp the office, to buy reprint rights from publishers in highly competitive bidding, and to oversee everything that goes into the editing and design of Dell Books.

Frank says that the most significant thing he's seen on this job is the recent growth of mass demand for quality paper-bound books. This does not mean highbrow books. All of the Dell titles in this field are carefully edited to make exciting and understandable presentations that would interest the average reader. The list now includes anthologies of the best literature of information ([Robert Penn Warren and Albert Erskine's] *Six Centuries of Great Poetry* [Dell First Edition #FE69] or [Leonard Engel's] *New Worlds of Modern Science* [#B102], "authoritative modern abridgments" of classics that are too long for modern taste ([Leo Tolstoy's] *War and Peace* [#F53], [Fyodor Dostoyevsky's] *The Brothers Karamazov* [#F55]), and beautifully illustrated books on subjects where illustrations count (Sam Hunter's *Modern French Painting* [Dell First Edition #FE98] and *The New Hammond-Dell World Atlas* [Dell First Edition #FE84]). The Dell line has now not only broken into this field, but taken the lead. Dell puts out the best quality books available in the mass market.

These books have helped Dell to open up *new* markets. As late as 1947, some bookstores were refusing to stock paper-bound books, but the new quality paperbacks have created large and growing bookstore sales. With books like these, Dell's Special Sales force has now been able to find and expand outlets in bookstores, college stores, religious shops, libraries and school systems. But the majority of copies still sell to the far wider newsstand audience, for which these books were created. And such books don't go out of date; they form a permanent active backlist for the Dell line, selling (and reprinting) year after year. Each title is expected to reprint at least 50,000 copies a year; in three years, Western has printed 450,000 copies of [Robert Penn Warren and Albert Erskine's] *Short Story Masterpieces* [Dell First Edition #F16].

To make these books more easily available, the third Dell line is being established—Laurel Editions. The new line will make it easier for book dealers and educators to order from a separate list, and for readers to identify these books on separate racks. In 1957 Laurel Editions will bring out *Great English Short Stories* [#LC102] edited by Christopher Isherwood, Sam Hunter's *Modern American Painting and Sculpture* [#LY102], and six other titles. Under the new imprint, the books will still be produced by the Dell Book staff. Each editor is working on one or more Laurel projects. Frank Taylor will continue to lead the program, and a new Laurel Editions Managing Editor, Dick Fisher, will co-ordinate work on the books under Frank's direction. Dick is a relatively new Westerner; he came over from the Paper Editions Book Club last October 15. He's a former college history instructor, and the office Ph.D. His job—to help keep Dell's quality books on top.

The oldest Westerner on the book staff—in point of service—is Allan Barnard, recently named Managing Editor of Dell Books. Allan joined the Dell Book Division in Racine in 1948—he'd previously been on the research staff of the *New Yorker*. He handles detail work on publisher negotiations and contracts, and inter-office liaison on contracts, purchase reports, and sales statistics.

Allan's main responsibility is mysteries. He reads all the promising hard-cover mysteries, and selects and edits about 36 mystery reprints a year. He helps to keep Dell Books by far the leading mystery line in reprint publishing. About 500 mystery titles have appeared as Dell Books, written by about 180 authors, printed to the tune of some 115,000,000 copies. In January [1957], Dell announced The Dell Great Mystery Library, a series of mystery classics either never reprinted before, or long unavailable in soft covers. Dell will now offer not only the best in new mysteries, but also the best mysteries of all time.

Glen Robinson has specialized in western novels since he came to the Dell Book Division in 1952. Yet until Glen went to a 1956 western writers' convention in Santa Fe, he'd never been west of Parsons, Kansas. . . . Glen is now in charge of all western reprints for Dell Books, about 18 books a year; he reads, selects, buys and edits them, writes cover copy and suggests cover art work.

These Dell westerns are among the top sellers in paper covers; they consistently sell upwards of 225,000 copies each. Dell Book western writers include Wayne D. Overholser, two-time winner of Western Writers of America awards, Eugene Cunningham, Norman A. Fox, Elmore Leonard, and, of course, Luke Short, far and away the best-selling western writer today. Today's westerns are selected for their values as realistic and authentic novels, and there's an annual $1,000 Western-Dell award to encourage writers to live up to these standards.

John Ferrone came to Western in August, 1953, from the Stanford University Press (he's a Stanford M.A.). He reads and makes preliminary selection of nearly all the general fiction that comes in, working closely with Allan Barnard. He writes Dell Book copy, and edits his share of original non-fiction.

The expansion of Dell Books recently brought two new Westerners to the staff. Joan Lamm came last October 3, to design inside typography for all three Dell Book Lines. Joan has been in paper-bound publishing for twelve years; she was formerly with New American Library and with Penguin Books. Peggy Dunleavy came in last November 12, to write copy for the covers and front pages of Dell Books; she has been a copy writer for the publishing house of John Wiley, and was publicity director for Pageant Press. Peggy was brought in to take up some of the slack left by the transfer of Pete Margolies and his assistant, Mildred Kapilow, to the Commercial Sales Division. Pete and Milly had specialized in the editing of original Dell non-fiction and had written much of the Dell Books cover copy. In their new jobs they will continue to develop the growing industrial book program which they started about two years ago.

The Dell Book editorial department has an impressive secretarial staff—two girls. Yolande Fortier, who's been with the office since January, 1955, is Allan Barnard's secretary; she's from Montreal and answers the phone with Gallic courtesy and charm. She also does some reading and copy writing. Barbara Markowitz, a cheerful young lady who came to Western in June, 1956, is Frank Taylor's secretary. Frank says she's the best secretary he's ever seen or heard of; Barbara just smiles.

These are the people who edit Dell Books. Sharing the new offices with them is a separate editorial staff that puts out the Dell First Editions—about thirty titles a year, a quarter of Dell's book output.

Knox Burger has headed the staff, as Editor (Dell First Editions), since the founding of the line in October, 1952. Knox was a *Yank* correspondent during the war, and was Fiction Editor of *Collier's* for three and a half years. One of his primary jobs is to supervise the editing of the First Editions novels. The other is to get hold of good original manuscripts. Knox maintains contact with a great many writers and with a couple of dozen literary agents (who are the source of most publishable novels), and with story editors of the movie studios.

Knox says that "soft-cover originals" pay off for both writers and readers. The type of hard-hitting, fast-paced action story that is the staple of paper-bound fiction seldom does very well in hard-cover editions, and many of the best writers in this vein prefer to publish directly in soft covers. The writers are paid in royalties—and the reader in satisfaction.

Dealing with original manuscripts, First Editions editors are able to keep close control of the quality and readability of their books. Manuscripts are gone over section by section, and frequently sent back to the writer with detailed suggestions for improvements in style, plot, character development and background. The editors give the same detailed supervision to the department's occasional anthologies and non-fiction, all of which means extra work for authors and editors. But it's worth it. Nearly all soft-cover lines are now putting out originals, but printings and sales demonstrate that Dell First Editions are the best in a crowded field.

Dell First Editions have sold some 20,000,000 copies in three years; T. T. Flynn's *The Man from Laramie* [Dell First Edition #14] has printed 700,000 copies, Walt Grove's *Down* (the first title of the line, now in its fourth printing) has 400,000 copies in print. Several First Editions have gotten the plus sales that result from movie tie-ins; *The Man from Laramie, The Body Snatchers, While the City Sleeps* and other films have been based on First Edition novels (*The House of Numbers* and *The Bravados* will soon hit the screens). Other First Editions have been written from screenplays (*The Great Locomotive Chase* was a Walt Disney production, and Clark Gable appeared in *The King and Four Queens*). From the corner newsstand to Hollywood studios, First Editions quality has paid.

Don Fine, Managing Editor of Dell First Editions, is Knox Burger's senior associate. He came to First Editions in October, 1952, after working as an editor at Doubleday and at Goodman Publications. He is the principal First Editions copy writer. Editorially, he develops manuscripts from outline to final draft. The part of the job that Don—in common with all editors—likes best is discovering and developing new writers.

Arlene Donovan works with Knox and Don on the editing of First Edition manuscripts. Arlene's known as the fastest reader on the staff; she goes through twenty to forty manuscripts a week, complete or partial, and never passes up a good one. Arlene also writes copy, contacts agents, and is in charge of getting First Editions reviewed—which they are, in papers all over the country.

Paul Kuhn joined the First Editions staff in October, 1952. Paul reads manuscripts, and writes copy, in addition to his job as Knox Burger's assistant, which involves correspondence on contracts, copyrights and authors' payments, also handling manuscript traffic, and hovering over the production schedule with an eraser. His assistant is Dori Schmidt, who arrived from Radcliffe College last June; she's a reader and copy writer and general secretary to the department. Dori's 22, which, by the way, was her father's age when he went to work as an artist for Western at Racine in 1916.

Both Dell First Editions and Dell Books share the services of the Dell Book Art

Department, headed by Art Director Walter Brooks. Walter has been Dell Books Art Director since January, 1952. He is responsible for the covers of Dell Books and Dell First Editions, developing the cover ideas and sketches in consultation with the editors and assigning and buying the final cover paintings. He is also responsible for the typography and layout of each book and for illustrations, working with the editors concerned, and he works with the Pokip plant on any special production problems.

Walter is very proud of the covers, and with good reason. In 1954 the Dell line won a Mystery Writers of America award for general excellence of covers. Over the last four years Dell covers have pioneered a revolution in paperback art work. The average early Dell cover was, like all other paper-bound book covers, an illustration of a key "situation" in the text, crowded with figures and detailed background. While this gave the reader a general idea of the book's content, it was usually cluttered, and pretty much like every other cover on the stands. For the last four years the Dell Book Art Department has been developing simpler, bolder, cleaner and more eye-catching covers, by simplifying backgrounds, reducing the number of figures, and organizing color schemes for a unified over-all visual impact. These covers are less like paintings, more like posters. This gets the passing readers' attention for each book, and for the whole Dell rack in every outlet. The new approach has definitely paid off in sales; Dell roadmen report amazing improvements in sales for old titles reissued with new covers. Dell's cover revolution is now receiving the sincerest form of flattery—imitation by other lines. Not surprisingly, the Dell covers are still the ones that stand out.

Walter's associates are proud of these covers, too. Jeanette Cissman will have an extra reason for this; one of her own covers will appear on a 1957 Dell First Edition ([Don Congdon's] *Stories for the Dead of Night* [#B107]). Jeanette is responsible for the layouts of all the back covers, follow-through, make-up, mechanicals and typography of both front and back covers. Jeanette's a Portland, Oregon, import and has been with the Art Department since August, 1952. Charles Walker arrived in August, 1956; he works up the roughs and contributes to the all-around operations of the Department, helping to keep up the high standard of Dell covers.

The men and women of all departments of the Dell Book Division are dedicated to producing the best books for the widest public. Dell Books and Dell First Editions lead the field on five counts—the best serious books for the mass market, the best original fiction, the best mysteries, the best westerns, the best covers. That's the heart of the record made by the Dell Book Division.[2]

The preceding account has the typically biased tone of a house organ (it even blasts the early covers!); it neglects a few people as well. Donald Frey had earlier checked through books to suggest cover situations; later he was librarian at Western in Racine. Edward Parone was an in-house editor who compiled several anthologies. And Stephen Becker, now a successful author, worked for Western for a short time:

I believe I started with Western/Dell in January, 1955, and left in about November 1956 after asking for a huge raise and being (properly) turned down. My duties, once I understood what was going on, were mainly to write headlines, cover copy and inside blurbs for a variety of paperbacks ranging from the ordinary mystery (and a lot of them were spectacularly ordinary) to quality items like *War and Peace* in its abridged edition and *The American Heritage Reader*. I was also expected to keep track of production schedules, proofread, make sure all front matter was in order, and occasionally flatter an author or make a contribution to an editorial meeting.

We were on the whole an intelligent bunch and had a fairly good time on the job. Some of the books I remember working on were the aforementioned *War and Peace;* Françoise Sagan's immensely successful *Bonjour Tristesse,* in handling which I committed my first real gaffe—I'm a translator myself, yet I somehow neglected to see to it that the translator's name [Irene Ash] appeared on the title page . . . ; and *The American Heritage Reader*. That quality magazine was in its early years, and working with their editorial staff we put together a nice collection. Joseph Thorndike, one of the ruling triumvirate there, suggested a picture-story on American frontier painting (Catlin, Bierstadt, Remington, etc.) that was a brilliant addition. It was the first book I had charge of from beginning to end, and when the finished product arrived in the office I was much puffed up—until I realized that I'd forgotten to specify the color of the stain on the top edge of the pages. The cover was naturally red, white and blue and our customary maroon stain would have been ghastly. Frank Taylor, the editor-in-chief, had specified a gold stain, thank God. I'd forgotten all about stain. Of such details is memory made.

About those headlines and blurbs—they were pretty damn silly. One headline I remember, for a murder mystery, went "They painted him a killer, and framed him to hang!" We used to amuse ourselves writing parodies, most of them obscene.[3]

Abridgments continued beyond 1952. Some were editorial—Theodore Sturgeon recalls hating to do the abridgment of Stewart Edward White's *The Long Rifle* (#D147, 1955).[4] Others were handled by the author, as William Donohue Ellis explains:

[*The Bounty Lands,* #F71, 1958] was abridged specifically for Dell reprints; Gerry Gross then editor. D. L. Couzens actually did the total abridgment. Her name is Dorothy Couzens; it was her first one; and I was afraid to tell Gerry Gross I had run out of time and turned the task over to a precocious young woman who had never abridged a book. However, upon receiving a telegram from him saying the abridgment was "remarkable and outstanding," I asked him to put her byline on the abridgment. Since then she has condensed two more of my novels.[5]

Editors made other changes: transforming the name of mystery writer William Campbell Gault to "Bill Gault" and Harold Q. Masur to "Hal Masur" and "Hal Q. Masur." Masur writes, "The use of the diminutive for my given name was Dell's idea. A mistake. And even though they have somewhat more money than I have, they ought not to be so familiar."[6]

And others altered book titles: Don Ward remembers a Dell executive changing the title of the western anthology *The Fall Roundup* (referring to the yearly fall roundup of cattle) by asking, "Suppose we want to schedule it in the spring or summer?"[7] The title became the unseasonal *Rawhiders and Renegades* (#D367), published in the summer of 1956.

In reference to title changes, the prolific author Donald Hamilton comments:

My original title for *Date with Darkness* [#375] was *Red Sector* (from the red sector of the lighthouse that figures in the final action) but I guess somebody at Rinehart (the hardcover publisher) thought I was talking about communists and people wouldn't be interested in a book about lousy reds. Well, we can't blame Dell for that change; but while I can't recall my original title for *Assignment: Murder* [Dell First Edition #A123], that wasn't it. I didn't mind that switch as much as the next one, though; when Fawcett reprinted the book a few years ago they changed it again—God help us—to *Assassins Have Starry Eyes.* (Seems there's a gent named [Edward S.] Aarons who writes an "Assignment" series for them and they didn't want a conflict there.)

Another book . . . was one for which I had a hell of a fine title, *The Two-Shoot Gun,* a fine old-fashioned term for the doublebarreled shotgun employed by the hero. Dell didn't like this, for some reason, and issued the novel as *The Man From Santa Clara* (First Edition B170), a title to which I objected strongly (but the book was already in print) because the guy wasn't coming from Santa Clara, he was going to Santa Clara; and those "man-from" titles are pretty damn' corny anyway. Also, the cover showed our hero wearing a sixshooter as well as carrying a two-shooter; and one of the things emphasized in the text was that he'd never carried a pistol, ever. Fawcett was nice about this when they reprinted it later; they gave me back my original title and took the holster off the hero's hip.[8]

Some Dell/Western paperbacks appeared in other countries as well—mostly Dell First Editions, some Dell reprints, even one Laurel book. Glenn Corbin's *Trouble on Big Cat* (Dell First Edition #25), for example, was also published in Great Britain (Viking #235, 1950's; same cover as the Dell) and in Australia (Star Western, no number, 1958; same text as the Dell, different cover). The other British publisher of Dell paperbacks was World; Australian imprints included Original Novels, Phantom, Regal, and Spur Westerns. Most editions used the same cover art, leased by Western. At least two Dell First Editions appeared in French: Harold R. Daniels' *In His Blood* (Dell First Edition #73) as *Jusqu'au cou*, translated by A. DuBouillon (Paris: Presses de la Cité #288, n.d.) and Victor Chapin's *Career* (#B148) as *En Lettres de Feu* (Verviers, Belgium: collection marabout #280, 1959?). The Laurel edition of *Guy de Maupassant* (#LC135), edited by Francis Steegmuller, was published in Britain by World (#C949, 1960; with the Dell text but a different cover).

Copy-editing proceeded differently than before. In 1955 James E. Hawkins went to the Western offices in New York City and Poughkeepsie, New York, to decide on the location for a new Production Editorial Department. Reluctantly, he chose Poughkeepsie. From then on, he assigned Virginia Hawkins, his wife, to copy-edit the Dell books, which she did until 1962. She worked as a free-lancer, more a "manuscript doctor" than a copy-editor, Hawkins remembers. She made whatever changes were necessary, from 15 to 3,000. If books required substantial changes, she contacted the New York office of Western or the author. She and Hawkins copy-edited the Laurel Shakespeare series; he did specification sheets (which noted all type requirements and other matter) for all these books. Hawkins once planned a book on editing, using the Dells as examples; unfortunately, he did not complete the work.[9]

After 1955, type was set in both Racine and Poughkeepsie; Hawkins believes it may also have been set occasionally at Western's plants in St. Louis and Cambridge, Maryland (the latter plant acquired by Western in late 1961). Frank E. Taylor pressed for larger books, but Western's equipment could handle only the smaller paperbacks, 4¼" x 6½". Only in 1961 did Western purchase equipment which could print the larger size, 4¼" x 7¼", which after 1966 became the standard size of Dell books and today is standard for most paperbacks of all companies. Letterpress continued to be used, except for those few books that featured black-and-white illustrations. Printing runs increased, the largest the 8 million plus for *Peyton Place* (#F61) and the smallest a possible reissue of Thomas Wolfe's *The Web and the Rock* [#LY103]—640 copies on December 30, 1960).

In July, 1957, the American News Co. disbanded its distribution system; Dell initiated its own system, as Dell Distributing, Inc., which handled books in the United States, and Dell International, Inc., which controlled books in Canada and abroad. *Peyton Place*, Dell's biggest seller, appeared just in time for Dell's new distribution system. The larger profits delighted Delacorte. Sales continued to be strong—even, according to Delacorte, in the paperback slump of 1954.

Dell used many promotional devices to increase sales. Bookracks became more elaborate, evolving from the earlier wooden racks with the familiar keyhole logo to lustrous metal and wooden racks. In August, 1954, Dell distributed 10,000 copies of the first *Dell Previews*, a 4-page promotional booklet, to newsdealers. A hanging "paper patch" in January, 1955, held copies of the bestselling *The Magnificent Bastards* (#D145), to provide extra display space for such fast-selling titles. In the mid-1950's, common sights were prepacked cartons of books—forerunners of the modern "dumps"—and elaborate posters and rack cards, especially for such successful movie tie-ins as *Elmer Gantry* (#S10) and *Bonjour Tristesse* (#D166).[10]

There were some legal problems. William Fuller's *Brad Dolan's Miami Manhunt* (#A158) used the name of a real-life Miami stripper, Zorita (changed in later printings to "Mirafa" and in the British edition to

"Laurette"); Zorita sued. And the once-scandalous *Peyton Place* attracted lawsuits; today the book seems tame. Earlier, in 1952, the Gathings Committee on Current Pornographic Materials had investigated the three S's in paperbacks—sex, sadism, and the smoking gun; the investigation prompted a decrease in lurid cover art and less emphasis on those three elements.[11] *Peyton Place* has a mild cover, not one that suggests any of the three S's. Its cover relies simply on the title to sell the book. In a sense, the cover is deceptive, promising less than it delivered. But readers knew what to expect from the barrage of Dell publicity.

In earlier years, Dell's internal censorship was mostly limited to James E. Hawkins' efforts and the occasional deletions by compositor Ralph MacNichol. Infrequently an item like "f---ing" would turn up (in, for example, Robert M. Coates, *Wisteria Cottage* [#371]). Hawkins remembers that every six months or so Dell felt there wasn't enough sex in the covers; six months later they took the reverse position. That shifting position might explain the two distinctly different covers on Ernest Hemingway's *Across the River and Into the Trees* (#D117, 1952 and 1956), one vibrant and lush, the other bland. The book was one of 57 paperback titles banned in Detroit in 1955; that action might also have prompted the mild reissue.[12]

Some books were vetoed altogether. Leslie Ford's *Honolulu Story* was planned in March, 1949, for the Dell series but rejected because of the book's anti-Japanese remarks (which were presumably acceptable after Pearl Harbor but not after Japan's surrender); the advance for the book was transferred to the author's *Murder with Southern Hospitality* (#505). Ursula Parrott's *The Tumult and the Shouting* may have been abandoned because of the resentment her other Dell titles caused among some Milwaukee ministers. And the former publicity director of Dell, Walter B. J. Mitchell, Jr., rejected a proposed Dell edition of Guy Endore's *The Werewolf of Paris*; Allan Barnard recalls that Mitchell "was a staunch Catholic and apparently resented things in the book."[13] The book is violently anti-Catholic.

The books' numbering system was Dell's idea. It was simple in the beginning: the 25¢ reprint series used consecutive numbers from 1 to 1020 (except 1011 and 1015-1018). Issue numbers closely followed printing dates, but in a few cases titles were unwisely scheduled; Brett Halliday's *The Uncomplaining Corpses* (#386, 1950) contains events that predate those in his *Blood on the Stars* (#385). The other series also used consecutive numbering systems, adopting a different letter prefix to denote the price of books in the series. Prices ranged from the conventional 35¢, 50¢, and 75¢ to the less common 40¢ and 60¢. The highest priced series had a 95¢ price. Frank E. Taylor advocated even higher prices, beginning with $1.00; Knox Burger wanted higher prices in the Dell First Editions. But Helen Meyer, of Dell, resisted increases.

3

Dell's Changing Contents

From 1942 to 1951, Dell paperbacks consisted primarily of genre fiction. Mysteries accounted for more than half of the books, westerns about 10 percent, and romances about 10 percent. The other books were general fiction and non-fiction. From 1951 to 1962, however, Dell shifted to less genre fiction, more general fiction and non-fiction. During that later period, mysteries accounted for less than half the books published, romances declined, westerns increased. The overall paperback field shifted in a sometimes similar fashion. Popular Library's titles almost mirrored Dell's changing contents. Bantam featured more or less equal amounts of genre fiction, then emphasized general fiction. Avon began with mysteries, general fiction, and science-fiction, even a few "literary" titles; later the firm brought in more general fiction. New American Library initially featured mysteries, westerns, and general fiction, later stressed unclassifiable fiction and non-fiction. Pocket Books, the largest of the paperback companies, always used a balanced format, perhaps with its basis in mysteries. Newcomers Ace and Ballantine (both in 1952) stressed science-fiction at first, gradually incorporating other types of books as well. Fawcett featured mysteries in its Gold Medal line of paperback originals, later stressed lurid fiction.[1] Overall, in the 1940's approximately 70 percent of all paperbacks were fiction, about one-third mysteries. In the 1950's about half of all paperbacks were fiction.

The emphasis of most paperback companies upon genre fiction is not difficult to understand. As an 1835 observer of American readers noted:

They prefer books which may be easily procured, quickly read, and which require no learned researches to be understood. They ask for beauties self-profferred and easily enjoyed; above all, they must have what is unexpected and new. Accustomed to the struggle, the crosses, and the monotony of practical life, they require strong and rapid emotions, startling passages, truths or errors brilliant enough to rouse them up and to plunge them at once, as if by violence, into the midst of the subject.[2]

Dell's paperbacks satisfied those requirements, by the brilliance and violence of their covers, and by the popular nature of the books' subject matter—mostly mysteries, romances, and westerns—the staples of genre fiction. Dell's mysteries included classic, tightly-constructed books (Agatha Christie's works, for example), hard-boiled stories (Dashiell Hammett, H. W. Roden, Henry Kane), Gothics (Mary Roberts Rinehart), "Had-I-But-Known" tales (Mignon G. Eberhart, Leslie Ford, Helen Reilly), mysteries dominated by madcap antics (Phoebe Atwood Taylor), literate novels (Rex Stout, John Dickson Carr), books with series characters (Brett Halliday, Baynard Kendrick, George Harmon Coxe, A. A. Fair, Frances and Richard Lockridge, Kelley Roos), and mysteries that defied pigeonholing (Matthew Head, Clayton Rawson, Dorothy B. Hughes, David Goodis, Cornell Woolrich). Some of these are police procedurals, Reilly's for instance; others involve private investigators or amateur sleuths.

Agatha Christie was well represented in Dell books. They featured such favorite characters as Belgian detective Hercule Poirot and amateur little-old-lady sleuth Miss Marple and included a few non-series books. Christie always plays fair with her reader, her plots always convincing and clear and her characterizations usually three-dimensional and realistic. In *Cards on the Table,* she even parodies both herself and her creation, Poirot. Her books were and are constant best-sellers for Dell. In 1982, Dell began reissuing her titles.

Hard-boiled stories sold as well, those involving tough private investigators, stark morality, and a heavy dose of sadistic play. The most literate example in Dell's line is Dashiell Hammett; imitations are H. W. Roden and Henry Kane. Kane's work is particularly uneven. His *A Halo for Nobody* (#231) is appropriately cynical and hard-boiled, a novel where everyone is guilty by the concluding sentence; on the other hand, *Edge of Panic* (#535) is fast-paced and morally complex, involving a wife who has to solve her husband's "mystery," in the larger sense of the term.

Mary Roberts Rinehart best exemplifies Dell's Gothic mysteries, which usually involve a naive young woman, a dashingly handsome man, and some hints of the supernatural or at least the preternatural. *The State versus Elinor Norton* (#203) is a prototypical Gothic, its ending particularly so.

"Had-I-But-Known" (or HIBK) is a term invented by Ogden Nash in his poem, "Don't Guess, Let Me Tell You." In HIBK tales, the narrator often reflects, at key points in the story, "As we were later to learn" or "Had we known." To many readers, such reflection seemed annoying foreshadowing. But the school gained many writers, notably, in the Dell line, Mignon G. Eberhart; her *Speak No Evil* (#25) is one of the more literate examples. Leslie Ford's Dell books provide less than perfect characterizations, but some of her novels, especially *The Hammersmith Murders* (#36)—written as by David Frome—have Christie-like craftmanship. Helen Reilly's police procedurals are difficult to defend; possibly appealing to the lowest denominator of the HIBK reading public, they offer hysterical women, police inspectors who talk like men in drag, and loose plots. Reilly's favorite line is "Darkness swallowed me. . . ."

Phoebe Atwood Taylor's mysteries involve madcap antics, almost imitations of P. G. Wodehouse's novels, but not usually as amusing. Some readers found "murder as fun" a bit forced, but she had a loyal audience. More literate mysteries are those by Rex Stout and John Dickson Carr. Many of Stout's Dell books feature Nero Wolfe, the enormous, eccentric genius recluse who solves most of his crimes in the confines of his New York brownstone house. Stout also uses a female sleuth, Dol Bonner, in two Dell titles, *The Hand in the Glove* (#177) and *Bad for Business* (#299). Atypical Stout is *The Mountain Cat Murders* (#28), a solid mystery with dark overtones. Carr's mysteries use fine plots and excellent, detailed solutions; the best example in the Dell line is *A Graveyard to Let* (#543), written as by Carter Dickson. Like Stout's one dark mystery, Carr's *Death-Watch* (#564) has disturbing elements.

Most of the Dell mysteries involve series characters. Donald Lam, a disbarred lawyer, and Bertha Cool, a Tugboat-Annie type, were invented by Erle Stanley Gardner, writing as A. A. Fair. Their antics are usually lightweight, but the books move quickly. Davis Dresser, as Brett Halliday, created Michael Shayne, one of the most popular and durable private detectives in mysteries. Later, other writers used the Halliday byline. One of them, Robert Terrall, explains:

Dresser wrote quite readily and easily when he was getting three or four hundred dollars a book, and he needed money, but when the pressures were off and the books were selling well, he began to have difficulty. . . . I wrote *Fit to Kill* [#D314], *Murder Takes No Holiday* [#D379] and *Target: Mike Shayne* [#D355]. This was arranged by the Dell people, but the deal was with Dresser. He was still writing every other one or so, but they were coming hard. *Target: Mike Shayne* was a particular hit, and Dresser was very relieved when Dell proposed that he stop trying and accept an annual check for the use of the byline.

The series was doing very well at the time, and Dell offered him a million dollars for all the titles and complete rights. It fell through for various funny reasons. This was '63, '64. The idea was that I would do three every two years. I always had other things underway, and I didn't keep to that schedule.[3]

George Harmon Coxe created series characters Kent Murdock and Flash Casey, both Boston news photographers. Most of Coxe's mysteries are standardized and indistinguishable from one another, not unlike Halliday's. But Coxe could do better: *Assignment in Guiana* (#321) and *The Groom Lay Dead* (#502) reflect a talent that showed promise when less restricted. Other favorite series characters of the 1940's were the "Mr. and Mrs." couples of Frances and Richard Lockridge, Kelley Roos, Delano Ames, and James M. Fox. All are literate and fast paced. Too few exist in print today; those by Roos certainly deserve more critical attention. Baynard Kendrick built his novels around a blind private eye, Duncan Maclain, whose two dogs reflect the dichotomy of good and evil. While the character's philosophical musings annoy some readers, the books are usually sound mysteries with interesting solutions.

Some of Dell's mysteries defy characterization. Art critic John Canaday, as Matthew Head, wrote too few mysteries, some of which appeared as Dell mapbacks. Noticeably atypical of 1940's morality, his books rely less on formula plots and more on character development to create psychological tension.

Clayton Rawson's central character is a professional magician, who allows Rawson to use unusual locales such as the circus. Although Rawson's solutions occasionally seem forced, his mysteries usually reward the effort. Dorothy B. Hughes created a kind of "male romance" genre; definitely not ordinary mysteries, hers are challenging and quickly paced. And darker thrillers were available in the Dell line, particularly in David Goodis' *Dark Passage* (#221) and Cornell Woolrich's *The Black Curtain* (#208). But such somber overtones are comparatively rare in Dell mysteries; most are light and determinedly unserious.

As are the romances. These began slowly in the Dell line, disappeared in the mid-1950's, then made a surprising comeback, perhaps influenced by the growing popularity of Harlequin Romances.[4] The romances are short on plot, long on formula; boy meets girl, woos her, marries her, then makes her quit work. The conflict between professional career and housewife reached prototypical perfection in Faith Baldwin's romances. Yet even she occasionally broke out of the mold. In *Rich Girl, Poor Girl* (#196) she creates an entertaining study of a small town; in *The Moon's Our Home* (#368) she fashions a frivolous story of the rich and beautiful, anticipating the light romances of the 1980's. The worst Dell romance may well be Lida Larrimore's *Robin Hill* (#119); it features puerile dialogue and no characterization. Some of the most adult romances are those by Mary Renault and Olive Higgins Prouty; Prouty's *Now, Voyager* (#99) provided the basis for the sensitive, romantic film with Bette Davis.

Westerns steadily increased in popularity, although they unexpectedly declined in the 1960's, perhaps because of the growing influx of science-fiction, which incorporates some of the western's ethics and morality. The usual western formula involves elements of mystery and romance, but in a frontier setting. A hero has a problem, perhaps with cattle rustlers, bandits, corrupt lawmen, or his fiancée; living by a strict code, he has to solve the problem. His enemies, bound by no such code, enjoy freer rein. Good examples of the genre include the Dell titles by Ernest Haycox, Wayne D. Overholser, and Norman A. Fox. Among the best are those by Dan Cushman, who often refuses to take the genre or his characters too seriously. Unusually pessimistic and political is Richard Summers' *Vigilante* (#471); uncommonly suspenseful is Walker A. Tompkins' *West of Texas Law* (#310). Disturbingly violent is Tompkins' *Manhunt West* (#551), where a character shoots a dying man in the head, then guns down a blind preacher, and later plans the murder of the preacher's sister.

After 1951, science-fiction still appeared infrequently in Dell imprints, even though Ace and Ballantine had demonstrated its appeal to readers. Dell experimented instead with "literary" endeavors: *Panorama* (#LC107), an anthology projected in several issues (it ran only one), the Laurel Shakespeare series, the Laurel Poetry series, and various author series such as the Laurel Jane Austen and the Laurel Hawthorne. All were the idea of Frank E. Taylor.

Two novels were inspired by comic strips—*Blondie and Dagwood's Footlight Folly* and *Dick Tracy and the Woo-Woo Sisters*. Of the latter, the ghost-author, Albert Stoffel, comments:

I did write this book, although I believe Chester Gould is credited as being the author. At the time I wrote this book the expression "woo woo" was one the boys hanging around the drugstore used when a good-looking chick went by. Later they used that familiar two-toned whistle.

Dick Tracy and the Woo-Woo Sisters really was written around the title. Lloyd Smith, who at that time was in charge of editorial preparation of Dell books, picked out the title and I took it from there. As I recall it now, the "Woo-Woo Sisters" were twins and became involved in some sort of fracas with a crooked night club owner. Dick Tracy of course came to the rescue.[5]

Many of the earlier Dell anthologies were "collected" by celebrities such as Orson Welles, Alfred Hitchcock, and Gene Autry. (Autry's rival, Roy Rogers, selling well in Dell comics, wanted a paperback anthology; none appeared.) These individuals were generally pleased by the ghosted anthologies, especially Hitchcock. Only Orson Welles changed any of the prefatory material—in his case, just one sentence.[6]

Later anthologies depended less on genre. Edward Parone comments:

Yes, I *did* edit *Six Great Modern Plays* [Dell First Edition #FE100]—*without credit*—since I was an in-house staff editor. I also edited & selected *Six Great Modern Short Novels* [Dell First Edition #F35]—also without credit. . . . The above . . . books I was totally responsible for. Among the other books I served as in-house editor on (that is, the books all had credited authors with whom I worked) were *Short Story Masterpieces* Edited by Albert Erskine and Robert Penn Warren [Dell First Edition #F16]; *Six Centuries of Great Poetry* Edited by Erskine and Warren [Dell First Edition #FE69]; *Thirteen Great Stories* Edited by Daniel Talbot [Dell First Edition #D99]—and to which I contributed the stories by Saul Bellow, Katherine Anne Porter (her second in paperback, after *Six Great Modern Short Novels*) and the then-new James Agee "The Morning Watch" which was his first reprint ever and the only way an "unknown" author like him could be reprinted in paperback in those days—(the same can be said about all the writers in *Six Great Modern Short Novels*) and *City of Love* Edited by Daniel Talbot [Dell First Edition #45]—to which my contribution was an original piece written at my request by the then-unknown James Baldwin, a friend, who was then living and broke in Paris.

There were others, of course, but only the few are still in print, which I find amazing—and these others because it was the first time many of these writers were for sale in drugstores and airports. It was just the beginning for paperbacks, and particularly for Dell—up to then a mass market reprinter of mysteries and crossword puzzles—to begin publishing literature. It was an exciting time.[7]

Motion-picture tie-ins occasionally appeared before 1952. One—Don Ward's anonymous novelization of Hitchcock's film, *Rope* (#262)—contains an inside joke, where two characters discuss actors in a Hitchcock film (see p. 62 of the book). Such tie-ins increased in later years, after a drought in the early 1950's. Three authors comment:

[Robert Terrall:] About *Moses and the Ten Commandments* [#B105]: that was a tie-in, of sorts, with a [Cecil B.] De Mille movie. Tie-ins have gone up and down over the years. . . . De Mille had a low opinion of paperbacks, so this had to be worked around him, through his PR people. A man named Paul Ilton had come to Dell with an idea for a novel about Moses' mother. . . . Ilton was a Viennese who claimed to have been a correspondent in Cairo. I doubt it. He had the Nile run from east to west, for example. He couldn't write English at all. I was supposed to turn his chapters into publishable prose as they came in—there was a big rush to get the book out to coincide with the release of the picture. He started writing about how corpses were embalmed. Five chapters later, he was still writing about how corpses were embalmed. It was completely unusable, and his facts were all wrong. He hadn't even bothered to read an encyclopedia article. The editors realized they'd been taken, and there was a lot of commotion for a time. An Egyptologist from Columbia was brought in. He was shown Ilton's manuscript and turned pale. Terrall was absolutely right, he declared. The Nile runs from south to north. So we threw out Ilton's stuff and I wrote the book as fast as I could. That was why the copyright was taken in Knox Burger's name. . . .

It didn't do very well, as a matter of fact, perhaps because the tie-in wasn't official. But Knox was grateful to me for saving them from something worse. . . .[8]

[Jean Francis Webb:] The three novelizations [*Little Women* (#296), *King Solomon's Mines* (#433), *Anna Lucasta* (#331)] were the only ones I did in book form for Dell. All of them were adapted from actual shooting scripts. In the case of

Little Women particularly, but also in the others, the studio had made many changes from the original. New treatments to jibe with the released films were thus made necessary. . . .

As to the three paperbacks, they were all done on tight deadlines because publication of each book had to coincide with the film's release date—much as they do nowadays, when novelization rights are unobtainable because studios demand a big slice of the action and the take. As I remember it, three weeks was about my allowed book-writing time. . . .

I was called in following *King Solomon's Mines* for a preliminary screening of another film I was to fictionize—a Ginger Rogers picture [*Storm Warning*] connected (incredibly) with the Ku Klux Klan. Before I began work, the project was called off with a blunt explanation that suddenly they had discontinued film novelizations. For a long time they indeed did none.[9]

[Victor Chapin, on his adaptation of *Career* (#B148):] I relied much more on the play. There was a certain amount of telescoping to do as the play covered a much longer time span than the film. Strangely, as it happened, I never saw either the play or the movie.[10]

Dell had many bestsellers prior to 1953. Representative titles, in order of sales, include Jack Lait and Lee Mortimer, *Chicago Confidential* (#D101), Lait and Mortimer, *Washington Confidential* (#D108), Lait and Mortimer, *New York: Confidential!* (#400, #440, and #534), Rosamond Marshall, *Celeste the Gold Coast Virgin* (#382), Edison Marshall, *Yankee Pasha* (#353 and #422), Dashiell Hammett, *A Man Called Spade* (#90, #411, and #452), Brett Halliday, *The Private Practice of Michael Shayne* (#23 and #429), Kathleen Rafferty, *Dell Crossword Dictionary* (#434), John Steinbeck, *To a God Unknown* (#358 and #407), Mary Roberts Rinehart, *The Window at the White Cat* (#57 and #506), Agatha Christie, *Sad Cypress* (#172 and #529), A. A. Fair, *Spill the Jackpot* (#109), Rex Stout, *Too Many Cooks* (#45 and #540), E. M. Hull, *The Sheik* (#174), Brett Halliday, *Murder Wears a Mummer's Mask* (#78 and #388), W. Somerset Maugham, *Mrs. Craddock* (#D106), Brett Halliday, *Murder and the Married Virgin* (#128 and #323), A. A. Fair, *Turn on the Heat* (#59 and #620), Edison Marshall, *The Upstart* (#233 and #341), and Edison Marshall, *Great Smith* (#D102).

Representative non-bestsellers include H. G. Wells, *The First Men in the Moon* (#201), Emile Zola, *The Human Beast* (#608), Gaston Leroux, *The Phantom of the Opera* (#24), Gottfried Leske, *I Was a Nazi Flier* (#21), Robert Trumbull, *The Raft* (#26), John MacCormac, *This Time for Keeps* (#32), Stanley Johnston, *Queen of the Flat-Tops* (#37), Samuel Hopkins Adams, *The Harvey Girls* (#130), Dr. Clifford R. Adams and Vance O. Packard, *How to Pick a Mate* (#224), Hervey Allen, *Anthony Adverse* (#281, #283, and #285), Kay Summersby, *Eisenhower Was My Boss* (#286), Sterling North, *So Dear to My Heart* (#291), Jean Francis Webb, *Little*

the 10¢ series. All books were saddle-stitched, had unstained edges and decorated single-sheet endpapers, and were 64 pages each (although not all were paginated). One welcome feature was an inside blurb about the author of each book, a feature Dell used in no other series.

Allan Barnard conducted most of the research and wrote most of the author blurbs. Barnard tried unsuccessfully to get one of James Jones' stories for the series; he believes Charles Scribner's Sons discouraged Jones. Other titles planned for the 10¢ series were James M. Cain's "The Girl in the Storm," which along with four other Cain stories was also planned as a Dell 25¢ book; both stories from Donald Hamilton's *Murder Twice Told* (#577); all three Rex Stout stories in *3 Doors to Death* (#626), although only the first appeared as a 10¢ book; A. G. Cronin's "Child of Compassion"; and some of Baynard Kendrick's Duncan Maclain detective stories. Also planned was Dashiell Hammett's "The Girl with Silver Eyes," from *Hammett Homicides* (#223). In fact, artist Victor Kalin remembers executing a cover for the proposed edition: "As I recall, the painting was of a blonde young lady firing a pistol from the position on the ground behind the front wheel of a car. I don't have any sketches for the cover and I can't recall ever having seen any proofs of it."[1]

In 1951, Western also printed a small series of "Catechetical Guild Society" books (also called Guild Family Readers), books similar in size and format to the Dell 10¢ books. One has a cover portrait of Moses by Stanley Borack, an artist frequently used by Dell. The books sold for 15¢. Another Dell 15¢ book similar to the 10¢ entries was *Gable's Secret Marriage* (1951), apparently a one-shot.

DELL FIRST EDITIONS

Western and Dell planned a line of first edition paperbacks as early as Spring, 1951, but did not effect such a line until 1952, and did not formally announce it until May 30, 1953, in *Publishers Weekly*. Knox Burger was the editor of Dell First Editions; he was hired by George Delacorte, who was impressed by the success of Fawcett's Gold Medal paperback originals. Burger had been fiction editor at *Collier's* until the summer of 1952. Initially there was some difficulty about hiring Burger; under the terms of Western's contract with Dell, only Western staff produced the books, so Burger had to be officially hired by Western.[2]

Burger planned four paperback originals every month. He wanted books "with some action in them, [books with] plausible plotting, books in which a non-literary reader could suspend his natural disbelief and keep on turning the pages." He was not interested primarily in genre fiction or in any "semi-pornography." The line stressed variety: collections of stories, anthologies, later some genre fiction, even science-fiction, which Burger and his associates "disguised" to pass through

Western and Dell. (Two such covers grace Jack Finney's *The Body Snatchers* [First Edition #42] and Kendell Foster Crossen's *Year of Consent* [First Edition #32.]) Arlene Donovan went to science-fiction conventions to scout for likely titles, and worked on the popular science-fiction anthologies edited by Judith Merril.[3] Mysteries included those by John D. MacDonald, whom Burger lured from Gold Medal with higher advances; later, when Burger left Western/Dell for Gold Medal, MacDonald went with him. Occasionally, Burger remembers, "we'd slip in something of a higher order," although those titles properly belonged to Frank Taylor's Laurel Editions. Some crossovers occurred: Burger did *Panorama* (#LC107, edited by R. F. Tannenbaum) for Laurel and prepared John Cunningham's *Warhorse* (#D177) for the 35¢ reprint series.

Burger pressed for a price higher than 25¢, but Dell executives vetoed the idea. Instead, the first run of Dell First Editions used mixed prices; most sold for 25¢, a few for 35¢ and 50¢. Some appeared simultaneously in hard-cover: "books which we originated and then planted in hardback, including a couple of awfully good books." Gordon Forbes' *Too Near the Sun* (Dell First Edition #D56) is such a title. A few of the titles were paperback originals only in the United States; C. S. Forester's *Plain Murder* (Dell First Edition #30) had earlier been published in England. The standard advance for First Edition manuscripts was $2,500-$3,000, somewhat less for non-fiction. Royalties were a standard 4 percent on printings. Printing runs averaged 200,000; returns averaged about 20-30 percent.

Many of the manuscripts originated from literary agents such as Scott Meredith, Don Congdon, and Max Wilkinson. Harold R. Daniels' *In His Blood* (First Edition #73) was the only manuscript to arrive with a knife attached to the text. A few books originated in-house: for example, *What, When, Where and How to Drink* (Dell First Edition #55), by Richard L. Williams, who worked on Dell magazines, and David Myers, his assistant. *Poker According to Maverick* (#B142), a bestseller, has a curious history: August Lenniger, the literary agent, had for sale a standard poker book by J. Hoyt Cummings, one that had been lying around for several years; Burger bought it for $1,000, had it thoroughly revised by Pete Margolies in the words of the television character Bret Maverick, then sold the book to Kaiser Aluminum, who added their advertisements to several editions of the book and used it in promotional giveaways. Burger also travelled several times each year to Hollywood to search out possible movie tie-ins: "I got them for practically nothing."

Burger pressed for printing dates as well as larger prices. He believes that Western did not include exact printing dates on the books' copyright pages (not until 1955) because "they operated on the assumption we could sell the same book to the same customer—or at least some of the same books to some of the same customers—a year or so later if we didn't put on 'second printing.'" This philosophy resembles Delacorte's early ideas about magazines. J. J. Barta of Western and Carl Tobey of Dell disagree; they believe the lack of printing dates reflected both firms' casual attitude toward such matters.[4]

All First Editions were sent in galley form to authors, as Knox Burger recalls:

We used to send long galleys (on the same crummy newsprint the books were printed on) to authors—usually with the admonition to get them back in a week. To California writers this meant proofing them & turning them around in a day or so. As I recall, the Western Printing typesetters were pretty good—more accurate than many typesetters for trade books at the time. I had come to WP&L from a national weekly [*Collier's*], and we tried to exercise more care in pencil-editing and copy-editing than some of those penny-a-word pulp writers had been accustomed to.[5]

The series included many writers who later became well-known—Kurt Vonnegut, Jr., Elmore Leonard, and Richard Jessup, for example. Burger remembers many readers and writers saying or writing to him that "when I saw a [Dell] First Edition I knew it was going to be up to a certain standard and I wasn't going to be terribly disappointed." One dissenter was Ralph Ellison, who complained to Frank Taylor about Fredric Brown's *Madball,* the second First Edition, which he thought in bad taste. In those days Brown was not well known; today his books are sought after by collectors, and *Madball* has the reputation of being an incisive drama of carnival life.

One bestselling author of Dell First Edition mysteries, Frank Kane, is not too well received today. Arlene Donovan edited Kane's books; Burger remembers him as

a kind of a vulgarian. But his books sold. . . . He was an entertaining fellow and wrote very fast, but not real well. I would try to get him to improve. He was a liquor salesman and he was a nice Irish roughneck from Brooklyn who pulled himself up by the bootstraps . . . but he was never going to write any better than what you read.

A few writers appeared only in Dell First Editions: O. G. Benson and Frank Sandiford, the latter as "Paul Warren." But most were seasoned writers, including E. Howard Hunt, whose Dell mysteries appeared under the byline "Robert Dietrich." Donald Fine believes that many writers learned their writing craft through Dell First Editions; he cites the case of Morris L. West, whose first manuscript, *Kundu* (First Edition #A116) came to Dell.[6] A few books in Dell First Editions received the added compliment of being reissued years later in hard-cover: Vonnegut's *The Sirens of Titan* (First Edition #B138, 1959; Houghton

Mifflin, 1961), Berton Roueché's *The Last Enemy* (First Edition #D90, 1956; Harper, 1975?), and James McKimmey's *The Perfect Victim* (First Edition #A159, 1958; T. V. Boardman, 1965), as well as several of John D. MacDonald's novels.

LAUREL EDITIONS

The Laurel Editions, named after Allan Barnard's daughter (born in 1956), were Frank Taylor's idea. Taylor, in the words of one writer, was "a slim, saturnine man who made an impression in the business everywhere he went, but never entered into lengthy alliances."[7] He had been at Reynal & Hitchcock and at Random House, and in Hollywood as a producer from 1948 to 1951. (In 1960 he produced *The Misfits*, with Clark Gable and Marilyn Monroe; in 1961 Arthur Miller's "film-story" was published as a Dell book.) Bennett Cerf advised Taylor to enter the paperback field, then the most active in publishing. Taylor, of a literary bent, sought to bring to Dell his varied, considerable experience. He wanted to prove with Laurel Editions that there "were serious people out there" who would buy pocket editions of good, non-genre books. But he had to secure the permission of both Western and Dell for his projects; and although Western supported him, Dell—particularly Helen Meyer—was hard to convince:

About one third of my staff's time was spent educating Dell to the fact that there was a world out there that *needed*, and would appreciate, such books. And by that time Pocket Books and other series had done all the classics—there was no need in re-tooling the classics (although later we did our share). . . . So at that time we were attempting to be more creative in what we put together.[8]

Taylor remembers that Dell was quick to take credit for Laurel's success. Delacorte bragged to Taylor, "You've made me a millionaire." Taylor began by buying reprint rights (arranged by Allan Barnard) to nine novels by Evelyn Waugh, for $40,000—the beginning of "quality in the line." Discarding genre fiction as much as he could, Taylor arranged for publication such items as an anthology of short stories edited by Robert Penn Warren and Albert Erskine, an anthology still in print.

Printing runs of Laurel editions varied a great deal, but in general they were less than for books in other series. Sales were at first difficult to estimate, but Taylor believes that Dell's placing fifth or sixth in sales (compared to other paperback publishers) in 1952, when he began, and second or third in 1962, two years after he left, was influenced by the sales of Laurel Editions.

John Ferrone edited the Laurel line; various individuals controlled the special sub-series. One of them, Richard Wilbur, discusses the Laurel Poetry series:

I was approached, regarding what became the Laurel Poetry series, by my friend Frank Taylor (who had been an editor at Reynal & Hitchcock in the latter 40's, when R & H published my first book) and his associate Richard Fisher. As I recall, they were not themselves on the staff at Dell, but thought up the idea of the series, enlisted my services, and then produced it for Dell. They were delightful to work with, and gave me free rein. At some point, Dell took direct control over the Laurel series, and I worked for some years with an agreeable man named Richard Huett. With Huett, however, I had or began to have less freedom to make decisions, and my impression is that his superiors had set limits to the series and warned him to keep it profitable. On one occasion Huett and I had lunch with one of his superiors: he was a young man who kept looking at his watch, and I think his name was [Ross] Claiborne; he did not seem particularly literary, and I blame not Huett but hustlers . . . for the fact that the poetry series never included volumes of such poets as Sidney or Burns.[9]

OTHER SERIES

The Sunrise Semester Library was a tie-in with the "Sunrise Semester" programs on WCBS-TV in New York in the 1950's. Floyd Zulli initiated the television series; David H. Greene edited the books. The Sunrise Semester editions, which were discussed or recommended on the programs, appeared in various price lines of Laurel Editions.

Visual Books began in July, 1959, when Western arranged contracts with Frédéric Ditis, of Switzerland, to publish a series of graphic books of general knowledge to be known as Alpha Books. They would be published by Dell and Golden Press. Nine books were planned; four appeared before mid-1962, two after that date. The series sold for 95¢ each and was published abroad as well: in France by Gallimard, in Germany by Droemer, and in Italy by Feltrinelli.[10]

Special Student Editions were published by various paperback companies as part of the Small Books Program of the Information Center Service of the U.S. Information Agency. Inexpensive reprints were made available in the Near and Far East, South America, and other parts of the world; the books sold through local bookstores. Dell contributed several books to the program.

Digest-sized books appeared occasionally under the Dell imprint. The most successful series was *Zane Grey's Western Magazine*; edited by Don Ward, it ran for eight years, from 1946 to 1954. The magazine featured stories and articles, abridged novels of Zane Grey (often abridged by Allan Barnard), and drawings and fillers. For a while, *ZGWM* had four pictorial covers: color on front and back, black-and-white on the front inside and rear inside. Artists such as Earl Sherwan and Robert Abbett painted covers.

Another popular series was the sports annuals, the best known the *Major League Baseball* annual, which began in 1937 as a radio premium book for P. Lorilard Co., which made Old Gold Cigarettes. The books first appeared under Western's Whitman imprint; in 1946 they became Dell books. The format changed considerably under the editorial staff of H. G. Salsinger, sports editor of *The Detroit News*; Harry Heilmann, former baseball star; and Don Black, of Western. In 1939 Western published a Centennial Edition, commemorating the 100th anniversary of baseball. Western sent the edition to fans who submitted by mail dimes and Old Gold wrappers.[11]

Western and Dell also experimented with various one-shot magazines or short-lived series. Most collectible today are the two "Told-in-Pictures" books, which are digest-sized comic-book adaptations of novels. Four books were planned for the series, but sales were low and the books difficult to market, too large for regular pocket-book racks and too small for comic racks. In 1950, Don Ward planned an "Alfred Hitchcock Suspense Magazine" as a Dell imprint, but it never appeared.[12]

5

Dell Paperbacks, 1962-1982

The unusual relationship between Western and Dell broke up in November, 1960. Dell assumed all editorial and artistic control of the books; Western became printers only, as they are today, under a new, non-exclusive contract dated November 17, 1960. Thereafter Western renewed its printing contract with Dell at regular intervals. Donald I. Fine feels that the earlier contract was the best thing that ever happened to Western, who produced books that were guaranteed sellers—to Dell, that is. Mark M. Morse remembers fighting at Western to get that company into production of its own line of paperbacks.[1] It had, after all, the considerable talents of Frank E. Taylor, Knox Burger, Walter Brooks, Marc Jaffe, Allan Barnard, and many others. But Western chose not to; the above-mentioned people left Western shortly after the break, and Dell brought in its own staff to produce the Dell books.

Morse thinks that *Return to Peyton Place* forced the break. Dell badly wanted reprint rights to the book, and Western was having trouble negotiating them, so Dell went after the rights by itself. After successfully doing so, Dell, primarily in the person of Helen Meyer, felt that it had grown up, that it no longer needed Western to do its editorial and artistic work. Delacorte remembers that at the time Dell personnel were gradually beginning to assume more and more control. Whether or not the Metalious book was the reason, the break seems to have been inevitable. In January, 1961, Western formally turned over to Dell all contracts and publishing rights to the books it had produced since 1942. For a while a semantic argument raged at Western over the actual identity of the publisher of those books—Western, who had edited and designed them, or Dell, who distributed them.[2] But it was decided that Western had bought the titles for Dell, who then published them under their imprint. Dell was thus indisputably the publisher.

After the break, Donald Fine became editor-in-chief of Dell Books.

Arlene Donovan was editor-in-chief of Dell First Editions, which lasted formally only until 1963; Ross Claiborne was editor-in-chief of Laurel Editions; Rolf Erickson was art director (replaced shortly afterward by John Van Zwienen); Robert Scudellari was production design manager. Most of the other names familiar throughout these chapters played little part in the production of Dell paperbacks after 1962.

A part of Western's 1962 annual report may shed some light on that firm's reaction to the break:

In July 1962, Western took over the publishing of comic books, which for many years previously had been created and sold on a commercial printing basis to an independent publishing company. Earlier, Western had discontinued as the originator of conventional pocket-type books for this same publisher and, under the terms of a ten-year printing contract, confined its activities to the printing of such books.[3]

The name Dell appears nowhere in that report.

Western continues to prosper today, both in its own consumer lines and in the commercial work it produces for other companies. It still prints the Dell books, still produces the popular Whitman books and Golden Press, still expands into new markets. In July, 1960, the firm adopted the name of Western Publishing, Inc., with its predecessor company, Western Printing & Lithographing, continuing as the principal operating unit of the company. In June, 1979, Western was bought by Mattel, the giant toy company that makes Barbie Dolls, for a reported $120.8 million.

Dell has also prospered, becoming one of the giants in mass-market publishing. After 1962, the company experimented with a variety of new lines and expanded previous lines. In 1963, "Every Child's First Color and Learn Book Series" was inaugurated, for members of "the crayon set." The books were 50¢ each, 8" x 10", 40 pages long, and included introductory material by Vera V. Vilirgas. For older children, the Home Activity Series was begun in 1979. Designed "to provide children with a truly exciting and original approach to learning basic educational skills," according to the promotional advertisements, the series featured striking graphics on such titles as *Paper Projects, Cats, Phonics, Spelling,* and *Metrics.* For ages 2-8 (in elementary grades), the Yearling Books provided classic and contemporary fiction. In a 5⅛" x 7⅝" format, the series spotlighted works by Robert Lawson, Kenneth Grahame, E. B. White, Lois Lenski, A. A. Milne, and Judy Blume, as well as the "Paddington Bear" series by Michael Bond. Prices ranged from $1.50 to $2.95; occasional oversized books were higher. In 1982, Dell boasted 75 million Yearlings in print.

A short-lived series began in 1963—Clover Books, changed to Dell Seal

Books when Dell learned that Grosset & Dunlap had earlier published a similarly named line of children's books. These were paperback originals, 4¾" x 7⅝", 35¢ each, for ages 8-12. At least eight titles appeared. More successful was the line of Harlin Quist, named after its editor and creator. Begun in 1964, these paperback juveniles (which appeared also in library binding) featured "quality format." The first title in this two-color series was Lewis Carroll's *Jabberwocky and More Nonsense*.

Older children were the market for Dell's Laurel-Leaf Library, an offshoot of Laurel Editions. Begun in March, 1963, for the 11-17 age group, the line was edited by M. Jerome Weiss. The first title was Weiss' *Men and War*; later books include fiction such as Nat Hentoff's *Jazz Country* and Paul Zindel's *The Pigman*. As of 1975, the leading title was S. E. Hinton's *The Outsiders*. Included in the line was George Bennett's *Great Tales of Action and Adventure*, in print since 1958. Most of the titles were well produced; one rare exception is *Pelé*, by Claire and Frank Gault; for 95¢, the 64-page book offered only about 7,000 words and unexciting illustrations. In 1966, Mayflower Books (no relationship to the British firm) was incorporated as part of the Laurel-Leaf Library. Edited by Weiss, Charles Reasoner, and Ned E. Hoopes, Mayflower Books began with titles by Rosemary Sutcliff. Intended as "a new series of leisure-line paperbacks for young people," they sold for 50¢ each. The latest addition to Laurel-Leaf (in mid-1982) is the "Young Love" series, tame romances for adolescents. Dell overlooked no age group and no interest of any age group.

High school and college students provided the primary market for Laurel Editions, begun in 1958 by Frank E. Taylor and continued by Richard Huett and Ross Claiborne. In 1961, Huett joined Dell as a senior editor of Laurel: "This was just after Dell's divorce from Western Publishing, and they had a publishing company with hardly any staff."[4] Huett helped to develop more series within Laurel, including the Laurel Language Library, with foreign-language texts for students; a six-volume series on *20,000 Years of World Painting*; the Laurel Classical series, edited by Robert W. Corrigan; and the Laurel Dickens series, whose editor, Edgar Johnson, restored original texts to the volumes. Some of the original Laurel series remained, including those on Shakespeare, Poetry, and the expanded short stories series from different countries. In 1972, two authors surveying the educational lines of paperback companies felt that "Dell has perhaps the most impressive record of all the mass market publishers for developing a number of series geared to student use."[5] In October, 1982, Laurel Editions incorporated a changed logo and new uniform cover formats.

As with all Dell lines, mass market or educational, Laurel required substantial sales, revealed in comments by its editor, Ross Claiborne:

The preponderance of the list is classics, our series of short stories, our Shakespeare and poetry series. These, of course, are widely used in high schools and colleges. Now that we are so well entrenched in the colleges and secondary schools, the Laurel line is real money in the bank. Every semester there are more reorders, and virtually no returns. Often the initial cost of a book is high, but the books pay off on continual reprintings. Many of our books have been on our backlist for six to eight years with sales increasing each year.[6]

Supermarkets became a prime market for another fast-growing line—Purse Books, tiny 64-page books that sold for 25¢, then for 35¢ and 49¢, today for 69¢. Most of the titles offered self-help for women: books on astrology, dieting, calorie counting, exercising, naming babies, and crossword puzzles. *Count Your Calories* and *3500 Names for Baby*, early titles, are still in print. Many were anonymously written; others featured writers like Dr. Joyce Brothers. Purse Books were challenged in the 1980's by Globe Mini Mags, selling for 59¢ and 69¢.

Dell experimented with other lines. In 1965, in connection with The American Heritage Publishing Company, Dell published a series of hardcover books on the 50 states, to be sold in supermarkets for 99¢ each. In the same year, Dell joined with Children's Hospital Medical Center of Boston to produce "Publications for Parents," a series of hard-covers (from Delacorte Press) and booklets (as Purse Books) on child growth and development. In September, 1966, Dell began Spot Notes, a not-too-successful imitation of Monarch Notes and Cliff Notes; 95¢ each, edited by Joseph Mersand, they were designed for use by high-school and college students. Another imitation flowered as Candlelight Romances, in July, 1967; these resembled Harlequin Romances in both content and cover art. Dell and Vineyard Books combined in April, 1974, to produce a series of paperback encyclopedias (e.g., *The Dell Encyclopedia of Dogs*); attractively designed and printed on durable paper, the books sold for $2.45. A year later, in June, 1975, Dell and Radcliffe College planned a series of autobiographies and biographies geared toward contemporary young women. This, the Radcliffe Biography Series (in paperback and as Delacorte Press imprints), was edited by Merloyd Ludington Lawrence. In 1978, Dell's Ivy Books appeared, spiral-bound books with self-help themes; $1.95 each, they apparently lasted only a short time, as did many of these series, with the exception of Candlelight Romances and the Radcliffe Biography Series.

More important innovations arrived in the form of Delta Books and Delacorte Press, both planned as early as 1962. Delta Books, introduced on September 26, 1962, featured paperbacks of larger format (5⅜'' x 8''), higher price ($1.45 to $3.75, initially), durable format (pages bound into linen spines), and sober, restrained cover art. Most of the titles were non-fiction, although the first two titles were Katherine Anne Porter's *The Leaning Tower and Other Stories* and James Baldwin's *Nobody Knows My*

Name. Delta Books was jointly conceived by Claiborne and Huett, in order to set up a rival for the paperbacks of Anchor, Vintage, and Grove. Aimed at the college market, Delta experienced its breakthrough when it published Eldridge Cleaver's *Soul on Ice,* for which Huett bought reprint rights for $2,000. Allan Barnard missed that one. Delta sales increased by inclusion of titles by Kurt Vonnegut, Jr. As of 1975, Delta planned little new fiction; it emphasized education and psychology.[7] Current Delta fiction authors are Vonnegut, Richard Brautigan, Thomas Berger, and Jim Harrison.

Delacorte Press, a line of hard-cover books, was set up in 1963 to allow Dell to retain reprint royalties, which Dell normally paid to hard-cover publishers. The move prompted similar actions from other paperback companies. The first Delacorte title was to be Louis Untermeyer's *An Uninhibited Treasury of Erotic Poetry.* But the more restrained *The Jet Set* by Burton Wohl replaced it, on February 18, 1964. Jointly overseen by Ross Claiborne and Donald I. Fine, Delacorte Press gradually expanded into a distinguished hard-cover line. One of its early hard-cover titles was *For Women Only,* by Dr. Bernard L. Cinberg, who had earlier written romances for Dell First Editions as "Russell Boltar." Two sub-imprints appeared: "A Seymour Lawrence Book—Delacorte Press" in 1965; "Delacorte Press—Eleanor Friede Books" in 1973. (Friede's first title was Richard Bach's *A Gift of Wings*; at Macmillan, she had discovered Bach's *Jonathan Livingston Seagull.*) In 1966 Delacorte Press began "Books for Young Readers," a line of original children's books. Current Delacorte Press titles are the Reinhart series (four books) by Thomas Berger and the newest novel by Kurt Vonnegut, Jr.—*Deadeye Dick.* The latter was available (in 1982) in a $14.95 trade edition as well as in a limited, signed, slipcased edition for $75—the most expensive Dell book yet published.

In 1964, Helen Meyer boasted of Dell's success and speculated on its future:

Our philosophy is to gamble, and our policy is to invest in new projects. As they take off, we look around to see what else we can do. For instance, although it's relatively new with us, we're in hardcover books to stay, and will let this end of the business go where it will. This is the pattern Dell has always followed.

We are the largest mass-market publisher in the world. We are the only publisher with mass-market paperbacks, higher-priced quality paperbacks, hardcover books, magazines, comics and even purse books.[8]

Dell's staple remained its regular series of Dell Books, the reprints. Genre fiction continued after 1962; in 1980 Dell initiated a dual series of "Scene of the Crime" mysteries and "Murder Ink." mysteries, each chosen by the proprietor of a bookshop specializing in mystery fiction.

The graphics were impressive (praised by Gerald Gregg, who painted most of the early Dell airbrushed covers), and titles were literate. Attractive art also combined with readable books in special science-fiction and fantasy lines, including some by Vonnegut, with whom Dell signed a million-dollar contract in January, 1972. Dell even began, in 1982, "Twilight," a series of horror novels "without the use of violence, religious overtones, or explicit sexual language" for young adults, ages 10-14. Candlelight Romances continued, adding a racy sub-line, Candlelight Ecstasy Romances. And westerns made a comeback; some of Wayne D. Overholser's books appeared with new covers using paintings by Frederic Remington. In February, 1974, Dell claimed that Overholser titles had sold in excess of 5 million.

Yet overall, the Dell books produced from 1962 to 1982 do not stand out significantly from the output of other publishers. Despite the varying books in Laurel, Delta, and Delacorte, all resemble the books of other publishers. Besides genre fiction, Dell published the expected number of unauthorized biographies of celebrities (Albert G. Gerber's *Bashful Billionaire*, about Howard Hughes), movie tie-ins (The Beatles in *Help!*, and D. M. Perkins' *Deep Throat*), titillating titles (Xaviera Hollander's *The Happy Hooker*), southern melodramas (Frank Yerby's *The Girl from Storyville*), and many trendy books, such as an exposé of *Playboy* magazine and *Generation Rap* (edited by Gene Stafford), the latter a Laurel-Leaf book.

More literate titles did appear. Reference works included the 2,016-page *Columbia-Viking Desk Encyclopedia*, selling modestly for $1.95 in 1964. It was the longest book then published.[9] Political titles included Theodore H. White's *Breach of Faith*, a study of Richard Nixon's downfall. Historical titles included Arnold Toynbee's *A Study in History*, attractively packaged in a two-volume boxed set. Even occasional offbeat titles appeared, such as *The Practical Cogitator or The Thinker's Anthology*, edited by Charles P. Curtis, Jr. and Ferris Greenslet. But for every volume on thinking or history or politics, Dell had dozens of lightweight titles. These were mass-market books, after all.

Dell was always proud of its bestsellers; like many paperback firms, it never tired of telling us so. In the mid-1960's, Dell began taking out advertisements in *Publishers Weekly* and newspapers to list its current bestsellers, beginning with 10, then expanding to 12, because, according to Walter B. J. Mitchell, Jr., vice-president of promotion and advertising, of "an embarrassment of riches."[10] In 1963, Dell bragged that its sales in September and October were the highest for that period in the firm's history; its bestselling book was then *Fail-Safe*, by Eugene Burdick and Harvey Wheeler. Other #1 bestsellers (for Dell alone), as recorded in Dell advertisements, included:

January, 1965 — Irving Shulman, *Harlow* (95¢)

February, 1966 — Morris L. West, *The Ambassador* (95¢)

August and October, 1966 — John Le Carré, *The Looking Glass War* (95¢)

June, 1967 — James Clavell, *Tai-Pan* (95¢)

May, 1968 — Ira Levin, *Rosemary's Baby* (95¢)

May and September, 1969 — Frances Pollini, *Pretty Maids All in a Row* (95¢)

September, 1970 — Michael Crichton, *The Andromeda Strain* ($1.25)

August, 1971 — Lois Gould, *Such Good Friends* ($1.25)

September and October, 1972 — Joseph Wambaugh, *The New Centurions*, and "M.," *The Sensuous Man* ($1.50)

November and December, 1973 — Marilyn Durnham, *The Man Who Loved Cat Dancing* ($1.75)

February and September, 1974 — John Godey, *The Taking of Pelham One Two Three* ($1.75)

April, 1975 — Lonnie Coleman, *Beulah Land* ($1.95), and Joseph Wambaugh, *The Onion Field* ($1.75)

September, 1976 — Irwin Shaw, *Nightwork* ($1.95), and Gerold Frank, *Judy* ($2.50)

August, 1977 — William Goldman, *Magic* ($1.95)

June, 1978 — Danielle Steel, *The Promise* ($1.95)

September, 1979 — John Saul, *Cry for the Strangers* ($2.50)

August, 1980 — John Saul, *Comes the Blind Fury* ($2.75)

February, 1981 — James Clavell, *Shōgun* ($3.50)

July, 1981 — Belva Plain, *Random Winds* ($3.50)

mid-1982 — James Clavell, *Noble House* ($5.95), Adam Smith, *Paper Money* ($3.95), and William Manchester, *American Caesar* ($4.50)

In 1982, Dell had three overall mass-market bestsellers—James Clavell's *Noble House* (#4), Danielle Steel's *A Perfect Stranger* (#5), and Irwin Shaw's *Bread Upon the Waters* (#5)—and one trade paperback bestseller—Danielle Steel's *Once in a Lifetime* (#12).

It would not be expected that all bestselling titles should reflect literary good taste, but in the 1970's Dell and others succumbed to what some critics saw as the nadir of bad taste. In 1971, for example, Dell took Pinnacle Books to court because the latter's *The Sensuous Male* echoed Dell's own *The Sensuous Man*. Neither title approached the explicit sexuality of Xaviera Hollander's *The Happy Hooker* in 1974. Dell had 6,600,000 copies of *Hooker* in print (not necessarily sold), compared to the following titles of other publishers: *Massage Parlor* (Ace; 1,500,000), *Jonathan Livingston Seagull* (Avon; 6,500,000), *The Guinness Book of World Records*, 11th edition (Bantam; 3,600,000); *Semi-Tough* (New American Library; 1,210,000), *The Winds of War* (Pocket Books; 2,200,000), and *Xaviera* (Warner Paperback Library; 3,572,000). One of Dell's overall bestsellers is *The Sensuous Woman* (9,000,000), but also *The American Heritage Dictionary* (10,500,000), *The Dell Crossword Dictionary* (10,400,000), Clavell's *Shōgun* (7,000,000+), and Joseph Heller's *Catch-22* (6,700,000).[11]

Always eager to cash in on what it included sex, Dell in October, 1978, signed as an author Judy Chavez, a "paid companion" to a Soviet defector. William R. Grosse, editor-in-chief of Dell Books, defended the signing, saying that "We have a fine tradition for that kind of book, but we hope this will have more substance."[12] Presumably serious, he may have been referring to Dell's past liaisons with "Happy Hooker" Xaviera Hollander and Elizabeth Ray, whose "novel," *The Washington Fringe Benefit*, provided a thinly disguised account of her sexual exploits on Capitol Hill. Ray had the dubious distinction of deadening both sex and politics. Chavez' autobiography, co-authored by Jack Vitek, was published in 1979, as *Defector's Mistress: The Judy Chavez Story.*

In January, 1978, Dell achieved what *Publishers Weekly* called "a publishing first."[13] Dell marketed John Rechy's *Sexual Overflow* in gay bars and bathhouses. Advertising managers Pat Cool and Scott Jacobson sent Sexual Overflow matchbooks and memo pads to the locales, noting the author as "an important author of homosexual subjects." Inhabitants' reactions are unrecorded.

Nevertheless, Milton Oehler, Dell vice-president, commented in 1980 that "We're very, very choosey about what types of things wear the Dell seal. We accept only clean, quality examples of publishing that we're proud to have carry our name."[14]

Production and distribution of Dell paperbacks became increasingly sophisticated in the 1960's. In 1965 Dell built a new distributing center in Pine Brook, New Jersey. Other centers existed in Chicago, Los Angeles, and Toronto.[15] In October, 1963, Dell had installed a 1410 IBM computer to process orders, so that by 1964 the machines processed an average of 2,000 orders per night.

Dell began to use other printers besides Western. Some in Europe produced their art books. Printers in the United States included Livermore and Knight (Providence, R.I.), Murray Printing (Forge Village, Mass.), Riverside Press (Cambridge, Mass.), Colonial Press (Clinton, Mass.), and Electronic Perfect Binders (Brooklyn, N.Y.). But Western remained the printers of the majority of Dell paperbacks; production of those books at Western's Poughkeepsie plant, in 1980, is described in a contemporary issue of *The Westerner*:

The production of a Dell paperback is unique in that all paper stock is supplied by Dell. Paper rolls arrive via railroad cars, are logged in and stored by material handling for later use.

. . . Dell-supplied paper is transported from inventory to one of four Strachan and Henshaw rotary presses. Outside waste is stripped off the roll and it is mounted onto the press infeed. Tabs and a little paste are used to splice the paper to the roll-on press in order to make a smooth changeover from one roll to assuming the duties of president. But she remained at Dell only a few months; in September, she left for Publishers Clearing House and was replaced by James R. McLaughlin, who remains Dell's president. At that time, Ross Claiborne, long-time Dell employee, left for Warner Books.

In the 1980's, there was reported trouble at Doubleday and Dell. Besides the loss of top people, authors such as Irwin Shaw were deserting or threatening to do so. In 1982, the contracts of Seymour Lawrence and Eleanor Friede were not renewed. And in 1983, across-the-board dismissals of 65-100 people occurred at Dell and Delacorte.[21] Doubleday, which in January, 1980, had acquired the expensive New York Mets baseball team, was, in the words of one observer, unable to keep up "in the expensive bidding wars for blockbuster books."[22] As of this writing (June, 1983), Doubleday and Dell are still together, still functioning, still producing the paperbacks that after 1962 assumed a uniform look. They have not changed substantially since the 1960's, despite the variety of imprints and lines. Gimmicks such as embossed covers and diecuts have appeared on Dell books, but also on other lines. As Oscar Dystel—a person long involved in publishing—comments, "There's a repelling look about the paperback racks today," partially because of "trend publishing, imitative publishing."[23] Nothing today makes the Dells stand out: so unlike the collection of Dell paperbacks of 1942 to 1962 *sui generis*. Part of the reason lies in the artwork and distinctive internal features of the early books; the earliest Dells (1942-1951) featured airbrushed covers, back-cover maps, and character lists, and the later books (1952-1962) used bold new designs.

6

Artwork: The Front Covers

The Dell paperbacks have three distinct periods: 1) the Racine period, from 1942 to 1951, when Western staff edited and designed the books; 2) the New York period, from 1952 to late 1960, when Western staff in New York edited and designed the books; and 3) the New York Dell period, from late 1960 to the present, when Dell staff assumed complete control over the editing and design of the books. Only the first two periods are of central concern in this chapter.

The Racine period features mysteries, westerns, and romances. At first, the books have vivid, vibrant airbrushed covers; later, action illustrations. They have back-cover maps and their title-pages and other front matter are busy and crowded with features such as character lists and "Things this Mystery is about." In the New York period, subject matter varies more; more "literature" is introduced. The books have more illustrative covers, are more varied in scope, but in general are less colorful. They have blurbs, not maps, on the back covers, which are more hastily done. The design and typography is more sparse, more sophisticated. After late 1960, in the New York Dell period, the books become assimilated into the general paperback melting pot.

Both of the central periods can be appreciated by readers and collectors, the first for its Fauvist display of color and more naive internal format, the second for its more subdued but also more sophisticated approach. Neither should suffer in comparison. Although all books produced during these periods bear the Dell imprint, they were produced by different staffs, with different philosophies.

Plans for the first Dell covers began in Racine's Creative Department on or before August, 1942. Gerald Gregg, one of Western's artists, remembers those days:

I will add everything I can remember about this account. Mr. William Strohmer was the Art Director and Mr. George Frederiksen was his assistant. It was decided that to make the books more oustanding a "design" approach would be used instead of the usual illustrative style and that full color airbrush technique would be the finished medium.

Bill and George did all the layouts (or designing) in comprehensive pastel on tissue. These were turned over to me (after an O.K. by Dell), for full color airbrush production paintings done double size. In the few instances where brush painting would be more suitable to the subject—Bill Strohmer or George Frederiksen did the finished art also.

All the lettering was hand lettered by our lettering specialist, Mr. Bernard Salbreiter, now retired.

I followed Bill and George's layouts closely. The use of airbrush in color was unusual then and very rare now. But for a period it was a very popular style. The airbrush is used primarily to retouch photos in black and white. So its use for color painting was unique. I found there was very little published material to help meet the problems in turning the airbrush to color work, so I had to improvise a lot.

Considerable interest developed in our work and it was decided to make a color movie of the techniques I used. The late Robert Bezucha did the photography using an Eastman 16mm. movie camera and telephoto lens for super close-ups. The movie follows the creation of one Dell cover from Frederiksen's designing of the layout to my doing the finish from making the "Frisket" right through every step to the final touch-up. This film was turned over to Western's Training Institute, headed by Mr. Lawrence Brehm (now retired) and soon went out on loan to scores of organizations—such as technical Institutes, Art Schools and Airbrush Companies all over the country. I heard it was even seen in Canada.

Regretfully, this film has disappeared—may have been "double-loaned" without the knowledge of Western.[1]

(The film Gregg mentions was made silent, with subtitles.)

In the 1940's, these four people created the Dell covers: William G. Strohmer, George A. Frederiksen, Gerald Gregg, and Bernard Salbreiter. (See illustration 3.)

Strohmer (1903-1980), art director of Western's Creative Department, was born in Germany and came to Western with newspaper and art studio experience.[2] He was considered by Gregg "the best art director in the country."[3] Strohmer spent a good deal of his time working with customers, although he always considered himself an artist first, then an administrator.

George A. Frederiksen was born in Copenhagen, arriving in Racine when he was four years old. After graduating from high school in 1929, he began work at the Harry Wilson Studios in Racine, then worked in Chicago, where he attended night classes at the American Academy of Art. In 1935, he worked for a studio in South Bend, then joined Western in 1940. He had done paste-ups for Strohmer in 1938 and was not particularly keen to work in his home town, but Strohmer persuaded him to remain at Western, in Racine.[4]

Gerald Gregg was born in Lamar, Colorado, in 1907. He graduated from Racine High School in 1925 and attended Layton School of Art in Milwaukee. After free-lancing in Milwaukee and Racine, Gregg met Ed Ritzman, Western's litho foreman, who introduced Gregg to Sam Lowe, president of Whitman (a subsidiary of Western). During the Depression, Gregg applied to Western for a full-time job, but was offered only a temporary position to fill in for a man on a six-month leave. But the man never returned, and Strohmer liked Gregg's work, so Gregg officially joined Western in May, 1935, as a full-time artist. At one time, he was offered the job of lithographer, because of his intimate acquaintance with color and value, but Gregg disliked the idea of being unionized and felt he could be a better finish artist.[5]

What both Gregg and Frederiksen term the "design" approach to art typifies the early Dell covers. Frederiksen remembers that "We thought the covers should *suggest* the title. . . . We illustrated the title" and that "We tried to make them simple and convey the idea and plot of the story."[6] Strohmer and Frederiksen, supplied by the editorial staff with three situations from each Dell book, made comprehensive layouts of each situation, using pastel on tissue, occasionally adding some pencil sketches of possible variations. After they settled on one sketch, Strohmer took it to Dell's New York offices to secure approval. Occasional rejections came from Fernando Texidor, Dell's art director, who took over from Otto Storch in the 1940's. But the rejections were infrequent; after securing approval, Strohmer returned to Racine, where the finished cover was prepared twice size, usually by Gregg alone. Final versions often differed dramatically from preliminary sketches.

In some cases, Strohmer or Frederiksen finished the cover. Even then, the finish suggested airbrushed work—on the cover of *Dreadful Hollow* (#125), for example, where Frederiksen rubbed in the pastels to give an airbrushed effect; the "eye" of the trompe l'oeil effect was executed in dry-brushed watercolor. (See illustration 4.) Another example of the "Frederiksen style" (Gregg's term) appears on *Blow-Down* (#156). But most of the early in-house work was by Gregg, in color airbrush, an idea suggested by Strohmer (and possibly also by Lloyd Smith) to avoid the usual illustrative approach and attain an eye-catching style. The airbrush was popular in Germany in the 1920's but not often used in color in the United States until the 1930's. The beauty of the airbrush is that, in Gregg's words, "[it] lets the artist paint with soft lines, giving the pictures a soft, full and flowing effect."[7] As a later critic notes:

Airbrush-rendering is tedious. It is a frustrating, elusive, deceptive, mechanical and laborious job. . . .

The attraction of the airbrush-rendering is that it reproduces so well. . . . A finished rendering has a fine grain in the tints and heavy-stain areas on the paper surface, and the color is so translucent and the density so clear that the result is a very refined image. The delicate shades overlap very lightly to create an evaporative highlighting that just sizzles as a finished piece of work.[8]

Gregg's attraction to the airbrush was a result of his mechanical interests and of fate. In the late 1930's, Gregg happened one day to watch a man using the airbrush to re-touch photos. Intrigued, he convinced Russell Stone, then Western's art director, to let him try the technique. Soon Gregg was using the airbrush for covers of Big Little Books, then adapting its use for the Dell covers. The technique was roughly as follows: on a drawing of the sketch on heavyboard paper, Gregg placed a "frisket" (transparent paper coated with one or two coats of rubber cement) over the drawing, smoothing out the wrinkles, then with a frisket knife cut the frisket paper (but not into the drawing), then lifted off the parts he wanted to airbrush, like using a stencil. The airbrush was fastened to an oxygen tank or compressed-air source. The needle on the airbrush he adjusted for air intake and for the amount of color. Applying the color he found time-consuming and very difficult, but rewarding. He soon found he had to use the best pigment (from Pelikan), since coarse color dried up the airbrush. Even the smallest grain presented a problem: if one speck got into the nozzle, the airbrush would spit, then he would have to start from scratch. He prepared one frisket for each color used, one after another. For a while, Gregg was the only artist at Western who would use the airbrush. He averaged three to five days for each Dell cover.

Gregg's wife, Nell, remembers that he often worked so hard on the artwork that he forgot quitting time at the abandoned shirt factory where the art department was temporarily located in the 1940's. Such "overtime" presented a problem because of the tight security at Western during World War II; in addition to using maps on the Dell books, Western prepared many maps used by the Armed Services—maps used for bombing runs over Germany, for example. The usual work schedule, Gregg recalls, was 8 A.M. to 5 P.M., a quick meal at a hamburger stand, then off to extra work in the shipping department until 11:00. (Men were in short supply at the plant, and the work was considered too heavy for women.) Finished covers were made into negative transparencies on aluminum litho plates at both the Racine and Poughkeepsie plants, and run off at Poughkeepsie. Original art was stored for a while at Racine, much of it later thrown away, and what remained given away to Western employees in 1976. (At least 41 paintings survive, including 20 by Gregg, 11 by Earl Sherwan, and one each by Strohmer and Frederiksen. I own 24 of these; Gregg owns the others, some of which he recently sold.)

Gregg calls the Dell covers he did "stylized realism." He names as influences on his work American realists such as Norman Rockwell, Winslow Homer, and Andrew Wyeth, as well as Ingres, Renoir, Monet,

Gauguin, and Grant Wood; their influence, however, is not always apparent in his Dell work, much of which is refreshingly new. Other influences seem to be Salvador Dali and the Art Deco posters of the 1920's and 1930's, particularly those by Cassandre (Adolphe Jean-Marie Moron). Gregg's work resembles in a sense Minimal Art, with its stress on simple color relationships and geometric forms; one could as easily label it Neoplasticism, since it often reduces form to simple movements and concentrates on primary colors; or even Surrealism, Magic Realism, or Neoromanticism. But it makes little difference. More important is to recognize the vibrant, intense movement in his work, the brilliant color, the varying approaches for different genres of fiction. Like earlier painters working within the patron system, Gregg's content was determined in advance, so he was free to concentrate on his medium.[9] And as Gregg notes, "I like to splurge in color and design." The Dell covers allowed such a splurge.

A common prejudice against illustrators, voiced by art critic John Canaday in *What Is Art?*, is that "an illustration [takes] second place to something else rather than existing as an independent creation"; Canaday objects to the works of Norman Rockwell, for example, because "enjoyment at their level is nothing more than a stirring up of stock responses to stock subjects."[10] But Gregg's paintings can exist independently from the books, and they certainly attempt new views of old subjects, in the process drawing on stock responses but always existing to tease, shock, and make the reader/viewer pay attention. What is offered for sale in the Dells is not just the paperbacks, but the covers—innovative, provocative, and bold, so unclassical and new in their appeal to the senses, in their suggestion of quick thrills.

Consider the following Gregg covers:

She Ate Her Cake (#186), one of the few "split covers" used by Dell. Gregg pasted a torn sheet of white paper atop the airbrushed cover to allow the lettering (by Bernard Salbreiter) to be done this size. The airbrushed woman—based, like most of Gregg's women, on one of the secretaries at Western—is a familiar figure on pulp and mystery covers: the femme fatale, scantily clad, armed with gun, simultaneously alluring and threatening. Gregg gives the figure new life by airbrushing a translucent shadow over part of the face and most of the body, softening the effect, even suggesting a veil. Such a presentation makes ordinary objects and people appear abstract and surreal. Like many Gregg paintings, this is naturalistic in its use of normal-size objects and of light; the focus is upon the person, through diagonal lines and warm colors. (Although the left arm may be in an anatomically awkward position, it does emphasize the jutting breast.) Color deceives: the background green, hardly noticed at first, gently complements and accents the female form. (See illustration 5.)

The Crooking Finger (#104), a classic mystery cover, where people are dwarfed by events and objects beyond their control, here by the title's literal "crooking finger" of the green skeleton hand (a common Gregg motif). Light strikes the hand from several directions but hits the threatened couple only from the direction of the hand, leading the viewer's eye to the diagonal contrast of the lines formed by the fingers. The complementary contrast of green hand and red dress might suffice for color contrast, the red of the title letters unneeded, and actually blending a bit awkwardly into the airbrushed background of low-value red-orange. Gregg thinks the color of the letters an error by Western's ink man. (See illustration 6.)

Half Angel (#118), for which Gregg pasted a paper doily onto the bottom of the painting—"resorting to tricks of the time to get the effects I wanted." Here, reflected light, soft lines, and analogous pastel hues give a softened effect. The champagne glass dwarfs the "half angel" (who is given an extremely sensual outline), the tilt preventing the painting from being too softened or too saccharine. (See illustration 7.)

Juliet Dies Twice (#68), showing Gregg's fascination with portraits of beautiful women. A deceptively simple arrangement of split tones, the cover was executed in both airbrush and drybrush, the latter used for the green hair and fringe outline.

Wiped Out (#165), a warm, arid cover, perfect for a book about the Foreign Legion. The analogous yellows and oranges of the sky reach to the face, hands, and rifle of the lone legionaire; the essentially diagonal lines of the soldier are offset by those of the title's letters, which Gregg thinks too scanty for the space he allowed for lettering. (See illustration 8.)

Fear and Trembling (#264), with a deliberately exaggerated approach, which to Gregg illustrates "the way you feel when you see one of Hitchcock's movies." Here the lettering fills up the space left by Gregg.

Appointment with Death (#105), one of Gregg's striking low-key covers. He painted the buildings first, then the red mountains, finally the figure—for the transparent effects. The cover succinctly expresses impending doom with its overcast sky, personified Death on a walkway, the suggestion of subtly disappearing features within the figure of Death. A perfectly balanced cover (in a classical sense), it is both balanced and cluttered, yet still vitally interesting and appealing. (See illustration 9.)

Jokes, Gags and Wisecracks (#152), for which Gregg followed Strohmer's cover sketch exactly. That he did and produced such an odd, chilling view of laughter suggests that Gregg's frequent departures from Strohmer's sketches may have been fortunate. (See illustration 10.)

Cold Steal (#142), a superb trompe l'oeil, suggests key items in the mystery novel. For the lipstick, Gregg formed surgical gauze into a lip-shaped stencil, through which he blew red watercolor onto the cover. The blue lettering on the original painting (owned by the artist) changed to white on the reproduction—one of the few color changes from painting to cover that can be verified. (See illustration 11.)

Bad for Business (#299), an exercise in colors and texture. Gregg photocopied a newspaper story, pasted it and a wash of the woman's face onto the cover, then airbrushed the umbrella, puddle, and background. A small flaw stains the red background (directly above the "X" in "FOX"); at the time, the Creative Department of Western was housed in an old shirt factory, where sparrows often sat on the overhead pipes and dripped excrement onto uncovered artwork. (See illustration 12.)

Gregg's two favorite works are *The Broken Vase* (#115) and *Candidate for Love* (#239), the first "because of the design, rich color, and dramatic contrast," the second because of the subject, a Western secretary. He calls *Candidate* "the toughest one I did," and also lettered the cover. Such portraits and flowers often appear on the covers.

Now, Voyager (#99) is the perfect romance cover, where complementary covers in the green outline and the pink-red camellia provide contrast and move the eye into the more analogous hues of yellow and blues in the "heart" inset. The repetition of the heart in the Dell logo and the lines of the ship contrast with the busy movement and colors inviting further inspection; they suggest, in the ship inset, romantic action of the shipboard variety. Altogether this is a spectacularly active, overlapping cover, for which Gregg also provided lettering. The camellia is one of his favorite devices, inspired by Dumas' *Camille* and by the film version of *Now, Voyager*, which Gregg saw and admired. (See illustration 13.)

Ill Met by Moonlight (#6) suggests the purity of the earliest Dell covers: simple color relationships, basic flowing lines, the emphasis on the sensuous texture of landscape and sky. (See illustration 14.) For *Death Wears a White Gardenia* (#13), Gregg blends two of his favorite objects— skeleton hand and flower. And for *The Boomerang Clue* (#46), he combines airbrush and drybrush, even pasting the body of the hypodermic needle onto the cover; this cover typifies the kind of ominous cover Gregg often favored.

He could be even grislier. *Curtains for the Editor* (#82) highlights impalement and flowing blood. A similar view of blood appears on *Judas, Incorporated* (#244), where the bloody knife and knife wound are framed by the casually outspread legs of the fashionably dressed woman: a Freudian delight. *Who's Calling?* (#151) has a grisly combination of airbrush and tempera, the latter for the severed ear, a feature that appears in Helen McCloy's novel. Gregg's most horrifying cover is *Bar the Doors* (#143), although the impaled monster hand does reveal as well a touch of humor in its obviously overdone proportions. *Bats Fly at Dusk* (#254) is horrifying in its simplicity, the trompe l'oeil overshadowed by the impalement of the woman's lips, its green and red providing the sparse but effective contrast. The battle-ax and severed head on *Odor of Violets* (#162)—elements mentioned in Baynard Kendrick's novel—create tremendous tone contrast and move the eye

3. Artists at Western's Creative Department, January, 1943. From left to right: Art Director William Strohmer, Assistant Art Director George A. Frederiksen, lettering specialist Bernard Salbreiter, airbrush artist Gerald Gregg, artist William Kaiser, artist Ben Hallam. From *Western at War* (1943).

. *Dreadful Hollow* (#125, 1946), cover by George A. Frederiksen, who rubbed in the pastels to give this an airbrushed look.

5. *She Ate Her Cake* (#186, 1947), cover by Gerald Gregg, who airbrushed this "split cover."

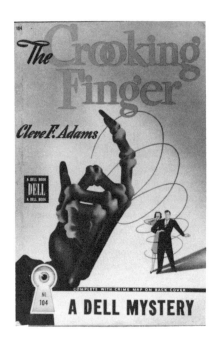

6. A sampling of Gerald Gregg's airbrushed work, *The Crooking Finger* (#104, 1946), a classic mystery cover.

7. *Half Angel* (#118, 1946), like many of Gregg's covers, a figure dwarfed by an object.

8. *Wiped Out* (#165, 1947), a warm, arid cover of Gregg's, perfect for a book about the Foreign Legion.

9. *Appointment with Death* (#105, 1946), one of Gregg's striking low-key covers.

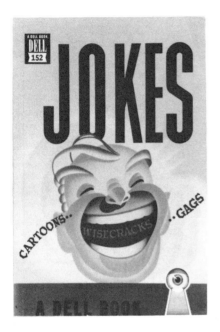

10. *Jokes, Gags and Wisecracks* (#152, 1947), for which Gregg followed William Strohmer's preliminary sketch exactly.

11. *Cold Steal* (#142, 1946), a superb trompe l'oeil, by Gregg.

12. *Bad for Business* (#299, 1949), a combination of airbrush and photography, by Gregg.

13. *Now Voyager* (#99, 1945), the perfect romance cover, by Gregg.

14. *Ill Met by Moonlight* (#6, 1942-1943), cover by Gregg. The early covers featured pure color and simple lines.

15. *Skyline Riders* (#250, 1948), original cover painting by Earl Sherwan (painting in the collection of the author). The Dell western covers often featured a horse and rider actively confronting the reader/viewer.

16. *The Bat* (#652, 1953), a silkscreened cover by Art Director Walter Brooks.

17. *Blood on Biscayne Bay* (#D342, 1960), cover by Robert McGinnis. A typical McGinnis feminine portrait, reflective of Dell covers in the late 1950's and early 1960's.

18. Robert Stanley and his wife and model, Rhoda, at Western's Poughkeepsie, N.Y., branch. Stanley was the most prolific Dell artist of the
1950's. From *The Westerner* (March, 1951).

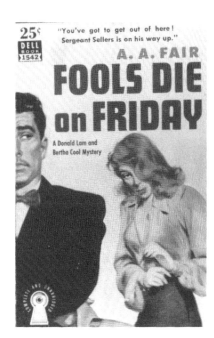

19a-b. *Fools Die on Friday* (#542, 1951; #1542, 1953). The only altered Dell
cover. Both covers are by Stanley.

67

20a. One of the few surviving examples of a rejected cover, *Quiet Horror* (#D325, 1959). The original cover, by Seymour Chwast, was considered too gruesome by Dell's Sales Department. The published cover (20b, c) is credited to the Push-Pin Studios, an innovative group to which Chwast belonged.

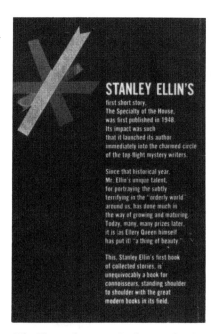

20b. The replacement back cover for *Quiet Horror*.

20c. The replacement front cover for *Quiet Horror*.

horizontally, to the left, like a film emphasizing contrast by right-to-left movement. (Such grisliness provides an ironic contrast to the conservatism of Western's editorial staff, who never suggested corpses on Dell *back* covers.)

Gregg's statement that "I like brilliant colors" is well demonstrated on *Gold Comes in Bricks* (#84) and on *Hammett Homicides* (#223), the latter a riot of hues pointing to the splattered red blood in the center. And on *Death Knell* (#273), the brilliant yellow and the flesh tone allow the black of the pistol and the blue of the woman's garment to evoke contrast. Combinations of color and texture appear on *The Corpse Came Calling* (#168), a simple yet cleverly arranged one-dimensional exercise, and on *House of Darkness* (#237), a three-dimensional work that is deceptively simple as it suggests the novel's emphasis upon topography.

It Ain't Hay (#270) is an interesting combination: marijuana smoke from an oversized joint aboard a coffin rowed by Death creates the illusion of a nude woman. It may be just a bit overdone, however, or an expression of Gregg's humor, which surfaces more clearly in *With This Ring* (#83), where a mannequin-groom is encircled by a wedding ring: not a happy view of marriage. Similarly, on *Honor Bound* (#116), a ring encircles both groom and bride, the groom tilting or falling.

The cover of *Too Busy to Die* (#185) suggests overkill, the nude woman on the cover both hanged and stabbed. Grisly, but stunning in its color and texture, the knife pinning the shower curtain to the woman's back is a grim, almost tender touch. An unusual bondage scene occurs on *The Continental Op* (#129)—Gregg rarely shows such obvious sadism. More gripping are the two fantastic creatures on *The Blackbirder* (#149), where an enormous taloned bird seizes human prey, and on *Great Black Kanba* (#181), where complementary blue and orange combine with swirling lines to create the metamorphosis of an Australian train into a winged, fanged, grinning dragon.

An early Gothic cover graces *The Case of Jennie Brice* (#40), where Gothic happenings are suggested through the focus—through light, tone, and line—on the candle and bloody rope. Later Gothic novels often transferred the light to the window of an old mansion. The classic contrast between career and domesticity in many Dell romances, especially Faith Baldwin's, emerges on *Self-Made Woman* (#163); while on *Western Stories* (#153) the two warring forces in western novels appear in simple visual synecdoche, the colors warm and cowboyish.

It is unfortunate that the later Western/Dell administration overlooked Gregg's work; he certainly did not decline in ability. *Dead Yellow Women* (#308), one of his last Dell covers, demonstrates skillful symmetry and use of color; and *Armchair in Hell* (#316) shows what he could do with simple lines and primary colors, perhaps the influence of Dell's art director, Fernando Texidor. (Model Ruby Hinds' legs were the basis for *Armchair*; they were a favorite with Western artists.)

Gregg continued to work for Western, but he did no Dell covers after 1950. At Western he devised the mechanicals for the more difficult "Pop-up" Whitman books and continued work on books that tied in with Warner Bros. and Disney—he is an accredited Disney artist. He also continued his interest in photography.[11]

His own private paintings range widely. In his private Racine studio hang the following: a work of abstract expressionism which he executed with cords dipped in thick colors then slapped on the horizontal canvas; figure drawings, some of which he creates on commission; watercolor landscapes; even an "op art" piece with a sliding kaleidoscope. One canvas contains "extra" paint left over from other work, the result a swirl of primary colors applied with a palette knife. Gregg makes his own frames from linen and wood and even designs many of the improvements in his house. Deaf since childhood, he communicates through his public and personal art.

Gregg also lettered some of his Dell covers, but Bernard Salbreiter was Western's lettering specialist. He did most of his work on acetate overlays, so that he could letter in black and white and then specify which colors the engraver should put in. If the Art Department wanted a really different color, Salbreiter lettered it directly onto the painting. His task was to utilize space to the maximum and complement the detail and effect of the cover paintings.[12]

Byron Gere (1898-1961), a member of Western's Art Department, may have done some Dell covers, or at least retouched a few. Ben Hallam, at Western for four years, airbrushed two Dell covers, *Blood on the Black Market* (#64) and *Death in the Back Seat* (#76). His work does not sparkle as does Gregg's, despite the similarity in technique, but the comparison is unfair in light of Hallam's relatively small contribution.

Some free-lance artists were used for the Dell covers before the New York shift. Earl Sherwan, a Wisconsin native, now a full-time sculptor, painted 18 Dell covers:

I do not remember ever having read any manuscripts or books before designing the covers. I was given titles and a verbal statement about the contents by the Editor-in-Chief [Lloyd Smith] at Western, with whom I worked as a free-lancer. Sometimes specific suggestions were made, sometimes not. It was pretty much up to me to come up with a design.

Sketches in full color same-size were submitted to Dell, and those approved were prepared as finished art, twice-size. My wife [Marguerite Sherwan] hand-lettered titles, authors' names and other data that appears on the covers. The lettering, of course, was an integral part of the original design sketch.

As to back-cover maps, I recollect only vaguely having done one for *Anthony Adverse* [#281, 283, and 285]. . . .[13]

Sherwan created bright pastel covers, executed in mixed media, including Shiva Casein paint, pastel (fixed), "and most anything that came to hand." *Hold Your Breath* (#206) shows a brilliant complementary contrast, the cover expressing a primeval fear. *Skyline Riders* (#250) and *Gun Smoke Yarns* (#217) are two of the best Dell western covers, where horse and rider actively confront and engage the reader/viewer. One of Dell's rare science-fiction titles, *The First Men in the Moon* (#201), has a Sherwan cover, a bright exercise in red using a clever see-through device. (The present author owns the only existing covers Sherwan did for Dell—11 canvases; see illustration 15.)

Identification of other free-lancers has been difficult. As Earl Sherwan notes,

Artists, as a rule, were not credited for their work on the Dell books. I was told that this was because "a signature would add clutter to an already cluttered front." Possibly an element of not announcing the artist's name to competitive publishers entered into this, because credit was not given inside either.

Nevertheless, through several sources, mainly the memory of Western staff, recollections of other artists, and the records at Western, some identification of other Dell artists is possible. Otto Storch (former Dell art director) may have contributed a painting. Free-lancers of this period included Alden McWilliams, George Prout, Bob Meyers, F. Kenwood Giles, Jean Des Vignes, H. E. Vallely, William George Jacobson, Victor Kalin, Roy Price, Van Kaufman, Bill Gregg, Reynold Brown, Louis Glanzman, William Shoyer, Harry Bennett, Ray Johnson, and Paul C. Burns. Meyers specialized in action paintings for Dell covers; Kalin also did many later Dell covers; the others contributed only a few pieces. James Bama, now a well-known gallery artist, painted one Dell cover, *Dead Sure* (#420), which he remembers because he had trouble drawing the right arm of the woman on the cover.[14]

Some photo covers also appeared on early Dell books. June Locke, daughter of William Strohmer, is the model used on *Out of Control* (#376), photographed by her husband, V. Locke; her photograph also appears on the January, 1960, issue of *The Westerner*. Frank Lewis may have done photo work for the covers. Some photo covers are movie tie-ins; the stills for these were supplied by the film studios in return for the resultant publicity.

By far the most prolific illustrator for the Dell books—besides Gerald Gregg—is Robert Stanley. A former pulp illustrator, Stanley executed covers for several paperback companies before Fernando Texidor, Dell art director, saw and admired his work. Following Texidor's sketches, Stanley concentrated on Dell westerns and mysteries, always with action covers of men fighting, cowboys riding, or women threatening or being threatened. His first published Dell cover, *Double Treasure* (#335), is typical Stanley: violent action with a rough-hewn hero and a beautiful, seductive woman. (The first Dell cover Stanley actually painted was #375, *Date with Darkness*.) Most of the men on his covers he patterned after himself: Mike Shayne (on *Blood on the Stars*, #385), Sam Spade (*A Man Called Spade*, #411), Kent Murdock (*Murder with Pictures*, #441), John Marshall (*The Inconvenient Bride*, #463), even Hercule Poirot (*The Labors of Hercules*, #491) and Zorro (*The Mark of Zorro*, #553). Stanley's men are serious, usually with tight jaws and unblinking eyes, and they are usually fully clothed; one odd exception is the "beefcake" cover of *Pirates of the Range* (#466), where a half-nude cowboy is caught bathing. Most of Stanley's women are modeled after his wife, Rhoda; they are alluring, with a hint of menace and laughing eyes (on *The Uncomplaining Corpses*, #386, for example), occasionally semi-nude (*The Demon Caravan*, #501). A few sadistic scenes occur, on *Date with Darkness* (#375) and *Murder Twice Told* (#577), for example. Occasionally, Stanley uses other figures: a Siamese cat on *The Congo Venus* (#605) and a rare Stanley Negro on *The Robbed Heart* (#512).

Overall, Stanley creates a strong plastic texture on his covers, has intelligent use of color—emphasizing primary colors—and uses light and line to create movement or action in his characters. On *Date with Darkness*, for example, primary colors and line cause violence; usually reds and yellows dominate, blue used more as background. One of his most striking covers is *The Creeping Siamese* (#538), where the pastel blue belies the mystery of the bloody dagger held by the alluring woman whose breast is partially exposed; the view is a Stanley trademark. A rare Stanley Gothic graces *The Web of Evil* (#479), where the Stanley woman (smiling?) attempts escape from a typically brooding mansion and darkening sky. His oddest cover is *Age of Consent* (#622), where a seemingly decapitated nude male torso, stroked by a disembodied female hand, dominates the cover, which was suggested by Richard Small, Allan Barnard believes. More typically Stanley is *Dividend on Death* (#617), where the cover provokes readers with a sample vignette of the book's action: why, the potential reader asks, is Mike Shayne kicking a pistol out of a nurse's hand?

The March, 1951, issue of *The Westerner* profiled Stanley:

Bob Stanley, an artist who furnishes Western with oil paintings which are used on the covers of the Dell 10-cent and 25-cent books, came to Poughkeepsie with Rhoda, his wife, to go through the plant and incidentally to see a window display in which they are featured.

Rhoda, who before her marriage to Bob was a ballet dancer, at one time lived in Poughkeepsie, and although she can't remember the city, she feels a closeness to Western because of its location and because of Bob's connections with the company.

Rhoda and Bob work as a team. We furnish Bob with a rough sketch of what we want. From this he makes a color sketch. After this has been approved, Rhoda plans and makes a photograph which Bob uses as a model from which he can paint the final picture. When Bob is the model, Rhoda takes the picture, and vice-versa. When they appear together, the modern camera with the delayed-action shutter is used. Other models are their seven-year-old daughter, Barbara, who combines the talents of her parents by painting and studying ballet; and Rhoda's father, Julius Rozenzweig, who also is brought into the picture at times.

Bob has a yearning to paint landscapes. As it stands now, though, we keep him so busy (he does about six covers a month for us), he hasn't found time to go off on his own. Perhaps some day he will be able to have a one-man show.

The Stanleys have bought a very new, very modern home in Westport, Conn., which faces the Sound. There are many windows and such a beautiful view, they find it hard to concentrate on their work. Along with this home, they have their own beach, which adds to the distraction.

Bob at one time worked on the Kansas City Journal and the Star and Times, so he was familiar with the set-up of a print shop. This was Rhoda's first trip through a printing plant and she thought Western was very impressive as far as layout and machinery was concerned, and she was also impressed with the cleanliness and orderliness of the premises.[15]

(See illustration 18.)

Stanley executed the only altered Dell cover—a painting which appears in two different versions. The first Dell edition of *Fools Die on Friday* (#542, 1951) features a view of a woman zipping up her dress in response to private detective Donald Lam ordering her out of his room. The suggestion is implicitly post-coital and rushed. The revised cover (#1542, 1953) has no such suggestion; Stanley painted over the revealed undergarments and the blurb was changed to a bland statement. The incident in the novel is considerably more innocent than either cover suggests. No sex is implied in the incident, and both blurbs distort the actual dialogue. Either the hard-cover publisher (Morrow) or the author (Erle Stanley Gardner) may have objected to the first version; the royalty cards of Western note that the revised cover was submitted to Morrow for approval. Stanley does not remember the reason for the change. (See illustrations 19a and b.)

Robert Stanley's covers gradually become more cinematic, as they begin to resemble stop-action freezes (on, for example, *The Red Tassel*, #565). Slowly, his later work for Dell becomes more subdued, influenced by Walter Brooks, as his work changes in scope and texture. On *Riding High* (#B209, 1961), his last Dell cover, Stanley's detail is still present, now a study in blue, a sign that Stanley could grow and change. But Art Director Walter Brooks used Stanley more sparingly in the 1950's; he believed Stanley had been overused on the Dell covers. Stanley did continue to work for other publishers, and today he paints for Las Vegas casinos as well as other clients. His Dell covers, however, stand as a remarkable collection for any artist.

1952-1962

The editorial and artistic changes in 1951 occurred partially because of conflicting interests between Dell and Western. Fernando Texidor, Dell's art director, favored an illustrative approach rather than Western's "design" covers. Texidor began to suggest the use of free-lance New York artists, often paying them slightly more than artists in the Racine/Chicago area. Texidor favored primary colors, especially for mysteries, and liked bold, block typefaces rather than the delicate lettering of Bernard Salbreiter. He wanted more of a hard-sell approach than the Gregg airbrushes represented.[16] So in the 1951 shift, responsibility for the Dell cover art transferred to Western's New York offices.

Edmund Marine was the first to assume artistic control, but only briefly:

In 1952 I was hired as art director of the division of Western Publishing which handled the Dell account. At that time Fernando Texidor was Dell's art director. We at Western, the editorial and art departments, worked through Helen Meyer, President of Dell, for editorial, and with Texidor on the art. I worked on the paperbacks for only a few weeks. I was so burdened with the other Dell projects I could not handle them. We then put Walter Brooks, my assistant, on the paperbacks exclusively.[17]

Brooks began as an employee of Western in January, 1952. Earlier he had free-lanced for Avon paperbacks, RCA records, and Dell comics. He worked in close conjunction with Dell's new executive editor, Frank Taylor. Both wanted to break away from the early "funny art from Racine" (in Taylor's words) and change the whole package of the books. They felt they could satisfy both Dell and Western by instituting new styles for different genres, even assigning one artist to one author's works when possible.[18] At this time many paperback covers imitated the style of James Avati's New American Library work. But neither Brooks nor Taylor wanted a copied format.

Their interest in graphics led them to "reform" the books' overall design, especially the cover. Brooks, says Taylor, "implemented my dreams." The two strove to put together a whole book, not just a separate text and jacket as in the books of the 1940's. Taylor discarded the back-cover maps, the keyhole logo, the decorated endpapers—"They weren't very exciting to me." And he began serious reform of the covers, "which I thought were embarassing."

In pursuit of this reform, Brooks read manuscripts of the Dell books, finding little help from free-lance reports in his attempts to visualize possible cover situations. Brooks first prepared a color sketch of the projected cover, secured approval from the Sales Department and

Editorial Department, then gave the sketch to the artist for the finished version. This procedure allowed for fast production of the artwork and allowed a larger budget for the artists. Artists usually had about a month to prepare the covers, which were done two or two and one-half times cover size (Robert McGinnis and William Teason actually wanted to work smaller); the size was specified by Western. Artists received from $200 to $250 per painting in 1952, the price gradually rising to an average of $500 in 1960, when Brooks was replaced as art director by Rolf Erickson.

Brooks describes the process for Dell covers in the 1950's:

When the artist finished the cover painting, a same size mechanical was prepared. This included a photostat of the art reduced to the size it was going to be used along with type or lettering—logotypes or any other elements that were going to appear on front & back cover as well as spine made up the bulk (number of pages) of the book. Color was marked up for titles and other type.

The art and mechanical was shipped to the Poughkeepsie plant where color separations were prepared. I.e., the camera department made a film positive for a red plate—yellow plate—blue plate and a black plate. Each plate had the type stripped into position as indicated by mechanical in colors specified. When separations were finished, plates were made (a set of four for each title involved—one plate for each color) and proofs pulled. These proofs were sent to me for final checking of color balance and for checking with editors and customer for any last minute changes in copy. When the proofs were marked up for any changes and essentially approved, they were returned to Poughkeepsie for plate making and printing. From the film positives, printing plates were made by a repeat process which allowed the covers to be printed 32 times up—or 32 covers to a sheet. Presses had a station or cylinder for each color involved. Of the 32 covers on a sheet there might be 6 of one, 12 of another, etc. made up to supply the total number of books (quantity) involved in a given order by the customer Dell.[19]

All typography, including type for covers, was done in-house, by Brooks, his assistant, Jeanette Cissman, and the staff—Charles Walker, Harry Lemay, and Richard Eiger. One feature they initiated was the use of keyed prices on the front cover: circles or other devices surrounding the price and issue number represented the book's genre. The idea was developed in response to the Sales Department, who wanted dealers to have a quicker system with which to identify returns for cash credit. (Later, Dell began an alternate system, using an IBM number on the inside of the front cover for similar purposes. The system foreshadowed the now-familiar UPC code on back covers.)

Brooks' own artwork is sparse, lean, and simple, a more polished, less naive form of commercial art than the early Dell covers. For example, *The Bat* (#652) was silkscreened with three different day-glo colors in fluorescent ink on the covers and spine—the first such paperback cover.

The Sales Department resisted this idea, afraid that the colors would fade and that dealers would return the faded copies. So Brooks tested the process by hanging a sample from his office window for three months; no fading occurred. This cover presents a simple but effective mystery design: flowing lines and basic color. (See illustration 16.) Brooks had other ideas, including the use of a highly reflective metallic cover (now a standard paperback feature), but at the time production problems existed with the inks necessary for such a feature.

Brooks was also indirectly responsible for the single dust jacket on a Dell paperback (*Go Down to Glory*, #D114). He believes the Sales Department thought up the idea; they thought the earlier cover, by Brooks, "too provocative." (In general, the Sales Department of Dell seems to have had a heavy hand in artistic decisions.)

Brooks considers his career at Western extremely satisfying, and all the artists I contacted thought him creative and knowledgeable. Mitchell Hooks recalls that Brooks "was responsible for the unique look of Dell covers, and was a major contributor to upgrading the quality of paperback covers in general."[20] During his tenure at Western, Brooks brought in a wide variety of talent, including the following artists:

WILLIAM GEORGE. Brooks remembers that George had conscience problems regarding his paperback assignments and finally left the field. George specialized in action covers, most of them for the later books in the 25¢ reprint series.[21]

MITCHELL HOOKS. Brooks feels that Hooks' style changed dramatically from that used on the early Dell covers; Bantam's art director notes that Hooks "had been doing low-key, emotional art, very rarely using pure color. He will use beautiful browns and grays—a very limited palette. . . ."[22] Hooks' Dell work includes excellent character sketches in pastel. He feels that

Walter [Brooks] was encouraging an adventurous approach for Dell's covers, and that period of his art direction coincided with the time in my career when I was trying to work out a personal and original style of my own.

It was most fortunate for me that—at a time when I needed to experiment—Walter Brooks as well as Knox Burger, the editor at Dell, was encouraging me to do so. I feel we produced some fresh and innovative covers during that period, and I certainly got lasting benefits from it in terms of developing my work.[23]

Much of Hooks' Dell work reflects Brooks' own; *The Last Enemy* (Dell First Edition #D90), for example, is sparse, like Brooks' covers, but also darker and more filled in. Much of his Dell work is somber, like the subjects of the books he illustrates.

ROBERT ABBETT. Abbett's style ranged from pulp-influenced covers to landscapes and portraits of beautiful women. He comments:

I enjoyed many of the books for which I painted covers, and the art director, Walter Brooks, gave me a wide range of subjects to deal with. The pace of trying to do enough covers fast enough to maintain a good income was terrifying and I'll have to be honest . . . my present schedule is much more human. But Walter was fun to work with and I feel that that period of my career enabled my craftmanship and basic "picture making" to mature, a fact which makes my success as a gallery artist possible.

In retrospect, I can see that many of the cover paintings that were the most successful had a quality which is present in my present painting, even though the subject matter is far different. Walter encouraged me to paint in a full painting style, in contrast to many of the flip, faddish ways which come and go so quickly in illustration.[24]

HARRY BENNETT. Although Bennett had painted two earlier Dell covers, Brooks re-introduced him. Bennett feels he was later used sparingly because Dell thought he was "too esoteric for them."[25]

VICTOR KALIN. Kalin used a wide variety of styles, from early pulp covers (*The Lady Regrets*, #338) to later ones of a Robert McGinnis-style (*Go, Honeylou*, #B215, a beautiful study in orange-red). Kalin comments:

Concerning your inquiry about influences; I really didn't have any in the paperback field. I admired the "slick" magazine illustrators (Coby Whitmore, Al Parker, Jon Whitcomb, etc.) but when I started painting covers for paperbacks the field was so new that there were very few examples to use for inspiration. I got started because some of the art directors liked the illustrations I had been doing for *Esquire* magazine and contacted me. At the time I considered it beneath my talent and aspirations, but it has served me quite well for a good many years—long after the market for illustration was taken over by the photographers, and the "slick" women's magazines allowed television to offer the nation's housewives the romantic fiction that they had featured.[26]

ROBERT MAGUIRE. Maguire is well known for his exotic paintings on the covers of other paperback publishers (especially Berkley), but his Dell covers are comparatively uninspired. Brooks remembers that Maguire became disillusioned for a time and retreated to a greeting-card company.

BARYE PHILLIPS. Phillips did some early pulp-style covers and later pastels, most derivative of others' styles.

SAUL LAMBERT. Brooks remembers Lambert working on light absorbent paper that faded quickly; the inks and dyes were "fugitive," that is, they faded fast, a process which allowed him to get blotted effects on the covers of some Laurel Readers.

RICHARD POWERS. Powers came to Brooks' attention through an agent. Brooks knew his work from other publishers (most notably Powers' science-fiction covers for Ballantine), but used him for a variety of covers, including pen-and-ink portraits of the poets in the Laurel Poetry series.

WILLIAM TEASON. Teason specialized in precise detail, giving ordinary objects a lustrous, sensuous texture and color. He later specialized in covers for Agatha Christie's books, often working in watercolor.[27]

PUSH-PIN STUDIOS. Now quite well known, Push-Pin, which included Seymour Chwast and Milton Glaser, executed designs in line and color for the Dell Great Mystery Library and other works, giving such books a "dignity" in this approach that resembled subdued Mondrian. Dell's Mystery Library won an "Edgar" award from the Mystery Writers of America in 1950. (See illustrations 20a, b, c.)

NICK EGGENHOFER. One of Eggenhofer's two Dell covers (*The Long Rifle*, #D147), was altered. Don Ward remembers that Eggenhofer's realistic portrait of a mountain man was too realistic for Dell, who had another staff artist re-draw the man's face. "The painting," comments Ward, "was too good . . . too authentic to be commercially appealing."[28]

ROBERT McGINNIS. McGinnis signaled a new era in paperback art. His subject was familiar—sensual, sultry, partially clad women—but his approach quite different. McGinnis' women flow and slide, in tight clothes and with sharply focused faces. All appear seductive, dangerous, sophisticated, often superficially amused. McGinnis' first paperback cover, *So Young, So Cold, So Fair* (#985), constitutes a surprising debut in its low-key arrangement of lines. But the McGinnis women evolve in the Dell covers, clarifying gradually until they reach predatory perfection in *Blood on Biscayne Bay* (#D342), a coquettish, aloof, vibrant portrait. The woman could also be brooding (*When Dorinda Dances*, #D359) or amused (*Double or Quits*, #D361), but even from the rear (*The Eighth Circle*, #D311) she is recognizable as a McGinnis woman, as are in earlier illustrations the "Petty Girl" or the Vargas portraits. (See illustration 17.)

McGinnis, a former fashion illustrator, remembers his beginning at Dell:

Regarding my affiliation with Dell Books, . . . Walter Brooks at Dell gave me my start in paperbacks and in a way Mike Hooks, the illustrator, also was instrumental.

Before this event, after arriving in N.Y. City from Cincinnati, Ohio, I worked for a couple of years at Chaite Studios. It was a good training ground; many of today's leading illustrators started there. There I met Mike, who later went on his own with a representative name of Don Gelb.

One day I ran into Mike and Don on the street. Mike introduced me and suggested I let Don show my work to some publishers. Dell was the first place Don went and Walter gave me an assignment. It was the break of a lifetime. After that I was averaging six books a month for Dell.

So much depends on an affinity between Art Director and artist. Walter liked the way I painted women and gave me complete freedom of expression. It was a tremendously creative and exciting period for me; for example, I think we did all the Mike Shayne books three times with differing formats.

This affinity did not occur with Walter's successor at Dell, John Van Zwienen, who methodically phased me out of Dell Books.

To answer your question about models. I did use my wife Ferne for many covers; she has ideal proportions and I drew heavily from her knowledge and taste of clothing and accessories. When the demands of young children and managing a home became too much I began using a professional model name of Lisa Karan who was proud of her beauty and enjoyed displaying it.

Later, Shere Hite became my steady favorite model for several years. She was of course exquisite but also creative. She contributed imagination and tasteful costuming to the posing.

Shere is better known now as the author of the bestselling *The Hite Report*.[29]

Brooks used McGinnis in one way to give a sense of identity to the Mike Shayne series (which retained, however, Robert Stanley's rough portrait of Shayne as its logo). McGinnis also painted a few western covers, even a landscape for *The Fiery Trial* (#F77), but none matched in appeal his feminine portraits for the Dell mysteries. A prolific illustrator for Dell and other lines, he even inspired an imitator, Ronnie Lesser. (Ted CoConis' style also resembles McGinnis'; even the signatures of Lesser and CoConis resemble that of McGinnis.)

AUTHORS' REACTIONS AND ACCURACY OF THE COVERS

Art directors often felt that authors were not necessarily the best judges of what sold books; so they rarely consulted the authors. But at least one author, Mary Renault, today has approval of the covers of her books. In the 1940's and 1950's, few authors had such a clause in their contract. On the subject of Dell covers, authors whom I contacted were varied in their comments. Martha Albrand thought her mystery covers gave away too much of the ending: "Here the author is more or less helpless. The author is not sent the blurbs, and therefore can do very little about it."[30]

Nicholas Monsarrat remarked about *Leave Cancelled* (#327), "I did not like the Dell cover, which I thought vulgar and ugly—but I think that about almost all my paperback covers, which never try to match the quality of the book, only a crude mish-mash of its least attractive parts."[31]

Donald Hamilton was more specific about *Mad River* (Dell First Edition #91):

I met the cover artist [George Gross] for *Mad River* at a Delacorte cocktail party and kidded him about having our hero holding some kind of a bastard Springfield musket when the text clearly specified a Henry rifle. He didn't think I was being a bit funny; and I guess I didn't really mean to be, at that.[32]

George Evans, one half of the pseudonym "Brandon Bird," went even further:

You touch a tender nerve when you ask about the cover of the Dell *Death in Four Colors* [#531]. It seems that these things must happen to someone who was a professional illustrator (you must guess that my experience as such inspired the murder of an art director, if only in fantasy) and considering the revolting quality of the front-cover drawing, the back cover didn't seem bad.[33]

However, Robert Terrall liked the McGinnis covers on his Mike Shayne novels and bemoaned the passing of those, replaced by the photographic covers in the 1960's and 1970's:

When the series began to go soft . . . the publisher decided to bring [the Mike Shayne series] into the world with photographic covers. The art director at the time was homosexual, and the model he hired was a friend of his.

The model was small, and he was photographed from an angle so that the women in the pictures would not tower over him.

He didn't look like the redhead readers had come to know.[34]

L. Sprague de Camp liked the cover of #600 "the best" of all the editions of his *Rogue Queen*. And Michael Gilbert thought the cover of *Death Has Deep Roots* (#744) "a remarkably spirited picture."[35] But on the whole, authors of the Dell editions seemed less than pleased.

Many of the Dell covers accurately illustrate the books. The cover of *Dance of Death* (#33), for instance, depicts an impersonation at a debut party, an incident central to the novel. The cover of *The Glass Triangle* (#81) corresponds well to pages 56, 131, 226-230 of the book; *Beyond the Dark* (#93) captures the spirit of the chase in the novel. The cover of *Murder Is a Kill-Joy* (#103) symbolizes the essence of the central character "Dolly," and *The Deadly Truth* (#107) depicts three key clues to the mystery. The corpse on *Name Your Poison* (#148) corresponds well to the description in the book, although the colors do not agree; the central female character is depicted accurately in her feline costume on *The Frightened Pigeon* (#204); *Cue for Murder* (#212) displays the key clue to the mystery—a fly and a bloody knife. The cover of *The Case of the Seven Sneezes* (#334) depicts a minor incident in the story, although strikingly; the woman pictured threatens to get the seated detective in trouble by simulating a rape. (She should rip her sweater "straight down," however; see page 149 of the Dell edition.)

The cover of *She* (#339) vividly represents the eternal Ayesha in her life-renewing flames; *Wake for a Lady* (#345) is suggested by the faked corpse of Gorgeous O'Hara in her bedroom (but in the book she is not in a coffin and she does not have green eyes). One of the most vivid Dell covers is *The Accomplice* (#346), which suggests the propped-up corpse described on page 200 of the Dell edition; the picture resembles the author's description, but the background should be Kansas City, Missouri, not Paris. The Eiffel Tower probably seemed more exotic than a Kansas City landmark. The cover of *Young Claudia* (#528) may seem too racy for a "Claudia" novel, but the cover is suggested by a scene in the book where Claudia innocently removes her shirt in order to clip hedges. (And the hard-cover publisher approved the Dell cover.) Similarly, the torture of a negligee-clad countess on *Passport to Peril* (#568) may seem too sadistic, yet it is based on an actual event in the (sadistic) story. An important clue to the mystery of *To Wake the Dead* (#635) appears on the cover, concerning the difference between the uniform of a policeman and that of a hotel liftman. *The Golden Eagle* (#D267) has a portrait of Hernando De Soto done by his lineal descendant Rafael de Soto. And a "Tabu" takeoff, intentional or not, appears on *Once in Vienna* (#524).

A cliché concerning paperback covers states that they often promise more than the book delivers, in terms of suspense, violence, or sex, and that they often distort the genre or atmosphere of the book. The complaint is occasionally valid. The cover of *Spill the Jackpot* (#109) promises violence, yet little occurs in the novel. The man on *The Visitor* (#132) cover should be a 17-year-old boy. On *Golden Earrings* (#216) the Colonel, not Lydia the gypsy, should wear golden earrings; she is described as an earthy, strong-limbed, sensuous Amazon with "black down over the upper lip" (p. 18), but Earl Sherwan transformed her into the romantic stereotype of a female gypsy—clean-shaven, almost angelic. The macabre portrait on *Bats Fly at Dusk* (#254) is completely false to the book; *Blind Man's Bluff* (#230), with the front-cover blurb, "A DOUGLAS MACLAIN MYSTERY," errs in the detective's name (Duncan Maclain). On *Alias the Dead* (#377) a serious blunder occurs by positioning the corpse face down (see pages 151-152, 235 of the Dell edition). And on *Jungle Hunting Thrills* (#468) artist Robert Stanley places a tiger in the trees, where a hunter might find a leopard, but never a tiger. The entire cover of *The Steel Mirror* (#473) incorrectly suggests the character of Ann as sadistic (she smiles at "Henry McEnroy" only to get him off guard); and *The Congo Venus* (#605) has a botched version of Botticelli's painting, *The Birth of Venus*, a distortion painful to the book's author, art critic John Canaday.[36]

One of the strangest covers is *The Boomerang Clue* (#664), painted by Fernando Texidor. The scene suggests a Dali-esque landscape, and although the setting in the book is an asylum, this representation approximates neither in details nor atmosphere Agatha Christie's novel.

Although Texidor accurately places the character Bobby in a chauffeur's uniform, the woman, Moira, should not faint, no tree exists in the area, and Bobby should have a moustache. What Texidor had in mind is inexplicable. It is his only Dell cover.

Of course, those who collect paperbacks only for cover art rarely care about accuracy in relation to the book. They appreciate the artwork for its own sake, as mass-produced works of art, almost as posters. Certainly Gregg's airbrushes, Stanley's action covers, and McGinnis' portraits are interesting in their own right.

Covers produced ˋafter 1962 resemble ones of the 1950's or early 1960's, or they become indistinguishable from those of other paperback companies. A statement in 1964 by Art Director John Van Zwienen (who joined Dell in September, 1961) might reflect as well the philosophy of the 1950's Dell books:

Our approach to art depends on the market. In the mass lines, *The Shoes of the Fisherman* is obviously treated differently from a mystery or romance. In many cases we use type covers for our bestseller reprints, letting the title or the author's name do the selling. Simplicity is the hardest thing to achieve in a book cover, especially when you're trying to express what's inside the books. Ultimately the designer has to make the decision of whether to go along with his own feelings or to bow to the requirements of the text.[37]

The earlier Dell covers, on the whole, represent much of the best in paperback art, even of commercial art of the period, although the covers do not necessarily typify the art of the periods. While Stanley's paintings are imitative to an extent, Gregg's airbrushes and McGinnis' portraits are essentially innovative. Color airbrushing became truly fashionable only in the 1970's, for record album covers, although H. L. Hoffman had used the process for many of the early Popular Library paperbacks. And McGinnis' paintings initiated a style much imitated by later illustrators. The trend was from the innocence of the "design" covers to the more sophisticated illustration approach. Taken together, as an entire collection, the Dell covers produced between 1942 and 1962 stand as a singular achievement, unsurpassed in variety. In a sense, they approximate André Malraux's "museum without walls."

7

Artwork: The Back Covers

Of all the interesting features of the early Dell paperbacks, the most immediately striking is the back-cover map or diagram. These four-color cartographic fantasies have caused collectors to refer affectionately to the books as "mapbacks." The maps were the idea of Lloyd Smith, whose philosophy was to fill up all the spaces on and in the books: to crowd character lists and other features into the front pages, to place head-of-title blurbs on the title-pages, to decorate the endpapers, and to put maps on the back covers.[1] The maps were an immediate success with readers, who could at any time in their reading simply flip over the books to consult the "Scene of the Mystery [or Romance, etc.]."

Before 1942, sketches of scenes of the crime often appeared in mystery novels. Those by Agatha Christie, Mignon G. Eberhart, and Ellery Queen often featured diagrams and maps, but they were placed on the books' endpapers, or worse, inserted haphazardly in the text. Such a device allows an author to dispense with digressive topographical information and proceed to develop character and plot. In Christie's *Murder in Mesopotamia*, for instance, she describes the place of murder, appends a map, and then moves on. On the other hand, a novel like Richard Burke's *Chinese Red*, cluttered with endless detail the reader does not need to know, could use a map badly. But only the Dell reprint edition has one. Some readers may argue that the existence of a map in a mystery is unfair, that a reader's being expected to solve a mystery by scrutinizing topographic details should be separate from the deductive reading process. Those readers have a point. But then so do those who enjoy the addition of another challenging dimension—a graphic one—whether it be required or merely decorative.

These "Scenes of the Crime" derive in spirit from those sketches and photographs made by police personnel to aid in criminal investigations. In *Modern Criminal Investigation*, Harry Söderman and John J. O'Connell discuss the usefulness of such sketches, dividing them into the sketch of locality (the scene of the crime and locality, including buildings and roads), the sketch of grounds (the scene of the crime and the nearest physical surroundings, e.g., house and garden), and the sketch of details (only the scene of the crime).[2] *The New York World* even used these devices to re-create photographically the "Scene of the Crime" of particularly lurid events.[3]

Readers who wish a touch of authenticity in police procedural mysteries may find such diagrams more appealing than will readers of other types of mysteries. Yet even in tales involving hard-boiled private eyes, a map of the locale can be useful—for example, to a reader of Dashiell Hammett who has never set foot in San Francisco. And readers of adventure novels may find extremely helpful a sketch of Budapest, Paris, or Shanghai. In some mysteries and adventures, characters in the novels even draw maps to aid themselves and others, although the maps described do not always correspond to those on the Dell back covers. (See, for example, Zelda Popkin's *Dead Man's Gift*, #190, pp. 153-155.) And occasionally characters consult maps to orient themselves (in Allan MacKinnon's *House of Darkness*, #237, pp. 84-86). Readers of science-fiction and fantasy may also enjoy maps, in this case usually maps of previously uncharted areas. As science-fiction and fantasy author Lester del Rey points out, "Without such a guide, the reader is often forced to attempt his own mental cartography, or to remain hopelessly vague about much of the development of the story."[4] But of course Dell's maps on westerns and romances have no such defense; Dell's back covers on such books rarely require constant reference. But the maps are attractive, decorative, often beautifully drawn, and can be appreciated on their own merits. What better defense do they need?

No other publishing company devised anything quite like the Dell maps. Avon's first 18 paperback titles featured a world map on the endpapers, but it was always the same map. And many of Bantam's first 99 titles were issued or reissued with endpaper designs, some of them maps; Bantam discontinued the feature but later, in 1965 and 1966, used small, arthritic-looking back-cover maps on its five "World's Great Novels of Detection." Only the Dell books used maps as a standard feature for a significant amount of time, 1942 to 1951.

Most of the maps were produced independently of the other artwork. Editors Allan Barnard and Don Ward noted scenes in the books that would be appropriate for a map. In many cases, proofreaders, free-lancers, and even secretarial staff helped as well; in the summer months, local teachers assisted.[5] Most of the descriptions and suggestions were passed on to Ruth Belew, a Chicago artist who drew at least 150 maps, probably much more, preparing line drawings of four to six of them at a time between 1942 and 1951.[6] She prepared the maps twice-size in black ink on white cardboard, complete with banners and lettering, then returned them to Western for approval. There, James E. Hawkins checked the maps against the texts to determine their accuracy. There were many mistakes, he remembers, especially on street maps, since the Dell authors were often unfamiliar with their locales. (Dashiell Hammett, recalls Hawkins, was an exception.) Using a file of Esso road and city maps (then printed by Western), Hawkins noted the errors. Occasionally, he had to return the drawings to Belew; more often, mistakes were corrected by Western's Art Department. Artists such as Robert Kissner often touched up the lettering, and apprentices like Gerald Poplawski noted colors, usually according to their own ideas.[7] (Only a few maps match colors to authors' descriptions, and only when the editor so specified.) In general, the Art Department, including Gerald Gregg, produced "fakes" of the maps: pastel tints on transparencies placed over Belew's line drawings showed the litho artist what dots to use, what colors to prepare.[8] The litho artist prepared four-color separation sheets; all color was flat, no shades.

In rare cases, other people prepared maps. Gerald Gregg drew the intricate map for *Crime Hound* (#34); Earl Sherwan designed the map for the three Dell editions of *Anthony Adverse* (#281, #283, #285); author and art critic John Canaday prepared sketches for two of his "Matthew Head" mysteries (*The Devil in the Bush*, #158; *The Smell of Money*, #219); and Henning Nelms planned the elaborate design for his "Hake Talbot" mystery, *Rim of the Pit* (#173). Byron Gere may have been responsible for finishing or touching up various maps.[9] The scant records at Western's Creative Center in Racine are a bit vague in assigning such credit. Ruth Belew, for example, is credited with doing maps for 92 specific titles from 1942 to December, 1947, but thereafter for only 58 maps, no titles of which are mentioned. The last map specifically credited to Belew is *Women Must Weep* (#482). The last map produced through the Racine Art Department is *The Congo Venus* (#605). Walter Brooks and others drew the few maps produced after 1952, in Western's New York office.[10]

In the 25¢ reprint series, 577 books had back-cover maps or designs. Twenty of the 4-digit reissues in the 25¢ series also used maps. Eleven other books in the 25¢ series employed other forms of back-cover illustrations. Eight books in the other series featured back-cover designs; many others used interior maps or diagrams, taken from the original editions or prepared especially for the Dell edition. Of those 577 original "mapbacks," 25 exactly duplicated previous maps, so there were 552 different maps in the series. Of these, 24 revised earlier maps, so altogether 528 original maps exist in the 25¢ series.[11]

A handful of the Dell maps were based—usually loosely—on sketches and maps in the hard-cover editions: for example, all of Clayton Rawson's mysteries, Carter Dickson's *The Unicorn Murders* (#16), Peter Hunt's *Murders at Scandal House* (#42), and George Worthing Yates' *If a*

Body (#159). But in a few cases the Dell artist ignored original sketches: the map on the endpapers of the first edition of Leslie Ford's *Ill Met by Moonlight* bears little resemblance to the back-cover map of the Dell edition (#6).

Not all of these back-cover designs are true maps—that is, flat representations of all or part of the earth's surface according to a set scale and a method of map projection (often the Mercator projection).[12] The Dell maps divide roughly as follows:

A) Maps of large geographical areas such as countries and continents. These appear on all types of books, depicting areas unfamiliar to many American readers, showing routes or trails in westerns and mysteries, illustrating historical parts of the world, or suggesting the immense scope of an historical adventure.

B) Maps of smaller geographical areas such as cities (similar to Söderman and O'Connell's "sketch of locality"). These are most appropriate for mysteries where a reader requires knowledge of the intricate arrangement of streets and buildings.

C) Maps or diagrams of even smaller areas ("sketch of grounds"), usually a building and the surrounding area—for example, a country estate or farm. These appear on mysteries and romances with one central setting or one important setting.

D) Diagrams or floor plans of structures such as houses or apartments, or even single rooms ("sketch of details"). These, the bulk of the Dell maps, are most suited for mysteries.

E) Miscellaneous designs, such as charts.

MAPS OF LARGE GEOGRAPHICAL AREAS

The majority of these use the Mercator projection and are usually oriented northward. Some depict an area unfamiliar to an average American reader: the Pacific area, scene of World War II action, on *Queen of the Flat-Tops* (#37), or the nearby South Seas, place of Errol Flynn's tropical passions, on *Showdown* (#351). The entire continent of Australia appears on *Great Black Kanba* (#181), with handy labels of railroad lines; just as unfamiliar to some American readers might be the areas of Kentucky and West Virginia known as Hatfield-McCoy country, where the clans waged a long-running feud in the late 19th-century (*Their Ancient Grudge*, #435). One of the most useful and best-labeled maps illustrates a section of Scotland (on *House of Darkness*, #237; see illustration 21a).

Often maps of these areas show routes or trails described in the books. The map of the western United States on *Trail Boss of Indian Beef* (#97) features cattle trails mentioned in the novel; *The Pioneers* (#290) pictures the famous Oregon Trail; smaller sections of the West on *Outlaw on Horseback* (#284) and *The Bandit Trail* (#424) reveal outlaw hideouts. A sideways map of the United States on *If a Body* (#159) allows readers to flee along with an innocent couple across the continent; *Golden Earrings* (#216) follows the escape route of a downed World War II flier and his gypsy rescuer through Central Europe. The route of an expedition for sunken treasure explains *Men Under the Sea* (#265) (but the artist unnecessarily elaborated the route); that of Errol Flynn's freewheeling sea trip off Australia graces *Beam Ends* (#195). Air trips are occasionally sketched. On *Crows Can't Count* (#472) the drawing just shows the air hops Donald Lam makes in the course of his private investigations. But on *No Highway* (#516) the sketch illustrates the important flights between Great Britain and Canada, routes crucial to the point of a novel concerned with the detection of flaws in airplanes traveling repeated long-distance flights.

Some maps illustrate an area as it existed a century or more ago. The map on *Cleopatra's Nights* (#414) intends to present the known world in 37-40 B.C.—the world known to Cleopatra. The map on *The Upstart* (#233) of 15th-century England details cities and towns visited by the novel's strolling theatrical troupe. The map of Europe and Asia on *Yankee Pasha* (#353) follows the adventures of the book's hero in the year 1800. Although these last two maps have good intentions, they show current geopolitical divisions rather than ones contemporary with the novel's setting. Similarly, on western novels most maps of the western United States feature only current outlines of the states.

Some maps suggest the immense scope of a novel. The center inset of an airplane circling the earth (on *Virgin with Butterflies*, #392) aptly captures the fast-paced travels of the titular virgin. The map of the western hemisphere and the insets on *Now, Voyager* (#99) suggest the romantic journey through the book; and the split hemispheres on the three editions of *Anthony Adverse* (#281, #283, #285) reveal the enormous scope of Adverse's adventures. These are generally of limited usefulness, serving mainly as decoration. The view of Europe on *Crosstown* (#477) that shows "Where Honeymoon Is Spent" is hardly mentioned in the book, and the split views of Asia and Africa on *Jungle Hunting Thrills* (#468) are unsettling because of the largely unidentifiable animal insets that serve as decorative touches on the map. (Ruth Belew drew diagrams very well, but not animals or people.) The map of the United States on *Fact Detective Mysteries* (#332) accurately places the scenes of the various stories in the book, but *Zane Grey Western Award Stories* (#523) places stories that reveal no details about their locale.[13] Both are only decorative, yet the map of Europe and North Africa on *Eisenhower Was My Boss* (#286) allows readers to follow Eisenhower's travels during World War II; in fact, one may have difficulty following the book without a map as guide. The first edition, surprisingly, has no map; only the Dell edition creates one.

Several of the most striking decorative maps depict islands. A few are even based on maps in hard-cover editions: *The Iron Spiders Murders* (#50) and *The Footprints on the Ceiling* (#121). Others, sketched from authors' descriptions in the books, feature elaborate pictorial embellishments. The map of the crescent-shaped South American island on *The Goblin Market* (#295) suggests the varied intrigue in the novel. Stone Island (*The Savage Gentleman*, #85) presents cluttered pictures that suggest the richness and diversity of the area, an inviting view for an undecided reader. And *Cave Girl* (#320) features a delicate rendition of a stone-age island, in the style of the book's author, Edgar Rice Burroughs.[14]

Only twice do extraterrestrial locales appear. The visible side of the moon decorates *The First Men in the Moon* (#201), although author H. G. Wells mentions none of the map's details in the novel. Wells prefers to build his story on character, perhaps even intentionally ignoring the topographical detail in his satire on human ignorance. The other extraterrestrial Dell map appears on *Invasion from Mars* (#305); the small section of Mars contains for careful readers a clue to the ending of Ray Bradbury's story, "The Million Year Picnic."

Many of the Dell maps combine with maps of smaller locale or with diagrams. Some appear only in outline in order to give the locale of a more important inset: India provides the background for a hotel on *Wives to Burn* (#134) and for a railway car on *Bombay Mail* (#488); northwest Africa highlights an Arab desert camp on *The Sheik* (#174); and Texas bears various insets on *Treasure of the Brasada* (#253), as do South Africa on *The Man in the Brown Suit* (#319) and the northeast United States on *The Moon's Our Home* (#368). Other maps are split with related smaller-scale ones: a section of California *and* a view of Palm Springs on *Enchanted Oasis* (#255); Sussex *and* one of its villages, Iping, on *The Invisible Man* (#269); Alaska *and* one of its (fictitious) islands, *Forlorn Island* (#364); Bermuda *and* the city of Hamilton on *Yours Ever* (#446). The dividing line between the split maps is usually clearly horizontal or diagonal, although occasionally a semicircular split occurs (as on *Castle in the Swamp*, #487). Occasionally the line of division is initially confusing (on *The Gaunt Woman*, #312).

In some cases an inset of a smaller area connects to that of a larger area: on *The Baited Blonde* (#508), the Suez Canal is skewered into a larger map of the Middle East. Conversely, some views of large areas appear only as insets in views or maps of smaller areas: Africa on *The Cabinda Affair* (#390), the Wyoming Hills section of Pennsylvania on *The Miracle of the Bells* (#474). Unfortunately, some maps connect awkwardly: floating suspended in the sky are the states of Virginia, above a farm on *Hunt with the Hounds* (#546), and New Mexico, above a ranch on *Murder Begins at Home* (#552). Some of the best-planned back covers offer comprehensive diversity: *Return to Night* (#394) displays a map of England, a map of the Cotswolds in England, and insets of buildings in a town in the

Cotswolds; *The Farmhouse* (#397) exhibits a map of Dutchess county, N.Y., a map of a smaller section of the county, and a view of a farm in the area; *She Walks Alone* (#430) shows a large map of the United States and the Caribbean, a view of a ship traveling in the Caribbean, plans of the ship's decks, and even a view of houses in the United States. These maps all present important locales of the books.

The scale of the larger areas varies from roughly the astronomical 1:13,147,200 (for the tiny globe on *Virgin with Butterflies*, #392) to the more usual one that allows a geographical area to neatly fit the Dell back cover—for example, 1:80,000 for Spain on *Blood and Sand* (#500); 1:2,000,000 for the continental United States on *If a Body* (#159). Although none of the maps give scale, the lack of scale rarely presents a problem, since maps of very large areas are recognizable as Mercator projections (e.g., the familiar hemisphere on the *Anthony Adverse* editions), and since those of smaller areas are usually familiar as political divisions of states or countries. One problem exists on *The Gaunt Woman* (#312), where the bottom map depicts the northeast United States and Canada on a scale of 1:1,360,000, but the top map shows the Grand Banks area on a scale of 1:217,500. The areas are not clearly labeled, and the division is complicated by a wavy, inexact line that conforms only vaguely to that of the Grand Banks.

These large-scale maps guide readers through the books' action rather than through actual areas, so a reader should not be too exacting. Thus, pictorial insets occur more often than do landform symbols (the latter, when they do appear, usually of mountains, plateaus, or cactus). The maps exist to help readers solidify their ideas of the areas they read about, to chart them through the imagination of the book.

MAPS OF SMALLER GEOGRAPHICAL AREAS

Most of the smaller maps show street maps of real cities, fictitious cities, and small towns and communities. Many of the street maps use a great deal of pictorial insets; others contain street arrangements with no frills. A few of these designs are angled views (that is, where the reader does not look straight down, as from a helicopter, but at an angle, of 30°, for example). The most useful appear on mysteries, where the arrangement of streets and locales is of more than passing interest to the reader. Romances rarely depend on topographical detail; westerns rarely use street maps.

New York City dominates both mysteries and other genres. Many mystery writers think of New York as the hub of the civilized world. Henry Kane, Stewart Sterling, and Helen Reilly, for example, often forget that there are readers unfamiliar with New York. So maps of Manhattan and surrounding areas are most welcome when they figure in mysteries where characters shuttle endlessly between Manhattan and Brooklyn, between 42nd Street and Harlem, across bridges and through tunnels, often at such a breakneck speed as to bewilder a non-New Yorker. The definitively fast-paced chase of *Beyond the Dark* (#93), much like that of a 1940's Hitchcock film, is made comprehensible by the beautifully detailed map of Manhattan that notes locales ranging from the northern "Inspiration Point" to the Battery in the south. The map also presents the main arteries in the novel, along with attractive and intriguing small views of key places. (See illustration 21b.)

One of the best New York City maps appears on *Armchair in Hell* (#316), its detailed street map pinpointing the 14 key locations of the "Rough and Bloody Action" in the book. Another useful map decorates *Staircase 4* (#498), and an elaborate set of connecting insets adds to the succinct Manhattan map on *Death Draws the Line* (#457). On the other hand, maps which non-New Yorkers might find too sketchy appear on *Murder within Murder* (#229), *Where There's Smoke* (#275), and *Brandy for a Hero* (#306). And on *Hell Cat* (#521), all we are offered is a large inset of the New York skyline.

Other kinds of novels set in New York City rarely require maps. Romances such as *Self-Made Woman* (#163) have them anyway. Attractive at first glance, few are really useful; the map on *The Heart Remembers* (#288), for example, has nicely-colored, well-drawn insets, but the map adds nothing. Similarly unhelpful are the New York City maps on fiction titles such as *Anna Lucasta* (#331), although the pictorial representation of Harlem on *The Robbed Heart* (#512) provides a nice decoration. The oft-reprinted *New York: Confidential!* (#400, #440, #534) displays a useful map of midtown Manhattan, surprisingly not present in the hard-cover edition. The map contains more accurate detail than the popular but flimsy "exposé."

San Francisco is almost as popular a Dell locale for mysteries as is New York. All of the seven Dell editions of Dashiell Hammett use San Francisco, at least in part. Hammett's topographical descriptions are excellent in their detail and accuracy. He evokes in his stories, often through such detail, a sense of the seaminess and decay in the San Francisco of the 1920's and 1930's, but makes us like it, as we follow the nameless Continental Op in his dogged chases through the city. To read Hammett without understanding his locale is a bit unfair; the Dell maps help in bringing the city to graphic life.

Consider, for example, the story "Fly Paper" in *The Continental Op* (#129), which features a chase through the city. We begin at the apartment at 601 Eddis Street, proceed down Market Street, Taylor Street, Sixth and Mission, down to Fifth, over to Mission, back to Sixth, up to Ninth, down to Harrison, down Harrison to Third, up Bryant to Eighth, down Brannan to Third again, over to Townsend, then across the street from the Southern Pacific passenger station, southeast down Third, finally to the trainyard. Could anyone follow that without a map? Similar chases occur in other Hammett stories—all exciting, all complicated, most helped by the Dell maps. (See illustration 21c.)

The Hammett San Francisco maps, though similar in scope, feature different arrangements. *The Continental Op* has extremely detailed routes through the city for three of the stories, with numbered points running consecutively. *The Return of the Continental Op* (#154) features flags pointing at key locales in the city, the flags' colors keyed to the five stories. *Hammett Homicides* (#223), however, adopts an eccentric and confusing system to illustrate its four stories: different numbering systems exist for each of the stories, but the places are not further labeled or keyed to a legend. Even the most careful Hammett follower may experience frustration here. *Dead Yellow Women* (#308) uses separate color-coded numbering systems for each of its six stories. The last Hammett collection Dell reprinted—*The Creeping Siamese* (#538)— uses only a small inset of the city, with seven other insets, all confusingly arranged.[15] *Nightmare Town* (#379) has only a map of the fictitious city of Izzard, to illustrate the title story. The one Hammett novel Dell re- printed—*Blood Money* (#53 and #486)—uses a sketchy San Francisco map in the latter edition.[16] San Francisco did occur in other Dell works, but not nearly as effectively as in the Hammett books.

Los Angeles provides the locale of surprisingly few Dell novels—only seven mysteries and one romance. The maps of greater Los Angeles on *Benefit Performance* (#252) and *The Lady Regrets* (#338) adopt so similar a scale that a reader can easily superimpose one upon the other. Both are helpful, although James M. Fox provides such detailed place descriptions in *The Lady Regrets* that one wishes for more connecting insets to round out the map, which features more of Los Angeles than we need. The map of the city on *The Gentle Hangman* (#526) is not particularly necessary, but the skeleton hand clutching the map does frame it dramatically. The one romance with a Los Angeles map erratically blends part of the city (in 1905), featured in the background, into the 12 insets of *Celeste the Gold Coast Virgin* (#382).

Miami and Miami Beach appear 12 times on Dell back covers, all illustrating Brett Halliday's Mike Shayne mysteries. Most of the maps are helpful, especially *The Private Practice of Michael Shayne* (#23) and *Marked for Murder* (#222), but *Blood on Biscayne Bay* (#268) disappoints in its lack of detail, considering the wealth of detail given by Halliday. Like some New York City-based writers, Halliday frequently assumes readers to be intimately acquainted with the two Florida cities; the Dell maps thus provide a welcome feature for readers concerned with Mike Shayne's repetitive exploits.

A reader might assume that London would provide the setting of many mysteries, but not of many Dell mysteries; the city appears on only three back covers of mysteries (and four romances and one work of general fiction). The pictorial map on *Scotland Yard: The Department of Queer Complaints* (#65)—one of the most detailed and ornate maps in the series—evokes a breathtaking, graphic view of the city. But the map is useless in connection with the collection of stories; author Carter Dickson mentions little topographical detail except the location of New Scotland Yard. (See illustration 21d.) The map on *Death-Watch* (#564) has an odd arrangement: the north side of the Thames has what it should, part of London, but the south side features a view of a house and clock shop. The disproportionate scale confuses. Dell's non-mysteries certainly do not require a map of London, yet the back cover of *Satin Straps* (#309) is attractive, and *Student Nurse* (#234) has intriguing legends such as "Mrs. Bleston Gets Dope." The latter book is not nearly as lurid as that legend implies; on the other hand, *Night and the City* (#374) needs a map that suggests more the novel's cheap London low-life.

Dell maps use other cities. U.S. locales include Pittsburgh; Central City, Colo.; Las Vegas; New Orleans (Mike Shayne's other habitat); Broken Lance, Kans.; Boston; Santa Fé, N. Mex.; El Paso, Tex.; Denver; San Antonio, Tex.; Palm Springs, Calif.; Washington, D.C.; Philadelphia; Centerville, Ky.; Natchez, Miss.; Annapolis, Md.; Charleston, S.C.; and Columbus, Ohio. The most useful are those of Boston (especially *Murder with Pictures*, #441), Philadelphia (*The Philadelphia Murder Story*, #354), and Annapolis (*Date with Death*, #547). The map of Centerville (*A Taste of Violence*, #426) has a particularly good attempt at a difficult layout. More exotic, non-American locales include Berlin; Calcutta; Mexico City; Hamilton, Bermuda; Merlinville-sur-mer, France; Vienna; Budapest; Nice; Bokabare, Madagascar; Juarez, Mexico; Shanghai; and Marseilles. All are good ideas, but the most useful are Calcutta (*Bengal Fire*, #311), with 16 numbered points, and Budapest (*Passport to Peril*, #568), extremely detailed. The map of Shanghai (*The Splendid Quest*, #188), though impressive, is sketchy and pertinent only to pages 25-81 and 217-240 of the novel; similarly, the map of Vienna (*Once in Vienna*, #524) has beautiful insets, but none required by the reader in order to follow the book's action.

Small towns—most of them fictitious—fare equally well on the back covers. Many, like April Harbor (on *Ill Met by Moonlight*, #6), use isometric projections of the houses (see p. 103); most, like the picture of Sudwich, Conn. (*Scarecrow*, #193), present the artist with an interesting challenge, to create an area never before graphically visualized. Scales vary from the very small town of Sandrock on *The Harvey Girls* (#130)—just a railroad stopover, an excuse for a "Harvey House" restaurant—to the larger area of Port Franklin on Long Island (*Double Treasure*, #335). All are imaginatively rendered and nicely decorative, though none as helpful as the street maps of real cities. In a few cases, though, the maps of these fictitious towns invite us to witness secrets: on *They Can't All Be Guilty* (#401), a magnifying glass enlarges a part of Detten, N.Y., to our gaze; on *The Sunnier Side* (#504) the inset of a church steeple gives little hint that in that locale in the story a homoerotic seduction takes place.

Fictitious cities include *Blue City* (#363), scene of political corruption and violence; the map is cleverly outlined, especially when one considers the intentionally lean descriptions of author Kenneth Millar. The map of Coaltown, Pa. (*The Miracle of the Bells*, #474), although not absolutely necessary, is accurately done, an earthy complement to a lofty best-seller. Exotic locales include the Sheik's City of Stones (*The Captive of the Sahara*, #402), a confusing choice for a map until the reader reaches the last section of the novel; and the lost Roman province Tarzan visits in *Tarzan and the Lost Empire* (#536), which presents a good selection of detail from Edgar Rice Burroughs' amazing and occasionally self-indulgent over-descriptions. Unfortunately, no Dell editions of other Tarzan novels appeared; a map of the ape-man's jungle dwelling would have been interesting.[17] Two areas in H. Rider Haggard's adventures appear in Dell editions, however: the ancient city of Kôr, home of She-Who-Must-Be-Obeyed (*She*, #339), and the jungle site of *King Solomon's Mines* (#433).

One of the more colorful and amusing maps of a possibly fictitious area discloses an aerial view of a small section of Hell (with an inset of Hell's "Civic Center") to illustrate Frederic Arnold Kummer's *Ladies in Hades* (#415). Most of this Virgilian guide is the artist's own effort. The author places Eve's home in Figleaf Park, near the Bottomless Pit, and Salome's Villa in the suburban Jezebel Farms, far from the Pit, but the location of Charon's Ferry, Lucrezia Borgia's house, the Gehenna Gazette, the Cloven Hoof Inn, and other colorfully named attractions is entirely the artist's contribution. In fact, not all of these places are even mentioned by Kummer: no Pluto Pictures, for instance, although (on page 37 of the novel) Satan mentions a picture studio named Famous Sinners, Incorporated. Despite the inaccuracies, the additions, and the mild pastel colors (the main map has no deep reds!), the back cover presents an entertaining graphic complement to a mildly amusing book. (See illustration 22a.)

The Dell street maps are quite varied. Beautiful pictorial maps adorn *The Lone Wolf* (#10) and *Murder Wears a Mummer's Mask* (#78); others use street positions. Some use compasses: *The Doctor Died at Dusk* (#14) employs a compass and shadows to illustrate the significance of the book's title. The only three angled views appear on *The Silver Leopard* (#287), *Until You Are Dead* (#580), and *Murder on the Links* (#454); the first two depict Manhattan, as an airplane would approach the city from low-level south. Most maps of fictitious cities and towns place streets and roads diagonally (rather than horizontally and vertically), an arrangement that allows the reader views of insets and that also dramatically cuts the map in two. On *Cactus Cavalier* (#406), for example, Main Street slices the town of Swayback, Mont. at a 90° angle. Street maps of real cities, on the other hand, particularly those of New York, favor the more conventional horizontal/vertical arrangement, usually of a northern orientation.

Of the smaller geographical areas, the most detailed fictitious example occurs on *Murders at Scandal House* (#42); based on the maps in the hardcover edition, this presents detail an artist would be hard pressed to capture just from a reading of the novel. Unfortunately, topographical wealth cannot save a dull book. One of the least useful maps of a smaller area adorns *The Swift Hour* (#141), of Chicago. A reader will search in vain for discussions in the book of places pictured on the map; Ruth Belew, the artist, a native of Chicago, apparently was carried away in her execution. Perhaps her intimate familiarity with this section of Chicago caused her to make a private contribution to the Dell series; she may have wondered if readers would ever discover the significance of the map, beyond its superficial relationship to the novel.

MAPS OR DIAGRAMS OF SMALLER AREAS

Maps or diagrams of areas such as country estates create the most challenge for the artist. Authors rarely give specific locations or relationships of such places. A swimming pool may be ''near'' the main house, or on the way to the lake, but usually no more precisely placed than that. Although few of these maps require readers' constant reference, they seem wise choices for mysteries or other types of books with one main setting.

Country estates usually have cute names like Ivy Hill, Broad Acres, or Belle Fleur. They usually include a main house, often outrageously large, and the accompanying items (such as a swimming pool) considered de rigueur by the characters on whose residences people are murdered (in the mysteries) or romanced (in the romances). The first Dell map (*Four Frightened Women*, #5) has a one-point perspective view of the estate, centered by a swimming pool, framed by house and beach—all important in the mystery. (See p. 103 for a discussion of perspectives.) The estate of Maple Hill (*Double for Death*, #9) is another elaborate one-point perspective drawing, here with rose garden and a cutaway view of the house's first floor. A more austere setting, actually a sort of grim castle, appears on *The Clue of the Judas Tree* (#61), its grimness tempered by gardens and tulip bed. Another suitably eerie estate (the setting for a vampire novel, *Dreadful Hollow*, #125), includes a strange pit in the estate, the result of the artist taking the English ''hollow'' too literally. (It is a ravine, not a deep pit.) A beautiful drawing of the Jennesma Estate illustrates *Midsummer Nightmare* (#150), based on the map and on the dust-jacket painting on the hard-cover edition. "Birchhaven" (*The Hand in the Glove*, #177) constitutes a demanding exercise for any artist, considering the complex and sketchy descriptions of author Rex Stout. The map of "Chimneys," the estate in Agatha Christie's *The Secret of Chimneys* (#199) shows a large assortment of—what else?—chimneys, a response to Christie's refusal (on page 77 of the Dell edition) to describe the house in detail.

The elaborate map on *The Smell of Money* (#219) was sketched by the author, John Canaday ("Matthew Head"), possibly finished by Ruth Belew. The best original map of a country estate—not derived from any source other than the book's descriptions—appears on *With This Ring* (#83), the plan of "Belle Fleur." This estate, just outside New Orleans, is framed by greenery and even includes a yacht harboring in a nearby bayou. Although the artist has been selective, she tries to be faithful down to the plethora of live oaks, the marble garden bench, the white pillars on the house, the flagstone porch, and the beds of water hyacinths entangled in the bayou. Two items the artist deliberately omits: on page 33 of the Dell edition, author Mignon G. Eberhart mentions a rowboat beside the pier, but on our view the rowboat would be hidden by the placement of the trees. And on page 173 of the Dell edition, the author brings in a second rowboat—much to the reader's surprise—which the artist does not include since its presence would tell the reader too much. (See illustration 22b.)

Few country estates occur in other types of fiction; the attractive views on *Robin Hill* (#119) and of Ashenden Manor on *Uncle Dynamite* (#469) are rare cases. None, however, rival the views on the mysteries. Western novels usually feature views of ranches—the Valle Verde ranch on *Jim the Conqueror* (#294), for example. Ranches also occur on non-westerns *She Ate Her Cake* (#186) and John Steinbeck's *To a God Unknown* (#358), the latter a gargantuan spread that is more the central character in Steinbeck's brooding novel than the people. A dainty farm appears on the romance *Dr. Parrish, Resident* (#215), complete with woodshed, buttery, and "bridal trees." Some mysteries feature ranches (*The State versus Elinor Norton*, #203), none too impressive.

The most painstakingly accurate view of another sort of ranch, a South American plantation, illustrates Carl Stephenson's story, "Leiningen versus the Ants," in the first Dell Hitchcock anthology, *Suspense Stories* (#92). This classic tale of a man confronted by an invasion of army ants is highlighted and enlivened by the map, which even notes the ants' advance towards the plantation. The horseshoe-shaped structure of Leiningen's defense, detailing outer water ditch and inner petrol ditch, suggests the intricate arrangement and the scope of the story's conflict. In fact, the film version, *The Naked Jungle* (1954), can be followed using the Dell map; one wonders if director Byron Haskin or producer George Pal knew of the map's existence. In one scene in the film, we glimpse a wall map of the plantation; a vague similarity exists between that map and the Dell version. (See illustration 22c.)

A few castles appear on the Dell maps, the most important on *The Case of the Constant Suicides* (#91), its cutaway view of a room in the castle tower crucial to the mystery's solution. A Chinese palace, regally drawn, graces *The White Brigand* (#144), and enormous castles appear on *Leave It to Psmith* (#357) and *The Code of the Woosters* (#393), both P. G. Wodehouse novels. Other structures and areas that encompass areas as broad as country estates include a golf course (*The Boomerang Clue*, #46; revised, #664), a mill (*Old Bones*, #127), a factory (mislabeled on *Alphabet Hicks*, #146), film studios (*And So to Murder*, #175), a carnival pier (*Innocent Bystander*, #461), a hospital and grounds (*One Angel Less*, #247), a sugar factory (*Assignment in Guiana*, #321), a zoo (*He Wouldn't Kill Patience*, #370), and various collections of houses and buildings (e.g., *While the Wind Howled*, #51). A beautiful view of a circus, slightly re-drawn from the author's map in the hard-cover edition, appears on *The Headless Lady* (#176), a superb complement to the entertaining text.

Small sections of New York City approximate areas discussed above; these decorate several Dell maps. *The Dead Can Tell* (#17) has a part of East River Drive; *Holiday Homicide* (#22) features a part of the East River waterfront; and *The Opening Door* (#200) shows Henderson Square and surrounding skyscrapers. The waterfront view on *Holiday Homicide* features buildings ominous in their simplicity, almost Bauhaus-inspired in its view of an apparently uninhabited city, made desolate by its lack of definable features. (See illustration 22d.) A useless and unnecessary view of a park illustrates *The Iron Gates* (#209); but another park, or a section of New York's Central Park, forms one of the best maps in the Dell series, on *Sailor, Take Warning!* (#155). The back-cover view captures the general impression of the area, as described by the author, Kelley Roos:

Jeff and I threaded our way through the nurses and their prodigies, the sun-seekers, the outdoor readers and the people who simply liked to sit and look at a little lake on which little boats bobbed merrily. A park attendant with a candy and ice cream store on wheels sent the children begging to their parents. Another khaki-clad employee with a pick-up stick busily rid the area of fallen papers. There was something fabulous about the scene, something operetta-like, and only the silhouette of the towering apartments and hotels fifteen blocks south on Fifty-ninth Street kept you from forgetting that this was New York. (p. 8)

Both the author's prose and the artist's scene are deceptively simple; both contain a subtle undercurrent of menace as well as a clue central to

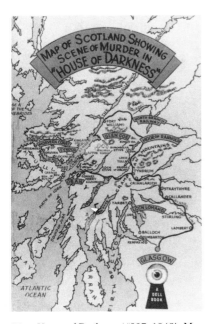

21a. *House of Darkness* (#237, 1948). Map by Ruth Belew. One of the most useful maps of a large geographical area.

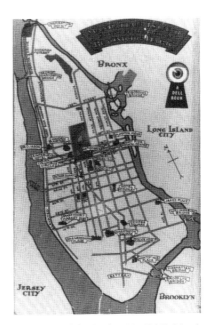

21b. *Beyond the Dark* (#93, 1945). Map by Ruth Belew. One of the best maps of New York City.

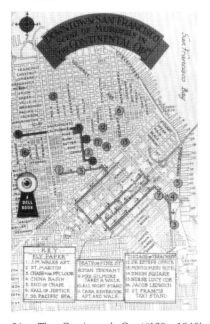

21c. *The Continental Op* (#129, 1946). Map by Ruth Belew. Detailed routes in Dashiell Hammett's stories.

21d. *Scotland Yard: The Department of Queer Complaints* (#65, 1944). Map by Ruth Belew. One of the most detailed and ornate maps in the series.

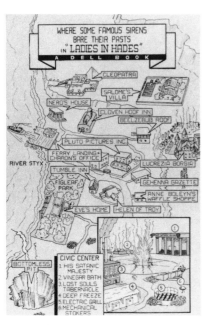

22a. *Ladies in Hades* (#415, 1950). Artist unknown. One of the few fantastic locales on the Dell back covers.

22b. *With This Ring* (#83, 1945). Map by Ruth Belew. The most detailed country estate map in the Dell series.

22c. *Suspense Stories* (#92, 1945). Map by Ruth Belew, illustrating Carl Stephenson's story, "Leiningen versus the Ants."

22d. *Holiday Homicide* (#22, 1943). Artist unknown. An almost Bauhaus-inspired view.

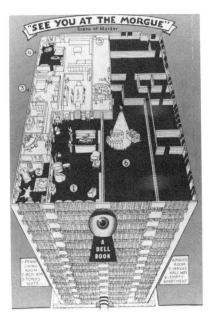

23a. *Sailor, Take Warning!* (#155, 1947). Map by Ruth Belew. One of the best maps in the series, with a subtle clue to the mystery.

23b. *See You at the Morgue* (#7, 1943). Artist unknown. A two-point perspective.

23c. *The Dead Can Tell* (#17, 1943). Artist unknown. A three-point perspective.

23d. *Dance of Death* (#33, 1944). Map possibly by Art Department, Western Printing & Lithographing, Racine, Wis. An excellent cutaway view.

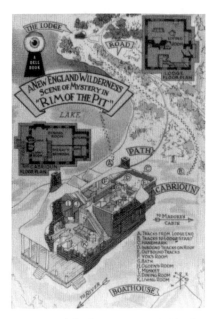

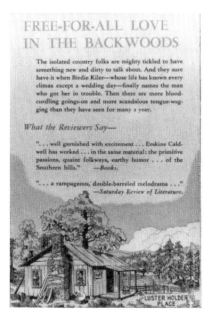

24a. *Rim of the Pit* (#173, 1947). Map by Ruth Belew, based on sketches made by the book's author, Henning Nelms ("Hake Talbot"), for the Dell edition. One of the most exact Dell maps.

24b. *Backwoods Woman* (#557, 1951). Artist unknown. The first "split back cover," with a view and a blurb.

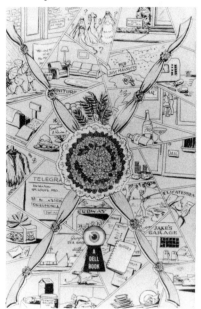

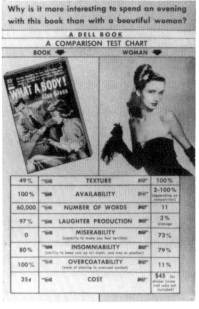

24c. *Week-End Marriage* (#73, 1945). Montage by Ruth Belew. One of the few back-cover montages.

24d. *What a Body!* (#483, 1951). Designer unknown. The most unusual Dell back cover.

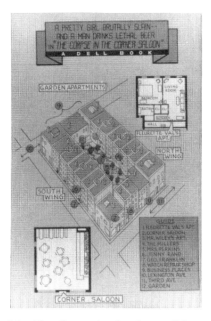

25a. *The Corpse in the Corner Saloon* (#464, 1950). Artist unknown. "[A] full floor-plan of the apartment [that] was the cover-artist's invention," in author Aaron Marc Stein's view.

25b. *The Crimson Feather* (#207, 1947). Artist unknown. Author Sara Elizabeth Mason wondered where the staircase was located on the map.

25c. *Q as in Quicksand* (#301, 1949). Artist unknown. Author Lawrence Treat thought the map "stark.'

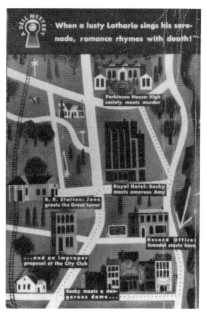

25d. *What Rhymes with Murder?* (#631, 1952). Map possibly by Walter Brooks or member of his staff. Author Jack Iams thought the Royal Hotel had "a kind of Kubla Khan feel to it (in Sheraton dress)."

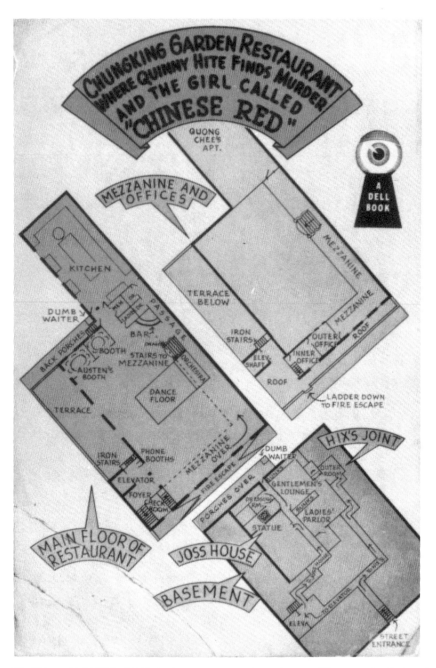

26. *Chinese Red* (#260, 1948), back-cover map, artist unknown. The most detailed and accurate of the Dell maps.

the mystery's solution. A careful reader should have no trouble finding the clue. (See illustration 23a.)

A few large hotels and inn complexes appear as well. The hotel/motel on *The Devil's Stronghold* (#395) is confusing and hides the important steps to Apt. 31-B; one of the poorest maps in the Dell series, it is not helped by author Leslie Ford's erratic descriptions. The cabin court on *The Hornet's Nest* (#79) exposes an interesting (and threatening) arrangement, like half an angry ellipse. The apartments on *The Murder That Had Everything* (#74) are good ideas; even a careful reader might have difficulty following the story without a diagram of this complex arrangement.

Most of the maps of country estates and similar areas are drawn diagonally, to allow prominent presentations of objects. Occasionally, one is even larger than a section of a town—Blandings Castle, for example (*Leave It to Psmith*, #357), typical of author P. G. Wodehouse's tendency to exaggerate. But most of these maps are small, and smaller still in scale are the diagrams and floor plans that form the majority of the Dell maps.

DIAGRAMS OR FLOOR PLANS

Small-scale diagrams or plans of a house, apartment, or similar structure, usually the scene of murder in a mystery, appear on most of the Dell books with decorated back covers. Most appropriate for mysteries, the diagrams also illustrate some romances and other works of fiction, but few westerns. Roughly half of these are overhead (90°) views, resembling architectural plans; others are angled views that allow furniture to be drawn in familiar shapes, the angles varying a great deal, but averaging about 30° (as on *Death over Sunday*, #19). Views are frontal and side, the latter dominating; occasionally a view of a house has half its side vertically cut away.

The maps use one of two systems of projection. In isometric projection, all measurements are to the same scale, all lines that are parallel appear so, and the front, top, and side of the area are at a 30° angle to the vertical axis. But most of the maps use central projection, either a one-point perspective (where each object has only one vanishing point for a set of otherwise parallel lines), as on the first Dell map, *Four Frightened Women* (#5); or a two-point perspective (two sets of vanishing points for each object), as on *See You at the Morgue* (#7), or, rarely, a three-point perspective, as on *The Dead Can Tell* (#17). (See illustrations 23b and c.) Interestingly, perhaps predictably, most of the diagrams have New York City settings (nearly 150); the second most common, California (almost 100).

Houses and similar dwellings are well represented on the Dell maps.

The details of *The Golden Swan Murder* (#15) include the odd "swan bed" of Brentwood House. (The setting here is California, of course—southern California.) An excellent cutaway view of half the side of a house appears on *Dance of Death* (#33). (See illustration 23d.) A strange arrangement, one difficult to follow in the books, is clarified on the map of *The Man Who Didn't Exist* (#41), detailed down to the hidden gun in the shrubbery outside the house. The house plan on *Spring Harrowing* (#98) includes the collection of objets d'art of the eccentric Bart Paget—items important to the story's plot and character development. One of the most fascinating views occurs on *Death in the Doll's House* (#122), where the map depicts the details of the upstairs floor of the Starling house along with a scaled dollhouse of the same structure; careful readers can solve the mystery by using both the map and the dollhouse view. Three separate overhead plans appear on *Odor of Violets* (#162), as well as an exterior view of the house; similar comprehensive layouts decorate *Fire Will Freeze* (#157), *The Glass Mask* (#198), and *Haunted Lady* (#361). All are excellent; the arrangement of rooms on *Through a Glass, Darkly* (#519) even provides the solution to the crime.

Even the colors are accurate on *The Rat Began to Gnaw the Rope* (#180), but the most complex and accurate view of a house illustrates *Rim of the Pit* (#173), the back cover sketched by the author, Henning Nelms ("Hake Talbot"), possibly finished by Ruth Belew. The design includes not only an ingenious cutaway of the Cabrioun lodge, exposing essential parts of two floors and the rooftracks through the snow, but also overhead plans of the structure and the adjoining lodge. All details are painstakingly accurate, down to the cupboard under the stair landing. A picky reader could argue that the map should include details of the cluttered living-room closet, but the map excludes little else. Those rare occasions where an author sketched his own arrangements proved rewarding. (See illustration 24a.)

The comparatively few unexciting maps of houses and similar structures appear on *The Blackbirder* (#149), lazily labeled; *The Crimson Feather* (#207), with a major error; and *Dangerous Ground* (#248), unimaginative, considering the author's wealth of detail. Equally unsatisfying are the house plans on romances. *Candidate for Love* (#239), for example, is actually overdone; *Desperate Angel* (#462), though impressive at first glance, suffers from inaccurate, vague drawings of the four women central to the novel.

Apartments illustrate many mystery titles. A typical approach exists on *See You at the Morgue* (#7): a two-point perspective of a cutaway of the 14th-floor apartments, detailed down to a disembodied hand holding a flashlight on hidden chests in a vacant apartment, the lines converging at the bottom of the building and contrasting with the view of the apartment. Overall, a startling, tense, dazzling view. A similar view appears on *The Whistling Hangman* (#113), where the outward arrangement of balconies and terraces on other floors is vital to the story. Of all the odd plans of interior detail, that on *The Frightened Stiff* (#56) is perhaps the most interesting; here a visitor enters the Troys' apartment through the bedroom, then proceeds to living room and kitchen. Such an arrangement allows for suspenseful occurrences in the novel, intensified when we discover that the apartment was once a speakeasy. The author comments:

About *The Frightened Stiff.* The odd bedroom arrangement . . . was because we lived in that apartment. . . . it wasn't on Gay Street, it was 11 Charles Street [New York City] . . . and that's the way it was. And it had been a speakeasy and we could still see the mark on the floor where the bar had stood.[18]

Initial views of apartment diagrams can occasionally deceive. Only after reading the book will one discover that the seemingly detailed floor plan on *Death Knell* (#273) actually contains too many liberties or that the plans on *The Death of a Worldly Woman* (#365) do not incorporate correct detail (available from the sketch in the hard-cover edition). On the other hand, the diagram of Hardracker's office on *Mrs. Murdock Takes a Case* (#202) allows us to detect a character's lie when he mentions a detail of the office that we can see does not exist there.

Another case of colors corresponding to the author's descriptions occurs on *Dark Passage* (#221), a map quite different from the enormous apartment in the film version of the novel. Apparently accurate, and a bonus for fans of series characters, Mike Shayne's apartments appear on *The Corpse Came Calling* (#168), Kent Murdock's apartment on *Murder with Pictures* (#441), and Murdock's studio on *The Camera Clue* (#453). One can only regret that Nero Wolfe's apartment decorated none of the appropriate Rex Stout titles; such a plan would have been especially welcome on *Not Quite Dead Enough and Booby Trap* (#267).[19]

Some extremely small apartments, basically consisting of one room and attaching dinette and bath, appear infrequently on the Dell maps. The bare view on *Turn on the Heat* (#59) implies seaminess even in the room's disarray, clothes strewn casually about. Similarly, the bleakness of "The Kid's Room" on *Kiss the Blood Off My Hands* (#197) suggests the poverty of the central character. The diagram on *Dead Man's Gift* (#190) is actually too complex—Ruth Belew was carried away in placing (through initials and arrows) seven characters and dogs in the area at the time of Michael Carmichael's death, so carried away, in fact, that even the most avid lover of diagrams might feel satiated here. Despite the excellent detail (which includes even the whistle and hearing aid on Carmichael's table, items important late in the novel), readers may feel they are being led too much here. But the author, Zelda Popkin, relies more on topographical detail than on character motivation. The best map or diagram captures the spirit of the book.

Diagrams of smaller hotels and other renting structures include the complex, accurate, and necessary one of Surf House on *The Cat Saw Murder* (#35), based on the sketch in the hard-cover edition. A beautifully acrophobic view of a hotel appears on *Do Not Disturb* (#261), with a three-point perspective. The large inset of the hotel on *Dead Wrong* (#314) can be used by readers of any Stewart Sterling novels; it is the locale of most of his series titles. A particularly elaborate arrangement occurs on *Just Around the Coroner* (#337): an exterior view of the hotel combines with floor plans of the basement, main floor, and one apartment in the hotel. The reader may be initially confused by the last detail, however, since two such apartments (both gambling-places) occur in the novel, but the confusion should dissolve halfway through the book.

Offices and office-buildings are usually well detailed on the Dell maps. The plan of the newspaper office on *Curtains for the Editor* (#82) suggests the end-of-day routine by its scattered paper in the City Room; similarly, the cluttered look of *You Only Hang Once* (#102) reveals the results of a fruitless, clumsy search for a missing document. Poorly sketched is the SUDS office on *Pick Your Victim* (#307), and particularly bad is the eighth-floor plan on *Blind Man's Bluff* (230); although the latter appears well drawn, it contains a major error concerning the solution to the mystery.

Other structures appear as diagrams. The sports arena called the Colosseum graces the reissue of *The American Gun Mystery* (#4); a similar, more detailed map appears in the hard-cover edition, but the Dell map opts for a lazy sketch, cheating a bit on perspective. The arena's placement in space, however, connected loosely to a spot in Manhattan, presents an interesting paradox—a visual oxymoron—of a wild-west rodeo in civilized New York City. A section of a department store, sporting women's lingerie, is detailed on *Death Wears a White Gardenia* (#13), its cutaway look appropriate in relation to the implicit suggestion of the Dell logo, "the eye-in-keyhole." And the Paris Opera House appears in profile, as a sort of imitation blueprint, on *The Phantom of the Opera* (#24), its details deriving not from the descriptions in Gaston Leroux's novel but partially from an afterword printed in some editions of the book.

Nero Wolfe's visit to an elaborate feast provides the basis for two diagrams of Kanawha Spa, on *Too Many Cooks* (#45; revised, #540), detailed down to the pieces of squab waiting to be test-eaten.[20] Beauty salons grace *Painted for the Kill* (#87) and *The Accomplice* (#346), the first an exploded view of all six floors, the second an exterior view and plan of part of the odd house of *Mimi Decors*. The only Dell tomb occurs on *Red*

Threads (#235), striking and accurate, even with the holes in the wall "through which the morning sun could come, or not come" (Dell edition, p. 74). An anatomy laboratory, with concealed corpses ready for dissection, decorates the grim back cover of *Bitter Ending* (#289); an undertaker's parlor comprises half the back cover of *One Angel Less* (#247). Railroad cars appear on *The Man in Lower Ten* (#124) and *Bombay Mail* (#488), neither really necessary, and ships on *Holiday Homicide* (#22), *Midnight Sailing* (#43), and *She Walks Alone* (#430). The last is a complex, confusing, inaccurate diagram of the ship decks, its inaccuracy attributable to the inconsistent descriptions of author Helen McCloy.

A nicely accurate map of a prop room in a theater illustrates *Juliet Dies Twice* (#68), the map detailed even in the location of cigarette butts on the lawn. A more useful view of a theater graces *Cue for Murder* (#212), where a seemingly poor choice for a map turns out to be intelligent and helpful. Here, all the details on the cleverly done map allow the reader to follow the plot and to solve Helen McCloy's mystery.

The most detailed original Dell map appears on the back cover of Richard Burke's mystery, *Chinese Red* (#260), a map of the Chungking Gardens Restaurant. The novel does not represent the best example of either the mystery or detective genre; the central character, Quinny Hite, is an uninspired, lackluster creation, and the plot is thin. But Burke did work out the physical details of the restaurant very carefully—if he were a better writer, the restaurant itself could come alive and become the main character. That is not quite the case, but Burke's elaborate descriptions do allow the Dell artist to create an ornate, accurate diagram of the basement, main floor, and mezzanine of the restaurant. Detailed are routes through the complex arrangement of rooms, as well as such minutiae as a gilded railing and large Chinese statue in the room called the Joss House (Dell edition, p. 37) and the mezzanine ladder to the fire escape (pp. 73-74). Consider, for instance, having to follow these scenes without a visual guide:

Quinny walked on around the mezzanine to Quong's office. There was an outer office, with two windows overlooking the restaurant floor, and an inner office with just one window which opened onto a four-foot-wide strip of roof between the mezzanine floor (which had been added to the building later) and the street wall of the building. No view of the dining-room was to be had from this inner office. An enclosed, narrow stairway led from it to the checkroom in the foyer below, serving Quong Chee as a sometimes more convenient way to his office from the elevator. The door to these stairs was closed, and the detectives supposed it was a closet. (pp. 22-23)

Beyond the elevator structure [at the mezzanine] they found iron steps and climbed down these to the deserted terrace. . . . It was about twelve feet high and three or four times that in length, with a breast-high parapet enclosing its two outer edges. Three circular doors . . . opened onto the terrace from the main dining-room. (pp. 74-75)

The map even allows room at a dinner table for the required eight people (p. 48). Missing from the map are only a few details: an urn on the terrace, stairs to the second-floor back porch, a telephone closet in Hix's place. But these are certainly minor compared to the wealth of detail that does appear. Many details assume no particular importance in the novel, but they do conform to Burke's descriptions. And he does like to describe . . . and describe. Perhaps if Burke had appended a map to his book, as Agatha Christie does in *Murder in Mesopotamia*, he could have allowed it to speak for him and concentrated more on the reasons for moving people through places. He preferred instead to outline positions of windows. (See illustration 26.)

A few similar structures illustrate other kinds of fiction, none too successfully. An overhead view of the Harvey House on *The Harvey Girls* (#130) presents an undistinguished plan of the restaurant figuring prominently in that romantic adventure; a plan of the Longhorn Saloon provides an inset for the western, *Rutledge Trails the Ace of Spades* (#383); a kind of map of the action in a Spanish bullring decorates *Blood and Sand* (#500), the last helpful to readers unaccustomed to the sport dissected in Vicente Blasco-Ibañez's novel. The diagrams in the mysteries remain the most useful, occasionally even helpful, in following the plot; *Chinese Red* is the best example.

MISCELLANEOUS DESIGNS

Occasionally, when an author has extremely sparse descriptions or when a novel has a particularly unidentifiable locale, views (as opposed to maps or diagrams) of houses or other structures adorned the Dell back covers. *Blood on the Black Market* (#64), for example, features an inset view of a gas station, the initial scene of action in that mystery. *The Visitor* (#132) has a view of two houses central to the plot. A view of the March house on *Little Women* (#296) appears very similar to the view in the 1949 film version; perhaps the artist had access to a still from that film. Poor views of houses occur on *The Seven Deadly Sisters* (#412) and *Tender Mercy* (#444), neither resembling even slightly the authors' descriptions. And a beach scene decorates *This Is It, Michael Shayne* (#533), for no apparent reason except that Brett Halliday's Mike Shayne mystery is set in Florida, which has beaches. A small sign of the approaching demise (in the early 1950's) of the maps is apparent on *Backwoods Woman* (#557), which has a split back cover: a view of a house and blurbs. (See illustration 24b.) Blurbs soon replaced the decorations on the Dell back covers.

Some montages of scenes appear as well. The montage on *Week-End Marriage* (#73) is a better choice than a map, since Faith Baldwin's romance shuttles between locations without giving details. (See illustration 24c.) On Nicholas Monsarrat's *Leave Cancelled* (#327) small vignettes tied to clocks suggest the briefness of time of the novel. Monsarrat disliked the idea.[21] But Richard Powell appreciated the decorations on his *Shell Game* (#518), views tied to a shell, the left-handed whelk. Powell suggests that the artist chose this shell as center inset because of its sinister reputation.[22]

In some rare cases, Dell back covers lack any sort of decoration. The first four Dell books (and the twelfth) simply announce the new paperback line. (The fourth title was reissued with a map.) Cartoons appear on the early joke books, crossword puzzles on the puzzle books, a balance sheet on *Dividend on Death* (#617),   and War Bonds advertisements on *I Was a Nazi Flier* (#21), *The Raft* (#26), and *This Time for Keeps* (#32). A series of drawings illustrate a chapter in *How to Pick a Mate* (#224), and portraits of characters appear on *Message from a Stranger* (#515) and *Wait for the Dawn* (#544). The most unusual Dell back cover appears on *What a Body!* (#483)—a "chart" which explains why the customer (presumably male) should buy the book rather than spend an evening with a beautiful woman. (See illustration 24d.) Another chart adorns the back cover of *Francis* (#507), but its appeal hardly matches the incredibly sexist, vastly entertaining one on *What a Body!*

OTHER FEATURES

The small features on all the Dell maps often were meticulously drawn. When a map or plan (especially a street map) needed references to many key spots in the story, the artist placed numbers on the map, keyed to a legend. The labeling is usually accurate (one glaring exception is *Framed in Blood*, #578). Unfortunately, the numbered places do not always follow the book's chronology. Occasionally the labeling in other areas is inexact: on *Alphabet Hicks* (#146) the banner should read "R.I. Dundee Laboratory," not "Factory." And *Murder Wears Mukluks* (#259) has "Van" Voss for "Val" Voss. On *Pirates of the Range* (#466), the cattle brands placed on the map of the western United States provide too easy a solution to the book's "mystery." But such errors occur infrequently.

More serious is the lack of accurate color on the maps. Colors match authors' descriptions only occasionally. On *The Rat Began to Gnaw the Rope* (#180), the required red tiles appear on the terrace and a blue rug in the study. *Dangerous Ground* (#248) has the red sandstone and green roof, as it should. The story, "Suicide Is Scandalous," in *Report for a Corpse* (#330) features grey and gold walls, as the author wished. Only in a few cases did Western's staff jot down such color arrangements, thinking the matchup of little importance; Ruth Belew worked in black-and-white, so it was up to Western's staff artists to add notations of color. Some maps need exact coloring: *Appointment with Death* (#105) has as its central feature the famed red rocks of Petra, yet on the Dell map the rocks are yellow. The earliest maps used color backgrounds linked to the spine color (#1-9); #10 used yellow and red alone; #11 green and yellow. The full four-color process began with #13 (although it is more apparent on #14), increasing in sophistication thereafter to highlight details in the maps.

Most of the banners were done by Ruth Belew. Not all of them are accurate. "Scene of Murders" (plural noun) promises more than is delivered in *Strawstack Murders* (#62), *The Affair of the Scarlet Crab* (#75), and *The Crimson Feather* (#207)—in all of which only one murder occurs at each pictured locale. "Scene of Murder" is accurate for *Mourned on Sunday* (#63), but we do not discover that the death in the book is a murder until late in the book; "Scene of Mystery" might be less leading. Similarly, a suicide (and the murder of a cat) occurs at the "Scene of Murders" on *Dangerous Ground* (#248)—but no homicide. "Murders" is not apt on *The State versus Elinor Norton* (#203), since the first "murder," we learn, probably was committed in self-defense, and the second is pronounced justifiable homicide by a jury. Should we dispute the jury's finding? And the name of the book is incorrect in the banner of #329: *Young Dr. Kildare*, not *Calling Doctor Kildare*, an altogether different novel.

But overall the banners were aptly chosen, not revealing too much of the plot but stimulating interest: "Murder Runs Riot," for example, accurately explains happenings in Mary Roberts Rinehart's Gothic novel, *The Great Mistake* (#297); "Scene of the Mystery" is correct for *Murder for Two* (#276), where the murder occurs near but not at the scene on the map. Most of the maps on mysteries did use the scene of murder. One exception is *Who's Calling?* (#151): although a poisoning occurs in one house, the house where most of the action occurs ("Where Poltergeist Leaves a Trail") appears on the map. And although most of the maps are scenes of murder, the Dell maps show no exposed corpses; Dell and Western felt such displays would reveal too much and make too graphic a display.[23] For example, compare two editions of Rex Stout's *Bad for Business*: the front cover of a digest-sized edition (Century Publications #28, n.d.) has a corpse in an office; the back cover of Dell #299 has just the office.

AUTHORS' REACTIONS

Many of the authors of the Dell books found the maps a fine complement to their text—at least those authors still alive who responded to my letters. Frederic Dannay ("Ellery Queen") and George

Harmon Coxe, however, did not remember ever seeing the maps, nor did Mignon G. Eberhart, though she remembers doing pencil sketches of her own for her early novels. James M. Fox gave little thought to the maps: "Dell did a good job of merchandising these books, selling from 250,000 to 350,000 copies per title. [Why] quibble about the artwork on the jackets?" Similarly, Martha Albrand felt that "it is not a question if the paper-cover maps or backs are correct or attractive to our personal taste. You have to leave the decision to the people who sell the book. In most cases they know best."[24]

Ray Bradbury thought that the map illustrating his story "The Million Year Picnic" in *Invasion from Mars* (#305) "doesn't depict my dream of Mars at all." But more authors found the maps attractive and relatively accurate. Leslie Ford and Delano Ames were pleased with them, and Eaton K. Goldthwaite thought the map on *Root of Evil* (#442) "a fairly faithful portrayal of the automobile trip" which inspired the trip in his novel. Richard Powell considered the illustrations to *Shell Game* (#518) "quite good"; S. Omar Barker felt the map illustrated well the events in " 'They've Shot Jug Murphy' " (in the anthology, *Western Stories*, #282). John Canaday believed the maps on *The Devil in the Bush* (#158) and *The Smell of Money* (#219) good on the basis of his sketches. Jan Westcott, noting that publishers often do not use maps because of the added expense, was "pleased with . . . the effort Dell made [on *The Border Lord*, #439]." And Audrey and William Roos ("Kelley Roos") replied that they thought "the maps accurate and reliable for the most part."[25]

More detailed responses came from other authors. Paul Winterton, responding to my question about the locale of *No Mask for Murder* (#571), wrote:

The apparent confusion about the whereabouts of Fontego was deliberate. I had spent several months in one of the larger West Indian islands doing a report on conditions for the London *Economist*, and had met all the leading people, official and unofficial. My original US publisher was concerned about the possibility of libel, since several of the characters in the story occupied official positions. None was in fact drawn from life, but as a precaution I made various changes in the MS (such as mentioning Singapore and Honolulu) so that Fontego could not be positively identified as West Indian. . .the map on the back [of *No Mask for Murder*] was very nicely done. I can't remember now whether or not I contributed a rough sketch.

I have no copy of the Dell *Two If by Sea* [#634], but I see that the map of the section of Estonia was in the original UK edition and I probably drew it from the relevant chart—after which, no doubt, it was professionally tidied up. The map of Europe . . . must have been Dell's own contribution.[26]

Aaron Marc Stein remembered:

The Corpse in the Corner Saloon [#464] was written a long time ago and there have been too many books since for me to have remembered in sufficient detail just how much importance physical layout may have had in the story. After many years of not having looked at it I have now reread it and with special reference to the maps on the Dell edition's back cover. I find that it is as I was remembering it. I had not hung any of the plot or action on any description of the layout of the murdered woman's apartment. I established that it was a rear apartment with windows that overlooked the garden. I also established that because of the depth of the window embrasures, action that took place even right at one of the windows could not be seen from anywhere but one of the windows of the flats directly opposite or from that part of the garden that was directly beneath the windows of the Val apartment. Obviously, therefore, that full floor-plan of the apartment was the cover-artist's invention. He did not, however, intrude anything that contradicted the text. [See illustration 25a.]

I would say that back cover was an exercise in graphics for the most part irrelevant to the story. In comparison with the wild irrelevance of most paperback covers and many hard-cover jackets, this was nothing. It did not mislead the potential purchaser beyond possibly leading him to think that it would be one of those stories in which the plot was so intricately involved with the architectural layout that it could not be followed without the aid of floor plans. Such a story I do not think it is.

At the time the book was written Third Avenue [in New York City] was only just beginning to be transformed from what it had been before the elevated railway had been torn down. Fashion was edging toward it and it was undergoing culture shock. The culture of the old-fashioned saloon was being fractured by the intrusion of the cocktail-bar element. I had the whole area of the Sixties, Seventies, and Eighties in mind, nothing more specific than that . . .[27]

C. W. Grafton wrote:

There is little to say about the diagram on the back of *The Rope Began to Hang the Butcher* [#232]. The situs of the story consisted of an abandoned subdivision with only one house on it and two streets which crossed one another; so there was not much room for imagination. I would say that the diagram on the back was exactly what I had in mind.

The diagram on the Dell edition of *The Rat Began to Gnaw the Rope* [#180] is more difficult to comment upon. It is very near to a mirrored image of the house I had in mind. Actually I am surprised that anyone could come as close as this to the layout of the house where Mr. William Jasper Harper was slaughtered, because I was deliberately vague. . . .

This is a long way of getting around to the fact that in *The Rat Began to Gnaw the Rope,* I did not want anyone to be concerned about how many feet it was from X to Y, or how many steps there were between the first floor and the second floor.[28]

And Donald Hamilton:

All I can tell you with respect to *The Steel Mirror* [#473] and *Murder Twice Told* [#577] is that I don't recall being particularly disturbed by the artwork when it appeared. As for *Date with Darkness* [#375], the map does give a reasonable idea of the Chesapeake area; and since I deliberately did not locate some of the places mentioned with any great accuracy in the book for the simple reason that they never existed except in my imagination, it seems to me it would have been hard for the artist to do much better. Anyway, it's decorative, as is the bullet-riddled scrap of a Texas map on the back of *The Big Country* [#B115]. . . .

As you're probably aware, where covers and artwork are concerned, the poor novelist is often the last to know. The map of a small part of Arizona Territory in *Mad River* [Dell First Edition #91] was an exception; it was originally sketched by me, on request. A wholly imaginary terrain laid out to suit the demands of the novel; but I probably got the idea from Medicine Hat, Utah, which I researched—this was during the uranium rush—for another novel published the same year. . . . *Assignment: Murder* (First Edition #A123). Well, it has no maps, just a pretty girl on the cover.[29]

Sara Elizabeth Mason, on *The Crimson Feather* (#207):

Your letter prompted me to reread the book. The setting, of course, is vaguely Tuscaloosa where the University of Alabama is located. A residential area there called "The Highlands" corresponds just as vaguely to the homes of the Tollivers. I know I worked with a house plan when I was writing the book but that is long gone. From the book, the entrance is a hallway with a stair to the second floor (bedroom area); the library to the left, the drawing room to the right. The second murder took place upstairs, so why a diagram of the lower floor?

and later:

What struck me as odd as soon as I looked at the diagram of the house was no stairwell upstairs. People would have to rise ghost-like through the floor. Surely it would be where the bath room adjoining Mrs. Tolliver's room is located. A small bath could be placed to the front, but somehow that staircase has got to lead to the center of the second floor.

The banner over the cutaway should certainly read "murder" rather than "murders."[30] [See illustration 25b.]

Lenore Glen Offord:

Comments: the map on *Skeleton Key* [#96] is indeed peculiar, and made me feel disoriented, as if my own house had been swung around to face the other way. Grettry Road ran downward, but the houses in the picture are all on the wrong sides. If I were in a truly nitpicking mood, I'd say that the Freys', Hollisters' and Gillespies' should look almost exactly alike, only "differing aggressively in detail." The three here pictured on the left, or east side, would have the valued view of the Bay from across the canyon. There now, I've boggled my mind again, just looking at that map.

I don't know why the artist insisted, in the design for [*My*] *True Love* [*Lies*]

[#476], on including the Federal Building and City Hall, unless he had some idea that the headquarters for police were housed in one or another. . . . The rest is all right.

The artist did very well with the complicated description of the Tillsit house . . . it does give the general idea.

(The author added that the map on *Skeleton Key* "makes me feel like Alice as she came through the looking-glass—everything familiar but turned the wrong way."]31

And Dorothy B. Hughes:

[*The So*] *Blue Marble* [#100] is really a good job. I stayed in that apartment; it was my brother-in-law's and he and his wife off on a cruise. The book describes it quite accurately. *The Cross-Eyed Bear* [*Murders*] [#48]—I remember next to nothing about that story and nothing about the scene except that it was expensive. As it was not a real place, I would say that the map artist did okay by it. [*The*] *Fallen Sparrow* [#31]. This too I think is well done, the old house made over into flats. . . . *The Blackbirder* [#149], I like. It gives the feel of Tesuque and the snow. . . . *Ride the Pink Horse* [#210] is the only one with a couple of noticeable flaws. Number 14, the Cross of the Martyrs, is north of Hillside; it should be over to the East, quite a bit over. I also cannot understand why they made a label for Number 6 "Church," when anyone knows a Church and a Cathedral are different, and Santa Fe's Cathedral is historical, it having been built by Archbishop Lamy (*Death Comes for the Archbishop*—Cather) and it being (in my opinion) perhaps the ugliest Cathedral extant. Also they have in the scene faced the Cathedral towards the Alameda (and it's some distance north of the Alameda) and what is irking is that the Cathedral faces west, down San Francisco Street, and that must have been clear in the book as it is so much a part of the Santa Fe scene to anyone who's been there—you look up the street and there it stands on a small terrace, looking over the town.

Of course I never protested any of this at the time nor would I do such a thing. Any more than a writer protests a book jacket—it is not in his province to do so. It's like having a book into a film or TV script—certain changes are necessary as they are different mediums from book writing, and who am I to criticize the experts, in their fields.32

Wayne D. Overholser:

My early Dell books all had the maps on the backs and I think it's an excellent idea because it orients the reader. I don't know why they stopped doing it unless it's just an added expense in putting the book out and with costs what they are, I suppose they're doing all they can to keep them down. I thought the map on *Buckaroo's Code* [#372] was good. The names of streets would have been a good addition, but maybe they thought they didn't have the room. I liked the maps on *West of the Rimrock* [#499] and *Draw or Drag* [#556]. I have no idea why they mention a twenty-cow spread. I've always used the term ten-cow spread meaning a small outfit, but I don't remember ever calling a ranch a twenty-cow spread.[33]

Lawrence Treat:

As for the accuracy of the "maps," you've checked that, and there's no need for me to double-check, except that I just happened to notice that the Gobelin Main Street [on *Q as in Quicksand*, #301; see illustration 25c] had concrete buildings—hardly such, in the map. But in a more general way, I think I can respond to the questions you've asked.

I don't like the kind of cold, stylized art represented in the maps or on the covers. I think sometimes of the great illustrators of the nineteenth century, like Frederic Remington, Howard Pyle, Thomas Nast. So much of book and magazine illustration runs from the cold to the smart-Alec. There are, of course, some fine abstracts. But this is not what I'm talking about. The maps seem to me to have little to do with the lived-in places I tried to write about. Gobelin was a New England community with charm, and its plant breathed of activity and movement. These maps are stark.

In looking over your analyses, I'm amazed at the detailed descriptions I wrote. Today, I like to give the feel and mood of a place or a person, and let the reader construct his own image.

As for your questions, neither book [*Q as in Quicksand* and *H as in Hunted*, #218] was based on a real town or apartment, and, to the extent I can remember, neither map has much relationship to what I had in mind. To all of which I have no objections. A publisher's job is to sell books, and if these maps helped, then why should I comment?[34]

The bluntest, most critical response came from Mary Renault—first, before she saw the copies (Dell apparently never sent copies to her home in South Africa):

The maps you describe sound perfectly idiotic. None of these books [*Kind Are Her Answers*, #189; *Promise of Love*, #298; *Return to Night*, #394] has a plot in any way dependent on topography. Are the front covers absolutely ghastly? I bet they are.

and then, after I sent her copies of the Dell editions:

Very many thanks for sending me Dell's horror-comic. After one stunned look I wrapped it well up and concealed it in the trash-can before my maid came back on duty. She would never have thought the same of me again. . . . You will be doing me a kindness, should any come into your hands, by directing them to the incinerator. If anything of the sort should appear in the drugstores *new*, then I'd be truly grateful to be advised of it so that I can get after them. Nowadays I get approval of all my jackets, but this book is more than 30 years old, and I hadn't yet managed it. But—honestly—what kind of person would *want* to read a book with that kind of jacket? Depressing.[35]

The reverse sentiment was expressed by Jack Iams, concerning his mysteries and adventures:

I can only say that I was, in general, very pleased with the Dell maps and appreciative of their having gone to such pains. They gave me the feeling that somebody at Dell cared. They also showed that whoever had designed the maps had read the books reasonably closely (which is frequently not the case with jacket designers).

As to the city in the two later books [*Do Not Murder Before Christmas*, #514, and *What Rhymes with Murder?*, #631], I did not have any specific city in mind. I wanted it to be of manageable size, and I rather liked the idea of creating my own city. Gave me a sense of power. (Somewhat akin, I imagine, to the fascination exercised by the game of "Monopoly.")

Later, after re-examining the books, Iams added:

. . . the map of the Caribbean on *Love—and the Countess to Boot* [#139] was a useful one, though I think it might have been more so if it had shown the relation of the islands to the U.S. mainland. The view of Charlotte Amalie had a nice feel to it, and saved the back cover from being too textbookish.

The map of Hilary Judd's house on *The Body Missed the Boat* [#274] is . . . not really necessary. It is decorative and an accurate enough picture of what the house might have looked like, but it doesn't help the reader relate the events of the story to the setting. The map of Africa doesn't strike me as particularly helpful either, though it does show the relationship between the three towns mentioned. Mind you, I have no serious objection to the back cover. It just could have been better.

Merry Point, on the other hand, on *Girl Meets Body* [#384], is like a rebuttal to the foregoing. It *does* help the reader relate events to setting, and does so accurately and with a sense of atmosphere. As a combination of decoration and usefulness, it's probably the best of the lot.

Also very good, I think, is the one of Manhattan on *Death Draws the Line* [#457]. For a reader unfamiliar with New York, it would be extremely helpful, and the insets convey a good sense of what the different scenes were like. The way they handled Zeke Brock's studio seemed to me particularly effective. In direct answer to your question, the insets do indeed correspond to my visualizations of the places involved.

The picture of the toy shop on the back of [*Do Not Murder Before*] *Christmas* [#514] does indeed correspond to my description, though I'm not sure that the pastel colors are right for it. Nor is it helped by the headlines. As you point out, the biggest one was supposed to have appeared in the Eagle, not the Record—in fact, it had a bearing on the story. The others have the amateurish quality that seems invariably to attach itself to supposed headlines written by non-professionals. (I find this particularly true of headlines in movies.) They aren't offensively bad for their purpose—they do make it clear that this is a newspaper story—but I feel it's the least successful of the back covers.

The map on *What Rhymes* [*with Murder?*] [#631] furnishes an example of how memory can play tricks. I had thought of it, in retrospect, as a good, detailed presentation of my imaginary city. Like Merry Point but on a larger scale. Now, having it in front of me, I realize that it is a far from satisfactory effort, one that is of virtually no help whatsoever to the reader. Decoratively, it is not bad. In fact, there is perhaps more imagination in it than in any of the others. The Royal Hotel, for instance, has a kind of Kubla Khan feel to it (in Sheraton dress). But the various spots are located more or less at random.[36] [See illustration 25d.]

POSTSCRIPT

Overall, the Dell back-cover maps and diagrams present an extremely decorative, often accurate feature, one which readers might wish more publishers adopted. When one map expert comments that "A map is a graphic document in which location, extent, and direction can be more precisely defined than by the written word," he might be justifying the Dell mapbacks.[37] Although the most accurate of the Dell maps are those based on sketches in hard-cover editions, many of the others, especially *Chinese Red*, are excellent original maps, helpful for a reader who takes his mystery seriously. Only one map tips off the reader too unfairly: *Octagon House* (#171) places a well on the map, thereby giving away a clue to the location of an important substance in the novel.

Occasionally the artist takes too many liberties, as on *Candidate for Love* (#239), where Ruth Belew invents an entire floor plan. But without some invented plans and maps, editions such as *Scotland Yard: The Department of Queer Complaints* (#65), *She* (#339), and *The Circular Staircase* (#585) would be comparatively drab. And odd arrangements are rendered well on *The Man Who Didn't Exist* (#41), *The Birthday Murder* (#214), and *Just Around the Coroner* (#337). Some maps are drawn (and drawn out) from sketchy descriptions in the book (*Kiss the Blood Off My Hands*, #197, for example), but they retain the flavor of the book. Could they detract from the book's impact, as author Mary Renault suggests? Only if they suggest, as front covers sometimes do, a book so different in genre or scope than what is truly between the covers. Rather than suggesting a book dependent on topography, however, the maps, as a *series feature*, help to create an attractive book and, occasionally, aid the reader in his literary travels.

The first 200 maps are, in general, more skillfully done than the later ones, although not always as accurate. A particularly poor batch occurs from #268 to #271 and (from a standpoint of accuracy) in those after #605. The decline of the maps was part of an overall re-design instituted by the executive editor of the Dell Books, Frank Taylor. "I was the villain," he admits.[38] Taylor, in response to readers complaining about the omission of the maps, considered adapting them to other series but decided against it for several reasons. Essentially, the kinds of books he was bringing into Dell did not need maps—Evelyn Waugh's novels, poetry volumes, Shakespeare plays. And having an in-house artist prepare the maps was expensive. Yet the maps were "revived very briefly in a more decorative form" by Walter Brooks, under some pressure from Helen Meyer, who wanted them used at least occasionally. Brooks used them "if the books demanded them" (on mysteries); either he or a free-lance artist drew and colored them.[39] But they never became a standard feature after 1951; collectors thus have only 577 books with maps on the back covers.

In 1980, Dell launched two new mystery lines: "Murder Ink." and "Scene of the Crime." Dell editor Peter Guzzardi wrote to me on October 17, 1980, that he would, as a believer in tradition, consider reviving the mapback feature. It has not yet happened, however.

8

Other Dell Features

Besides distinctive front covers and back-cover maps, Dell paperbacks also had a number of other interesting features, including an "eye-in-keyhole" logo, front-cover blurbs, character lists, lists of key items or events in the book ("tantalizer-pages"), crowded title-pages, and special chapter titles.

LOGO

Pocket Books used a kangaroo; Bantam, a rooster; Avon, Shakespeare's head. Dell adopted an unusual "eye-in-keyhole," which despite slight changes through the years remained Dell's impossible-to-mistake insignia from 1942 to late 1951. The idea may have been Lloyd Smith's; George Frederiksen thinks Otto Storch may have designed it. The symbol of the eye commonly represents omniscience, or scrutiny; it is particularly familiar in the "We Never Sleep" logo of Pinkerton's Detective Agency (which gave rise to the phrase "private eye") and the CBS logo. The keyhole suggests mystery—most of Dell's early books were mysteries—and often appeared on covers of pulp and detective magazines of the 1930's (*Whisper*, for example). The eye/keyhole combination, suggesting approved close-up voyeurism, was a brilliant idea, one George Delacorte predicted would be "firmly implanted in the minds of dealers and customers."[1]

The logo appeared on the spines of most Dell books until late 1950, on the covers until August, 1952 (a modernized version re-appeared briefly in the mid-1950's), and on the back covers until July, 1949. Seven types of logos appeared. The main logo served on all spines and back covers; on front covers it identified mysteries but served also for science-fiction and general fiction titles. A romance keyhole substituted a heart for the eye; westerns used a cattle skull; adventures had a steamship; historical romances featured a quill and pen; and two puzzle books used a puzzle.

Three books use a blank keyhole.[2] The disappearance of the logos was the result of Frank Taylor and Walter Brooks' overall revision of the Dell books format. A keyhole device re-appeared in later years on at least two Dell books: Norman Bogner's *Seventh Avenue* (1968) and *The Intimate Sex Lives of Famous People,* by Irving Wallace et al. (1981). (See illustrations 27 a-f.)

After 1951, variations of the word "Dell" appeared as logos. None were really distinguished, although the boxed "A DELL BOOK/DELL/A DELL BOOK" of the early 1950's apparently impressed Toby Press, who imitated it in 1953 and 1954. Some of Dell's lines used small, unobtrusive logos (a yearling colt for Yearling Books, a laurel-leaf for Laurels), but "DELL" remained the main logo, rivaling in uniform, unimaginative consistency the logos of most other paperback companies of the 1960's and the 1970's.

FRONT-COVER BLURBS

What we today call a blurb paperback historian Frank Schick defines as a "skyline," which he traces back to eighteenth-century printed sermons. He terms it "a short sentence or phrase printed on the outside covers above the title, summarizing the book's content in a striking way and indicating why the book should be bought."[3] Like those of some other paperback publishers, Dell's blurbs usually explained the type of book or identified a series character in a mystery title. Occasionally the blurb nearly replaced the title—for example, THEIR ANCIENT GRUDGE/ A HATFIELD AND McCOY NOVEL ABOUT/HILLBILLY FEUDING AND LOVING (#435), the last four words prominently featured in yellow letters; and ONCE IN VIENNA/HE HAD THREE LOVE AFFAIRS (#524), the last phrase in shocking pink. (Some dealers' catalogs actually use the later phrases as titles; the dealers never inspected beyond the covers of the books.)

Most of the Dell blurbs are accurate or at least inoffensive. A particularly misleading one, however, occurs on *That Girl from Memphis* (#548), where the blurb quotes a scantily clad woman descending stairs as saying, "Look me over, gentlemen. Would any of you have a fancy to call me theirs?" Both the front-cover painting and the blurb suggest the woman is a prostitute; in the book, however, the quote ends, "Their wife, I mean. In marriage" (Dell edition, p. 71). And occasionally the blurbs exaggerated too much: Luke Short's *Bold Rider* (#A134) boasts "over a million copies in print," but only 657,000 copies existed.

In 1950, and then in 1952 and 1953, Dell experimented with spine blurbs. But the spines of most books could not accommodate such a feature; the obtrusive feature was dropped after appearing on the spines of 49 books.

27a-f. Representative Dell keyhole logos. From left to right: the original Dell "eye-in-keyhole," a later version, and keyholes adapted for other genres—romance (heart), western (cattle skull), adventure (steamship), historical romance (quill and ink). Keyhole photos by *Paperback Quarterly*.

27g. Four of the logos patterned into the Dell endpapers.

28a-b. The evolution of Dell's title-pages. The early books used cluttered but informative title-pages, as on *Anthony Adverse in America* (#285, 1949). Later title-pages, under the direction of Walter Brooks, used sparse, lean designs, as on *The Operation* (#F171, 1962).

29a-b. Two of Dell's advertisements in the 1940's. The advertisements stressed Dell's distinctive features: airbrushed covers, keyhole logos, character lists, lists of key items (tantalizer-pages), and back-cover maps.

CHARACTER LISTS

Some hard-cover publishers thoughtfully included brief lists of the main characters in their books—especially in mysteries—to allow readers to keep characters straight. Occasionally paperback publishers, especially Pocket Books, retained the feature or initiated it. Pony Weldun paperbacks (a Canadian imprint of the 1940's) used character lists in some books; the format of the lists copied that of Dell's. One Pony Weldun book, Douglas Stapledon and Helen A. Carey's *The Corpse Is Indignant*, even featured a map on the *verso* page of the character list. But only Dell used character lists (or character-indexes)—"Persons this Mystery [or Romance] is about"—as a standard feature in all books. Devised by Lloyd Smith, these lists were individually compiled by the editorial staff of Western, with occasional help from free-lancers and secretarial staff.

The earliest lists were selective, usually only one page long. Characters usually appeared in order of importance, their descriptions often taken verbatim from the books. The first two-page list occurs on *The Harvey Girls* (#130); later lists vary from one to two pages, depending on the novel's complexity and length. Beginning in late 1950, most lists began with a teasing synopsis of the book's plot. Occasionally, the lists are borrowed from the hard-cover edition (*The Case of the Seven Sneezes*, #334, for example); *Made up to Kill* (#106) reproduces the list of characters in a stage play featured in the novel as well as the special Dell list; and *Little Women* (#296) adds the actors who played the roles in the film version. The strain of the compilers' task shows in the synopsis in *Death in Four Colors* (#531), which features "Hamp Stone" (a pseudonym of Dell author Aaron Marc Stein) rather than the character "Hamp Hume."

Obviously, the lists could not be all-inclusive. But lively, readable lists exist on *The Clue of the Judas Tree* (#61), *Murder Is a Kill-Joy* (#103), *Golden Earrings* (#216), *Alias the Dead* (#377), and *The Neat Little Corpse* (#560). Keeping the characters separate in *Judas, Incorporated* (#244) would be unnecessarily difficult without such a list. The list in *Skyscraper* (#236) is actually overdone. On the other hand, some Dell lists omit important characters. *The Footprints on the Ceiling* (#121) neglects the narrator; *The Lady Is Afraid* (#147) lacks the principal suspect, among others; *The Corpse Came Calling* (#168) excludes the character about whom the novel revolves; and *Where There's Smoke* (#275) misses the real villain. One list, in *Wiped Out* (#165), a collection of stories, places the characters in random order—confusing for anyone reading the stories in the order in which the book arranges them. Occasionally, an author will crowd so many characters into a book that no two-page Dell list can accommodate them. Helen Reilly is particularly guilty of this habit. And occasionally a list will omit a character for good reason; *The Woman in Black* (#447) justly lacks Betty Livingstone, the first murder victim, since her identity is supposed to be kept secret for a while.

The character descriptions are usually succinct, playful, and witty, in keeping with the style and sense of the particular book:

HELEN JETTWICK,
Bruce's mother, who looks like a motor job that's been in a bad traffic accident and has been put together again, too quickly. (Rufus King, *Holiday Homicide*, #22)

ZENOPHEN ZWICK,
the author of three clever, witty, well-written sardonic detective stories that prove to be very popular; he lived and died in mystery. (Geoffrey Homes, *The Man Who Didn't Exist*, #41)

SUE MARSHALL,
Max Hale's secretary . . . a pale, slender girl with straight, yellow hair, worn long and pulled severely back in a compact knot. She could be a knockout if she took off the horn-rimmed glasses and fixed her hair. (George Harmon Coxe, *Murder for the Asking*, #58)

MRS. CLIFFORD MEREDITH, SR.,
an elderly woman with untidy gray hair and a hard and suspicious face. She doesn't seem clever. (Anna Mary Wells, *A Talent for Murder*, #66)

LILY ROWAN,
a rich and predatory blonde who is not at all faded. She's a vampire, with unusually good legs. (Rex Stout, *The Red Bull*, #70)

MAGNOLIA,
a wizened, small, very black old Negress, wears two large gold hoops in her ears and looks like an elderly and rather malignant monkey. . . . (Mignon G. Eberhart, *With This Ring*, #83)

MISS MITZI PLUMMER,
a very stout lady, cheerful, amiable and dark-haired, is quite definitely masochistic, and would love to be tortured. (Elisabeth Sanxay Holding, *Murder Is a Kill-Joy*, #103)

TONY MURILLO,
a flashy, knife-carrying lad who beats Mamie up when she annoys him. He smokes marihuana and once did two years for peddling reefers. (Margaret Millar, *Wall of Eyes*, #110)

CHAO-YUAN,
loyal henchman of Prince Kiang, has a big body, a middle-sized mind and
a small soul. This son of a Mandarin is ruthless, realistic, cruel, and he
bears small love for any member of the white race. (Edison Marshall, *The
White Brigand*, #144)

LEROY,
a slender and sharp-featured gunsel, has thin lips and a thin voice. . . .
(Brett Halliday, *The Corpse Came Calling*, #168)

SANTIAM JONES,
a buckaroo whose sober judgment Cotton deeply respects, is a man to
ride the river with when the chips are down. (Wayne D. Overholser,
Buckaroo's Code, #372)

KENT MURDOCK,
top-flight young news photographer, is loyal, square, and intelligent and
has a virile hardness mixed with a certain refinement in his make-up. He
can talk nearly anyone's language and he is equally at home balancing a
cup of tea or busting his way through a danger-crammed situation.
(George Harmon Coxe, *Murder with Pictures*, #441)

FOX THE DIPPY,
. . . is a beggar by day and a man about town by night. Before he lost his
legs, Dippy was a gang leader and pick-pocket, but now he has a legal
racket. (John Held, Jr., *Crosstown*, #477)

(Obviously, the descriptions could occasionally be offensive and silly,
again in keeping with the style and sense of a book.)
    The Dell compilers seem to have been prejudiced against animals, few
of whom appear in the lists. *The Red Bull* (#70) lacks Hickory Caesar
Grindon, the book's title character; *Skyline Riders* (#250) omits the
important horse, Rosinweed; *The Lady Regrets* (#338) deletes the dog,
Khan (pictured on the front cover); *He Wouldn't Kill Patience* (#370)
neglects the tree-snake, Patience. And *Tarzan and the Lost Empire* (#536)
excludes the great apes with whom Tarzan fraternizes (although it
includes the monkey, Nkima). All the Dell editions of A. B. Cunningham's
mysteries omit the dogs, who figure as prominently as do Cunningham's
humans. One of the few Dell books to include an animal is *Death of a Tall
Man* (#322), which has Mr. and Mrs. North's cat, Martini. *Treasure of the
Brasada* (#253) wisely includes the horse Africano, since the book's main
character, a cowboy, fears horses.
    The character list lasted almost ten years; occasionally, an alternate

"Report" substituted, as on *The Philadelphia Murder Story* (#354). In early 1952, the new art director, Walter Brooks, eliminated the lists, replacing them with a page of blurbs, which imitated that of most other paperback companies. A few of these interior blurbs included character descriptions, but never as a standard feature, and never as cleverly as the compact character lists that readers of Dell books had come to expect.

LISTS OF KEY ITEMS (TANTALIZER-PAGES)

The second or third page of most Dell books was termed by some Dell advertisements the "tantalizer-page." Until 1946, it began with "Things this Mystery is about" (or a paraphrase), including selected items of vital interest in the book. Rarely in any particular order, or rarely very helpful to a reader, they were intended only to provoke, not to inform. Two lists included items they should not: in *Greenmask* (#111), the inclusion of one article gives the reader too much information; in *The Case of the Constant Suicides* (#91) the inclusion of two items completely gives away the solution to the mystery.[4]

Fairer, more provocative entries were:

- A blood-stained TOWEL. (James Francis Bonnell, *Death over Sunday*, #19; Brett Halliday, *Michael Shayne's Long Chance*, #112)

- Three Black Widow SPIDERS. (Baynard H. Kendrick, *The Iron Spiders Murders*, #50)

- BLOOD on a fender. (Helen Reilly, *Mourned on Sunday*, #63)

- A CORPSE who TELLS HIS OWN STORY. (Carter Dickson, *Scotland Yard: The Department of Queer Complaints*, #65)

- Rare ORCHID PLANTS. (Rex Stout, *The Red Bull*, #70)

- At least two grams of CYANIDE OF POTASSIUM. (Bruno Fischer, *The Hornets' Nest*, #79)

- A few MARIHUANA CIGARETTES. (Baynard Kendrick, *The Last Express*, #95)

- A bloodstained SWORDSTICK-UMBRELLA. (Carter Dickson, *Death in Five Boxes*, #108)

- A stuffed WEREWOLF in an English library. (Irina Karlova, *Dreadful Hollow*, #125)

- A spitted AIREDALE DOG barbecuing over a fire. (Dashiell Hammett, *The Continental Op*, #129)

- An OPIUM DIVE in a Mexican border town. (Brett Halliday, *Murder Is My Business*, #184)

- A sinister PINHOLE in a can of rattlesnake meat. (Zelda Popkin, *Dead Man's Gift*, #190)

- A savagely slashed PORTRAIT. (Agatha Christie, *The Murder at the Vicarage*, #226)

- ARSENIC-SEASONED BANBURY TARTS eaten by 200 people. (Phoebe Atwood Taylor, *Banbury Bog*, #251)

Beginning with #123, the feature changed to "What this Mystery is about" (including the "Things") combined with "Wouldn't You Like to Know [What this Book is about]" (or a paraphrase). Items still appeared in random order. But the newer lists were more detailed, more cleverly done, rarely gave away too much knowledge, and seemed more carefully prepared. In fact, the list on *Murder Wears a Mummer's Mask* (#78) makes a dull novel appear exciting. A few romances used this feature to summarize the book's plot, even tell the ending. One mystery, *Blow-Down* (#156), uses a synopsis instead of a list—in this case a poor choice, since it reveals too much of the plot. In adventures, even in many romances, some element of the unexpected is necessary. The entire feature was dropped in 1950, giving way to larger character lists.

Until then, the feature asked readers, "Wouldn't You Like to Know—"

- How to boil an ape? And why is it boiled? (Ruth Sawtell Wallis, *Too Many Bones*, #123)

- Who kidnapped Peg and carried her into the swamp? (Herman Petersen, *Old Bones*, #127)

- Where to get the best spaghetti in New York? (Rex Stout, *Alphabet Hicks*, #146)

- Who the Whosis Kid was watching?

- Who was watching the Whosis Kid? (Dashiell Hammett, *The Return of the Continental Op*, #154)

- Why a battle-ax was used to cut off a pretty girl's head? (Baynard Kendrick, *Odor of Violets*, #162)

- What is behind the evil doings in the back alleys of Juarez? (Brett Halliday, *Murder Is My Business*, #184)

- How a wife outsmarts her husband and the British Intelligence? (Agatha Christie, *N or M?*, #187)

- Why the handsome doctor is racked with sobs? (Katharine Newlin Burt, *Lady in the Tower*, #191)

- What Jacob finally did with the horrible handbag? (Elisabeth Sanxay Holding, *The Innocent Mrs. Duff*, #194)

- Who was in the bathroom with Faith Ann? (Helen Reilly, *Murder on Angler's Island*, #228)

- Why dainty little Wesley Gorin is warned that he is fey? (Henry Kane, *A Halo for Nobody*, #231)

- What anyone would want with a pair of dead hands? (C. W. Grafton, *The Rope Began to Hang the Butcher*, #232)

- Why anyone would pelt a man with canned baby food? (Eunice Mays Boyd, *Murder Wears Mukluks*, #259)

- What happens when Mike Shayne, stark-naked, drives a car through the streets of Miami? (Brett Halliday, *Counterfeit Wife*, #280)

- What Lucas Quincey means by: *The solution lies in Eliot?* (Anthony Boucher, *The Case of the Seven Sneezes*, #334)

- Why turkeys are fed whisky in Chile? (David Dodge, *The Long Escape*, #405)

TITLE-PAGES

Early Dell title-pages, before 1952, are utilitarian—compact, informative, entertaining, and certainly full—reflecting Lloyd Smith's philosophy never to allow unfilled space on or in the books. Blurbs at the top of the page (Head-of-Title Blurbs) often identified the book's series character or the book's genre. Occasionally, an over-enthusiastic editor noted a non-series character; *The Golden Swan Murder* (#15) proclaims itself "A Francis Grady Detective Story," although Grady was not, like Nero Wolfe or Hercule Poirot, a continuing character in any other novels.

Title-pages also included a listing of the author's other books, when there were any, the "etc." often used following the list even if the author had written only one other book. Such information usually appears on the verso of the half-title page in hard-cover editions, occasionally on dust-jackets as well. The Dell books disclaimed such conventional usage. On the title-page they included not only the publisher but even identified the executive staff of Dell Publishing Company (not of Western). The phrase, "Designed and Produced by Western Printing & Lithographing" appeared on only a few title-pages, then, with other data, on the copyright page, until its legitimate demise in 1961. By that time, Western was printing but not designing the books.

Walter Brooks re-designed the title-page in 1952. Using space more liberally and adding occasional illustrations, Brooks modernized the page, occasionally even extending it to include the verso opposite. He took complete control of what before had been more or less decided by Racine typesetters, "any way they wanted."[5] He brought new life to the Dell title-page. Yet the old version often told more. (See illustrations 28a and b.) As S. H. Steinberg notes,

More than any other single part of the book, the title-page has ever . . . been a true reflection of the general taste of the reading public—not only with regard to typography. . . . each art period has produced title-pages in its own image.[6]

CHAPTER TITLES

Most of the Dell books before 1952 added chapter titles (without authors' knowledge) to the texts. In a few cases, the books retained titles from hard-cover editions. Added titles occur in Dorothy B. Hughes' *Ride the Pink Horse* (#210, 1948), for example, although that edition eliminates Hughes' original three-part format. The reprint (#D225, 1958) drops the chapter titles and restores the author's format. In ten years Western staff had begun to demonstrate more care in dealing with authors' intentions.

Although the feature seems a serious violation of editorial integrity (although not as serious as the early abridgments), at least one author commented favorably:

Dell deserves full marks for the [*Do Not Murder Before Christmas*, #514] chapter headings. They don't *quite* come off—some are decidedly forced—but it was one of those things that made me feel . . . that somebody at Dell cared.[7]

OTHER FEATURES

Early Dell paperbacks used laminated covers and decorated endpapers. Lamination occurred on #97-285 (1945-1949) and on some later reissues; covers were sent to a plant in New York City, laminated, then returned to Western's Poughkeepsie plant for attachment to the texts. Other paperback companies had initiated the practice; most discarded it at about the same time. Dell endpapers were plain until 1949, then the four common keyhole logos—mystery, romance, western, and adventure—decorated the endpapers until 1953. (See illustration 27g.) Double-sheet endpapers appeared until 1949, single-sheets thereafter.

Typography on the Dell books varied. Walter Brooks often used Baskerville (on *Peyton Place*, for example). And he attempted to use the same type for series titles—all the A. A. Fair books, for instance. Earlier, Lloyd Smith and staff had allowed the text to run into the gutter of the books; on *Their Ancient Grudge* (#435), they even introduced a cumbersome double-columned text. Brooks cleaned up the typography.

During and just after World War II, a "Books Are Weapons" blurb usually appeared at the bottom of page 2 of the books. The blurb commanded readers to send the book to a soldier overseas. (Pocket Books adopted a similar feature.) In 1946 and 1947, Dell used a small issue number at the top left of the front cover; the practice helps collectors to distinguish between first issues and reissues. More clever was the system Walter Brooks devised for Dell's Sales Department: coded issue numbers on the spine and coded prices on the front cover identified genres. Circles indicated mysteries; triangles, non-fiction and science-fiction; diamonds, westerns; rectangles or squares, general fiction. The system lasted until 1959.

Until December, 1950, no Dell books had prices on the covers. Special racks announced the standard 25¢ price; everyone knew the price, anyway. But Bantam introduced the 35¢ book in 1950—its success promised the slow death of the quarter paperback. *Crows Can't Count* (#472, December, 1950) is the first Dell paperback to feature the 25¢ price on the cover. The last 25¢ Dell book is a thin volume of cartoons: *Nellie's Bedfellows* (#A209, March, 1960). It even had a second printing, in October, 1960. After that, the 25¢ paperback was a memory, the Dells among them.

Notes

N.B. References to interviews, telephone interviews, and letters appear in slightly abbreviated form; it is understood in all cases that I communicated with the sources. Personal interviews were conducted at the source's residence or office.

INTRODUCTION

1. Jean Peters, "Publishers' Imprints," in her edition of *Collectible Books: Some New Paths* (New York: R. R. Bowker, 1979), pp. 198-224.

2. Thomas L. Bonn, *UnderCover: An Illustrated History of American Mass Market Paperbacks* (New York: Penguin, 1982), p. 119. See also Bonn, "American Mass-Market Paperbacks," in Peters, ed., *Collectible Books*, pp. 118-151; this essay also appears in Bonn's *Paperback Primer: A Guide for Collectors* (Brownwood, Tex.: Paperback Quarterly Publications, 1981), pp. 9-44.

3. S. H. Steinberg, *Five Hundred Years of Printing* (Baltimore: Penguin, 1961), p. 184.

4. Alfred A. Knopf, quoted in Charles A. Madison, *Book Publishing in America* (New York: McGraw-Hill, 1960), p. 324.

5. Stephen King, *Danse Macabre* (New York: Berkley, 1982), p. 101.

6. Margaret Atwood, *Bodily Harm* (New York: Simon & Schuster, 1982), p. 218.

1. DELL PAPERBACKS, 1942–1951

1. Quotes from and information about George T. Delacorte, Jr., are, unless otherwise credited, from my telephone interview with Delacorte, October 1, 1980.

2. Max Hastings, "How I Popped the Million Dollar Question," London *Evening Standard*, July 13, 1976; quoted in John Tebbel, *A History of Book Publishing in the United States*, vol. 4, *The Great Change, 1940-1980* (New York: R. R. Bowker, 1981), p. 391.

3. Knox Burger, telephone interview, August 14, 1980.

4. "The Story of Dell Publishing Co., Inc.," *Book Production Magazine*, 80 (November, 1964), 34.

5. Frank Gruber, *The Pulp Jungle* (Los Angeles: Shelbourne Press, 1967), p. 21.

6. W. A. Swanberg, letters, September 14, 1978, and October 2, 1982.

7. Mort Walker, *Backstage at the Strips* (New York: A & W Visual Company, [1975?]), pp. 191, 194.

8. Information about the history of Western Publishing is from issues of Western's house organ, *The Westerner*, specifically the following articles: "The Western Story," No. 1 (March, 1949), pp. 3-8; "The Story of Western 1907-1962, Part III," No. 151 (June, 1962), pp. 2-7. Also helpful was the single issue of the earlier house organ, *The Western Breeze* (March, 1929).

9. Lou Nielsen, letter, June, 1978.

10. Knox Burger, telephone interview, August 14, 1980.

11. Information about Lloyd Smith is from Lou Nielsen, letter, June, 1978; the obituary on Lloyd Smith in the *Racine Journal-Times*, December 16, 1971; and Knox Burger, telephone interview, August 14, 1980.

12. Lou Nielsen, letter, June, 1978.

13. J. J. Barta, letters, March 16, 1979, and February 16, 1979.

14. Don Ward, interview, February 24-27, 1979.

15. James E. Hawkins, interview, December 10, 1980.

16. Allan Barnard, interview, August 7, 1980.

17. James E. Gunn, letter, August 24, 1978.

18. *Publishers Weekly*, April 22, 1957, pp. 22-23. See also the September 19, 1953, issue, p. 1203.

19. Anthea Morton-Saner (for Curtis Brown Limited), letter, February 13, 1979.

20. Mary Renault, letters, March 22, 1979, and October 2, 1982.

21. Don Ward, interview, February 24-27, 1979. See also "25¢ Books Lure Publishers," *Business Week*, No. 843 (October 27, 1945), p. 82. I lack specific information on Dell's advances and royalties after 1952; Dell refused me permission to quote such figures.

22. J. J. Barta, letter, December 4, 1980.

23. J. J. Barta, interview, October 27, 1980; letter, October 14, 1982.

24. Frank E. Taylor, interview, August 7, 1980. In general, most 25¢ paperbacks cost 10½-12½¢ to make; the wholesaler paid the publisher 15½-16¢ and received 19-20¢ from the retailer. See Frank E. Comparato, *Books for the Millions* (Harrisburg, Pa.: The Stackpole Company, 1971), p. 245; and J. K. Lasser, "Lessons from the Paper Covers: Part II," *Saturday Review*, 33 (November 18, 1950), 26.

25. Information concerning typesetting of Dell paperbacks is from my interview with Edwin Bachorz, October 28, 1980.

26. See Dave Lewis, "Christ No, Hell Yes," *Collecting Paperbacks?*, Vol. 2, No. 4, pp. 6-7.

27. John K. Hutchens, "Publishing's Lively Child, the Twenty-five Cent Reprint," *The New York Times Book Review*, May 5, 1945, p. 3.

28. "Pokip Streamlines Material Flow," *The Westerner*, No. 13 (December, 1950), pp. 20-23.

29. For an extended discussion of paperback distribution, see Roger H. Smith, *Paperback Parnassus* (Boulder, Colo.: Westview Press, 1976).

30. "Dell, Publishers of Magazines and Reprints," *Publishers Weekly*, May 19, 1945, p. 1992.

31. J. J. Barta, letter, December 4, 1980.

32. See the following issues of *Publishers Weekly*: May 19, 1945, p. 1992; January 14, 1950, p. 141; November 18, 1950, p. 2198; May 15, 1954, pp. 2084-2085.

33. J. K. Lasser, "Lessons," p. 26.

2. DELL PAPERBACKS, 1952–1962

1. James E. Hawkins, interview, December 10, 1980; Allan Barnard, interview, August 7, 1980.

2. "Western in New York," *The Westerner*, No. 88 (March, 1957), pp. 3-6. Some of the figures given in this account differ from those noted on Western's royalty cards. And according to my calculations, Dell published 635 mysteries by the end of 1956, not "about 500." For more information, see the charts and series listings in William H. Lyles, *Dell Paperbacks, 1942 to Mid-1962: A Catalog-Index* (Westport, Conn.: Greenwood Press, 1983).

3. Stephen Becker, letter, May 16, 1979. The blurb, reworded slightly, appears on Richard Powell's *Masterpiece in Murder* (#915).

4. Theodore Sturgeon, letter, July 7, 1979.

5. William Donohue Ellis, letter, July 3, 1979.

6. Harold Q. Masur, letter, November, 1979.

7. Don Ward, letter, July 6, 1979.

8. Donald Hamilton, letter, August 3, 1979.

9. James E. Hawkins, interview, December 10, 1980.

10. *Publishers Weekly* noted such Dell features in the following issues: July 17, 1954, p. 206; January 15, 1955, p. 242; January 27, 1958, p. 212; July 18, 1960, p. 61.

11. U.S. Congress, House of Representatives, *Report of the Select Committee on Current Pornographic Materials*, House Report no. 2510, 82d Cong., 2d sess. (Washington, D.C.: Government Printing Office, 1952). See also Frank L. Schick, *The Paperbound Book in America* (New York: R. R. Bowker, 1958), p. 85.

12. Schick, *Paperbound Book*, p. 115.

13. Allan Barnard, letter, September 2, 1980. Information about vetoed titles is from the Western Printing & Lithographing royalty cards.

3. DELL'S CHANGING CONTENTS

1. Information on other publishers is from my own collection of their books and from R. Reginald and M. R. Burgess, *Cumulative Paperback Index 1939-1959* (Detroit: Gale Research Company, 1973).

2. Alexis de Tocqueville, *Democracy in America*, trans. Henry Reeve, trans. rev. Francis Bowen (New York: Vintage Books, 1955), II, 62.

3. Robert Terrall, letter, October 26, 1979.

4. See Angela Andrews, "Pink for La Vie En Rose: Early Dell Romances," *Paperback Quarterly*, 5 (Spring, 1982), 3-12.

5. Albert Stoffel, letter, March 22, 1979.

6. Don Ward, interview, February 24-27, 1979.

7. Edward Parone, letter, June, 1979.

8. Robert Terrall, letter, October 26, 1979.

9. Jean Francis Webb, letters, June 16, 1979.

10. Victor Chapin, letter, June 21, 1979.

11. Information about bestsellers is from Freeman Lewis, *Paper-Bound Books in America* (New York: The New York Public Library, 1952), pp. 25-26; Frank Luther Mott, *Golden Multitudes: The Story of Best Sellers in the United States* (New York: Macmillan, 1947); and Alice Payne Hackett, *60 Years of Best Sellers 1895-1955* (New York: R. R. Bowker, 1956). See also James D. Hart, *The Popular Book* (Berkeley and Los Angeles: University of California Press, 1961). See especially the excellent bibliographies in Russel Nye, *The Unembarrassed Muse: The Popular Arts in America* (New York: The Dial Press, 1970) and M. Thomas Inge, ed., *Handbook of American Popular Culture* (Westport, Conn.: Greenwood Press, 1978-1981).

12. Knox Burger, telephone interview, August 14, 1980.

13. *Publishers Weekly*, April 4, 1966, p. 30.

14. Leslie Bennetts, "Advice to Girls, Then and Now," *The New York Times*, May 23, 1979, pp. C1, C11.

15. O. G. Benson, letters, April 30, 1979, July 25, 1979, and August 19, 1979.

16. James McKimmey, letter, November 20, 1979.

4. THE DELL SERIES: AN OVERVIEW

1. Victor Kalin, letter, February 18, 1981.

2. Most of the information about Dell First Editions is from my telephone interview with Knox Burger, August 14, 1980, and his letter of September, 1982.

3. Arlene Donovan, telephone interview, August 13, 1980.

4. J. J. Barta, interview, October 27, 1980; Carl Tobey, letter, August 22, 1980.

5. Knox Burger, letter, September, 1980.

6. "The Story of Dell Publishing Co., Inc.," *Book Production Magazine*, 80 (November, 1964), 34.

7. John Tebbel, *A History of Book Publishing in the United States*, vol. 4, *The Great Change, 1940-1980* (New York: R. R. Bowker, 1981), p. 392.

8. Frank E. Taylor, interview, August 7, 1980. Most of my information about Laurel Editions is from this interview.

9. Richard Wilbur, letter, June 30, 1979.

10. *Publishers Weekly*, February 26, 1962, p. 29.

11. "Neither Snow nor Rain," *The Westerner*, No. 14 (January, 1951), p. 18.

12. Don Ward, interview, February 24-27, 1979.

5. DELL PAPERBACKS, 1962–1982

1. Donald I. Fine, telephone interview, September 16, 1980; Mark M. Morse, interview, December 10, 1980.

2. Mark M. Morse, interview, December 10, 1980.

3. *Western Publishing Company, Inc. fifty-fifth Annual Report 1962*, p. 3.

4. *Publishers Weekly*, August 4, 1975, p. 37.

5. John T. Gillespie and Diana L. Spirt, *Paperback Books for Young People: An Annotated Guide to Publishers and Distributors* (Chicago: American Library Association, 1972), p. 24.

6. "The Story of Dell Publishing Co., Inc.," *Book Production Magazine*, 80 (November, 1964), 34.

7. *Publishers Weekly*, August 4, 1975, pp. 37-38.

8. "The Story of Dell Publishing Co., Inc.," p. 33.

9. The production of the Dell encyclopedia was featured in an article in *Publishers Weekly*, August 3, 1964, pp. 62, 64-65.

10. "The Story of Dell Publishing Co., Inc." p. 35.

11. *Publishers Weekly*, December 4, 1974, p. 51; and Judith Appelbaum, "Paperback Talk," *The New York Times Book Review*, December 26, 1982, p. 19.

12. *Publishers Weekly*, October 23, 1978, pp. 18, 20.

13. *Publishers Weekly*, January 9, 1978, p. 68.

14. "A Dell Affair with Western," *The Westerner*, 1 [New Series] (Fall, 1980), 10.

15. The opening of the Pine Brook facility was the subject of a feature article in *Publishers Weekly*, October 18, 1965, pp. 19-22.

16. "A Dell Affair with Western," p. 11.

17. *Publishers Weekly*, March 11, 1983, p. 14.

18. "The Story of Dell Publishing Co., Inc.," p. 33.

19. *Publishers Weekly*, May 24, 1965, p. 34.

20. George T. Delacorte, telephone interview, October 1, 1980.

21. *Publishers Weekly*, March 11, 1983, p. 14.

22. R[obert] H. H[arris], "Trouble at Doubleday," *Saturday Review*, 8 (November, 1981), 9. For a critical appraisal of the purchase of the Mets by Nelson Doubleday, Jr., see Joseph Durso, "Rebuilding the Mets," *The New York Times Magazine*, April 3, 1983, pp. 28-31.

23. Oscar Dystel, quoted in Judith Appelbaum, "Paperback Talk," *The New York Times Book Review*, October 24, 1982, p. 47.

6. ARTWORK: THE FRONT COVERS

1. Gerald Gregg, letter, November 8, 1978. Details were confirmed by George A. Frederiksen's letter, October 16, 1978, and my interviews with Frederiksen, October 29, 1980, and with Gregg, October 26, 1980.

2. George A. Frederiksen, interview, October 29, 1980. See also "The Art of Selling," *The Westerner*, No. 40 (March, 1953), pp. 2-7.

3. Gerald Gregg, interview, October 26, 1980.

4. George Frederiksen, interview, October 29, 1980. See also "Art Appreciation in Racine," *The Westerner*, No. 15 (February, 1951), pp. 14-15; "Westerner Wins Medal of Honor," *The Westerner*, No. 55 (June, 1954), pp. 12-13; "Let George Do It," *The Westerner*, No. 28 (March, 1952), p. 7; and "Saturday and Sunday Painters," *The Westerner*, No. 11 (October, 1950), pp. 16-17.

5. Gerald Gregg, interview, October 26, 1980.

6. George Frederiksen, interview, October 29, 1980.

7. Gerald Gregg, interview, October 26, 1980.

8. John Van Hamersveld, "Introduction" to Elyce Wakerman, *Air Powered: The Art of the Airbrush* (New York: Random House, 1979), p. 13.

9. See Clement Greenburg, "Avant-Garde and Kitsch," in Bernard Rosenberg and David Manning White, eds., *Mass Culture: The Popular Arts in America* (Glencoe, Ill.: The Free Press & The Falcon's Wing Press, 1957), p. 106.

10. John Canaday, *What Is Art?* (New York: Alfred A. Knopf, 1980), pp. 77, 12.

11. See Gerald Gregg, "This Is My Job," *The Westerner*," No. 78 (May, 1956), pp. 18-19. Gregg's plans for a promotional item appear in "Great Locomotive Chase," *The Westerner*, No. 82 (September, 1956), pp. 16-17.

12. Bernard Salbreiter, letter, March 17, 1979.

13. Earl Sherwan, letter, March 13, 1979.

14. James Bama, letter, July 17, 1979.

15. Jeanette Case, "Meet the Artist," *The Westerner*, No. 16 (March, 1951), p. 20.

16. George Frederiksen, interview, October 29, 1980; Robert Kissner, interview, October 28, 1980.

17. Edmund Marine, letter, February, 1979.

18. Frank E. Taylor, interview, August 7, 1980; Walter Brooks, interview, September 20, 1980.

19. Walter Brooks, letter, October 23, 1980.

20. Mitchell Hooks, letter, June 3, 1979.

21. All of Walter Brooks' comments about artists are from my interview with him on September 20, 1980.

22. Leonard Leone, quoted in Clarence Petersen, *The Bantam Story: Thirty Years of Paperback Publishing*, second edition (New York: Bantam, 1975), p. 66

23. Mitchell Hooks, letter, October 12, 1982.

24. Robert Abbett, letter, May 30, 1979. Abbett's gallery art is represented in *The Outdoor Paintings of Robert K. Abbett* (New York: A Peacock Press/Bantam Book, 1976).

25. Harry Bennett, letter, June 5, 1979.

26. Victor Kalin, letter, October 17, 1979. See also "The Artist at Work: Victor Kalin," *North Light*, 6 (November/December, 1974), 14-19.

27. William Teason's covers for Agatha Christie's books are discussed in Frank Eck, "Shadow Gallery: An Informal Survey of Cover Art of the Seventies; Exhibition One—A Cover Art Tribute to Agatha Christie," *The Armchair Detective*, 9 (June, 1976), 170-171.

28. Don Ward, letter, August 20, 1978.

29. Robert E. McGinnis, letter, October 11, 1982.

30. Martha Albrand, letter, June 15, 1979.

31. Nicholas Monsarrat, letter, February 24, 1979.

32. Donald Hamilton, letter, August 3, 1979.

33. George Evans, letter, May 25, 1979.

34. Robert Terrall, quoted in Bernard A. Drew, "The Mike Shayne Caper," *Paperback Quarterly*, 3 (Spring, 1980), 55.

35. L. Sprague de Camp, letter, June 10, 1979; Michael Gilbert, letter, July 5, 1979.

36. John Canaday, letter, August, 1979.

37. "The Story of Dell Publishing Co., Inc.," *Book Production Magazine*, 80 (November, 1964), 34.

7. *ARTWORK: THE BACK COVERS*

1. Don Ward, interview, February 24-27, 1979; George T. Delacorte, telephone interview, October 1, 1980. See also "Dell, Publisher of Magazines and Reprints," *Publishers Weekly*, May 19, 1945, pp. 1990-1993.

2. Harry Söderman and John J. O'Connell, *Modern Criminal Investigation* (New York: Funk & Wagnalls, 1935), pp. 80-82.

3. Elyce Wakerman, *Air Powered: The Art of the Airbrush* (New York: Random House, 1979), p. 21.

4. Lester del Rey, "Introduction: A Guide to Wonder," in J. B. Post, *An Atlas of Fantasy*, revised edition (New York: Ballantine, 1979), p.v.

5. Don Ward, interview, February 24-27, 1979; Allan Barnard, interview, August 7, 1980; J. J. Barta, interview, October 30, 1980; George Frederiksen, interview, October 29, 1980.

6. The name of R. Belew is credited on the royalty cards of Western Publishing; J. J. Barta and James E. Hawkins remembered her first name as "Ruth."

7. James E. Hawkins, interview, December 10, 1980; Robert Kissner, interview, October 28, 1980; Gerald Poplawski, interview, October 30, 1980.

8. George Frederiksen, interview, October 29, 1980; Gerald Gregg, interview, October 26, 1980.

9. Gerald Gregg, letter, April 19, 1979; Earl Sherman, letter, February 1, 1979; John Canaday, letter, August, 1979; Henning Nelms, telephone interview, January 26, 1979. Bryon Gere is credited on Western's royalty cards with some Dell work.

10. Walter Brooks, interview, September 20, 1980.

11. For details, including a list of Dell books with back-cover maps, see William H. Lyles, *Dell Paperbacks, 1942 to Mid-1962: A Catalog-Index* (Westport, Conn.: Greenwood Press, 1983).

12. A good introduction to map projection is Erwin Raisz, *General Cartography* (New York: McGraw-Hill, 1948).

13. Don Ward guessed at the locales for the stories (letter, June 6, 1979).

14. The Burroughs map is reproduced in J. B. Post, *An Atlas of Fantasy* (Baltimore: The Mirage Press, 1973), p. 189; in the revised edition (New York: Ballantine, 1979), p. 77.

15. Dell did not reprint the last two Hammett collections, *Woman in the Dark* and *A Man Called Thin,* although it had an option on *Woman.*

16. *Blood Money* is really a combination of two related Hammett stories. Pocket Books reprinted other Hammett novels.

17. For other maps of this area, see Alberto Manguel and Gianni Guadalupi, eds., *The Dictionary of Imaginary Places* (New York: Macmillan, 1980), p. 71; and Post, *Atlas,* p. 175 (revised edition, p. 65).

18. Audrey and William Roos, letter, February 19, 1979.

19. A sketch of Nero Wolfe's apartment appears in William S. Baring-Gould, *Nero Wolfe of West Thirty-Fifth Street* (New York: Bantam, 1970), p. 178. See also Ken Darby, *The Brownstone House of Nero Wolfe* (Boston: Little, Brown, 1983).

20. See Bill Lyles, "Nero Wolfe in the Dell Mapbacks," *Paperback Quarterly,* 2 (Winter, 1979), 13-25.

21. Nicholas Monsarrat, letter, February 24, 1979.

22. Richard Powell, letter, May 19, 1979.

23. Neither Western nor Dell wanted "to make waves," as James E. Hawkins remembers (interview, December 10, 1980).

24. Frederic Dannay, letter, February 22, 1979; George Harmon Coxe, letter, June 17, 1979; Mignon G. Eberhart, letter, July, 1979, and interview, August 6, 1980; James M. Fox, letter, July 26, 1979; Martha Albrand, letter, June 15, 1979.

25. Ray Bradbury, letter, November 30, 1978; Leslie Ford, interview, June 16, 1979; Delano Ames, letter, August 7, 1979; Eaton K. Goldthwaite, letter, February 27, 1979; Richard Powell, letter, May 19, 1979; S. Omar Barker, letter, November 27, 1978; John Canaday, letter, August, 1979; Jan Westcott, letter, April 16, 1979; Audrey and William Roos, letter, February 19, 1979.

26. Paul Winterton, letter, September 12, 1979.

27. Aaron Marc Stein, letter, April 1, 1979.

28. C. W. Grafton, letter, February 25, 1980. Grafton's comments also appear in Bill Lyles, "C. W. Grafton," *The Poisoned Pen*, 3 (December, 1980), 7-9.

29. Donald Hamilton, letter, August 3, 1979.

30. Sara Elizabeth Mason, letters, December 1, 1978, and February 11, 1979.

31. Lenore Glen Offord, letters, April 20, 1979, and September 28, 1982.

32. Dorothy B. Hughes, letter, November 3, 1979.

33. Wayne D. Overholser, letter, July 7, 1979.

34. Lawrence Treat, letter, January 9, 1979.

35. Mary Renault, letters, January 29, 1979, and March 22, 1979.

36. Jack Iams, letters, September 19, 1979, and October 18, 1979.

37. R. A. Skelton, *Decorative Printed Maps of the 15th to 18th Centuries* (London: Spring Books, 1965), p. 1.

38. Frank E. Taylor, interview, August 7, 1980. George T. Delacorte thought "they dropped a good feature for a bad reason" (telephone interview, October 1, 1980).

39. Walter Brooks, letter, November 1, 1978; interview, September 20, 1980.

8. OTHER DELL FEATURES

1. *Publishers Weekly*, May 19, 1945, p. 1992. Mickey Spillane, in *My Gun Is Quick*, terms reading books looking at "Life through a keyhole" (New York: New American Library, 1950), p. 5.

2. For a list of Dell books with the varying logos, see William H. Lyles, *Dell Paperbacks, 1942 to Mid-1962: A Catalog-Index* (Westport, Conn.: Greenwood Press, 1983).

3. Frank L. Schick, *The Paperbound Book in America* (New York: R. R. Bowker, 1958), p. 39.

4. "A fortune in EMERALDS" is the offending article in *Greenmask;* "A quantity of DRY ICE" and "A disjointed FISHING ROD" in *The Case of the Constant Suicides*. This author wishes to play fair with his readers.

5. Walter Brooks, interview, September 20, 1980.

6. S. H. Steinberg, *Five Hundred Years of Printing* (Baltimore: Penguin, 1961), p. 150.

7. Jack Iams, letter, October 18, 1979.

Bibliography and References

1. *PRIMARY SOURCES*

A. Correspondence and Interviews

Abbett, Robert. Letter. May 30, 1979.

Albrand, Martha. Letter. June 15, 1979.

Ames, Delano. Letter. August 7, 1979.

Bachorz, Edwin. Interview, Racine, Wisconsin. October 28, 1980.

Bama, James. Letter. July 17, 1979.

Barker, S. Omar. Letter. November 27, 1978.

Barnard, Allan. Interview, New York City. August 7, 1980.

––––––. Letter. September 2, 1980.

Barta, J. J. Letters. February 16, 1979; March 16, 1979; December 4, 1980; October 14, 1982.

––––––. Interview, Racine, Wisconsin. October 27 and 30, 1980.

Becker, Stephen. Letter. May 16, 1979.

Bennett, Harry. Letter. June 5, 1979.

Benson, O. G. Letters. April 30, 1979; July 25, 1979; August 19, 1979.

Bradbury, Ray. Letter. November 30, 1978.

Brooks, Walter. Interview, Norwalk, Connecticut. September 20, 1980.

––––––. Letters. November 1, 1978; October 23, 1980.

Burger, Knox. Telephone interview. August 14, 1980.

––––––. Letters. September, 1980; September, 1982.

Canaday, John. Letter. August, 1979.

Chapin, Victor. Letter. June 21, 1979.

Coxe, George Harmon. Letter. June 17, 1979.

Dannay, Frederic. Letter. February 22, 1979.

de Camp, L. Sprague. Letter. June 10, 1979.

Delacorte, George T., Jr. Telephone interview. October 1, 1980.

Donovan, Arlene. Telephone interview. August 13, 1980.

Eberhart, Mignon G. Letter. July, 1979.

––––––. Interview, Greenwich, Connecticut. August 6, 1980.

Ellis, William Donohue. Letter. July 3, 1979.

Evans, George. Letter. May 25, 1979.

Fine, Donald I. Telephone interview. September 16, 1980.

Ford, Leslie. Interview, Baltimore, Maryland. June 16, 1979.

Fox, James M. Letter. July 26, 1979.

Frederiksen, George A. Letter. October 16, 1978.

_____. Interview, Racine, Wisconsin. October 29, 1980.

Gilbert, Michael. Letter. July 5, 1979.

Goldthwaite, Eaton K. Letter. February 27, 1979.

Grafton. C. W. Letter. February 25, 1980.

Gregg. Gerald. Letters. November 8, 1978; April 19, 1979.

_____. Interview, Racine, Wisconsin. October 26, 1980.

Gunn, James E. Letter. August 24, 1978.

Guzzardi, Peter. Letter. October 7, 1980.

Hamilton, Donald. Letter. August 3, 1979.

Hawkins, James E. Interview, Hyde Park, New York. December 10, 1980.

Hooks, Mitchell. Letters. June 3, 1979; October 12, 1982.

Hughes, Dorothy B. Letter. November 3, 1979.

Iams, Jack. Letters, September 19, 1979; October 18, 1979.

Kalin, Victor. Letters. October 17, 1979; February 18, 1981.

Kissner, Robert. Interview, Racine, Wisconsin. October 28, 1980.

LaVoie, Dick. Interview, Poughkeepsie, New York. December 10, 1980.

McGerr, Patricia. Interview, Washington, D.C. February 16, 1979.

McGinnis, Robert E. Letter. October 11, 1982.

McKimmey, James. Letter. November 20, 1979.

Marine, Edmund. Letter. February, 1979.

Mason, Sara Elizabeth. Letters. December 1, 1978; February 11, 1979.

Masur, Harold Q. Letter. November, 1979.

Meyer, Helen. Telephone interview. August 13, 1980.

Monsarrat, Nicholas. Letter. February 24, 1979.

Morse, Mark M. Interview, Staatsburg, New York. December 10, 1980.

Morton-Saner, Anthea (for Curtis Brown Limited). Letter. February 13, 1979.

Nelms, Henning. Telephone interview. January 26, 1979.

Nielsen, Lou. Letter. June, 1978.

Offord, Lenore Glen. Letters. April 20, 1979; September 28, 1982.

Overholser, Wayne D. Letter. July 7, 1979.

Parone, Edward. Letter. June, 1979.

Poplawski, Gerald. Interview, Racine, Wisconsin. October 30, 1980.

Powell, Richard. Letter. May 19, 1979.

Renault, Mary. Letters. January 29, 1979; March 22, 1979; October 2, 1982.

Robinson, Robby. Telephone interview. September 4, 1980.

Roos, Audrey and William. Letter. February 19, 1979.

Salbreiter, Bernard. Letter. March 17, 1979.

Sherwan, Earl. Letters. February 1, 1979; March 13, 1979.

Stein, Aaron Marc. Letter. April 1, 1979.

Stoffel, Albert. Letter. March 22, 1979.

Sturgeon, Theodore. Letter. July 7, 1979.

Swanberg, W. A. Letters. September 14, 1978; October 2, 1982.

Taylor, Frank E. Interview, New York City. August 7, 1980.

Terrall, Robert. Letters. August, 1979; October 26, 1979.

Tobey, Carl. Letter. August 22, 1980.
Treat, Lawrence. Letter. January 9, 1979.
Ward, Don. Letters. June 8, 1978; August 20, 1978; July 6, 1979.
_____. Interview, New York City. February 24-27, 1979.
Webb, Jean Francis. Letters. June 16, 1979.
Westcott, Jan. Letter. April 16, 1979.
Wilbur, Richard. Letter. June 30, 1979.
Winterton, Paul. Letter. September 12, 1979.

B. Records

Dell Publishing Company, New York City. File cards at the Dell library.
Western Publishing Company, Racine, Wisconsin. Author & Title cards, at the
    Creative Center. Xeroxes of these cards are available at the Rare Book
    Room, Library of Congress, Washington, D.C.
_____. Royalty cards, at the Creative Center.

C. Collections of Books

Collection donated in 1976 by Western Publishing to the Library of Congress.
    The collection includes all Dell paperbacks printed between 1942 and 1976.
    The books are available at the Rare Book Room.
Collection of Dell Publishing, New York City. The collection covers all years and
    includes all publications that appeared under the Dell imprint. Most of the
    paperbacks are bound; unfortunately, in that process the books' spines
    were removed.
Collection of the author, Greenfield, Massachusetts. This collection covers
    the years 1942 to mid-1962, selectively thereafter. Unlike other collections,
    this includes reissues (almost 75 percent).

2. SECONDARY SOURCES; BOOKS AND PERIODICALS

Abbett, Robert K. *The Outdoor Paintings of Robert K. Abbett.* New York: A
    Peacock Press/Bantam Book, 1976.
Andrews, Angela. "Pink for La Vie En Rose: Early Dell Romances." *Paperback
    Quarterly*, 5 (Spring, 1982), 3-12.
Appelbaum, Judith. "Paperback Talk." *The New York Times Book Review*,
    October 24, 1982, p. 47; December 26, 1982, p. 19.
"The Artist at Work: Victor Kalin." *North Light*, 6 (November/December, 1974),
    14-19.
Ashe, Rosalind. *Literary Houses.* New York: Facts on File, 1982. Maps derived
    from works such as Nathaniel Hawthorne's *The House of the Seven Gables*
    and F. Scott Fitzgerald's *The Great Gatsby.*
Bennetts, Leslie. "Advice to Girls, Then and Now." *The New York Times*, May
    23, 1979, pp. C1, C11.
Bonn, Thomas L. "American Mass-Market Paperbacks." In Jean Peters, ed.,
    Collectible Books: Some New Paths. New York: R. R. Bowker, 1979, pp. 118-
    151. Also reprinted in Bonn, *Paperback Primer: A Guide for Collectors.*
    Brownwood, Tex.: Paperback Quarterly Publications, 1981, pp. 9-44.

_____. *UnderCover: An Illustrated History of American Mass Market Paperbacks.* New York: Penguin, 1982.

Canaday, John. *What Is Art?* New York: Alfred A. Knopf, 1980.

Carroll, John M. *Eggenhofer: The Pulp Years.* Fort Collins, Colo.: The Old Army Press, 1975.

Collecting Paperbacks? Edited by Lance Casebeer, 934 S.E. 15th, Portland, OR 97214. Published, 1979-present.

Comparato, Frank E. *Books for the Millions.* Harrisburg, Pa.: The Stackpole Company, 1971.

Crider, Allen Billy, ed. *Mass Market Publishing in America.* Boston: G. K. Hall, 1982.

"Dell, Publishers of Magazines and Reprints." *Publishers Weekly,* May 19, 1945, pp. 1990-1993.

Dell Publishing Company. Publishers' catalogs for Dell Books, Delta Books, Delacorte Press, and Laurel-Leaf Library, various years.

Drew, Bernard A. "The Mike Shayne Caper." *Paperback Quarterly,* 3 (Spring, 1980), 51-56. An interview with Robert Terrall.

Eck, Frank. "Shadow Gallery: An Informal Survey of Cover Art of the Seventies; Exhibition One—A Cover Tribute to Agatha Christie." *The Armchair Detective,* 9 (June, 1976), 170-173.

Gillespie, John T., and Diana L. Spirt. *Paperback Books for Young People: An Annotated Guide to Publishers and Distributors.* Chicago: American Library Association, 1972.

Gruber, Frank. *The Pulp Jungle.* Los Angeles: Shelbourne Press, 1967.

Hackett, Alice Payne. *60 Years of Best Sellers 1895-1955.* New York: R. R. Bowker, 1956.

Halsey, Ashley, Jr. *Illustrating for the Saturday Evening Post.* Boston: Arlington House/The Writer Inc., 1951. Includes biographical sketches of illustrators.

Hancer, Kevin. *The Paperback Price Guide.* Cleveland, Tenn.: Overstreet Publications/New York: Harmony Books, 1980.

_____, and R. Reginald. *The Paperback Price Guide No. 2.* New York: Harmony Books, 1982.

Hanratty, Thomas F., and Daniel P. King, eds. *Crime Scene Sketches.* Privately Printed, 1976. Crime sketches of scenes in Arthur Conan Doyle's Sherlock Holmes stories.

H[arris], R[obert] H. "Trouble at Doubleday." *Saturday Review,* 8 (November, 1981), 9.

Hastings, Max. "How I Popped the Million Dollar Question." London *Evening Standard,* July 13, 1976. Quoted in John Tebbel. *A History of Book Publishing in the United States.* vol. 4. *The Great Change, 1940-1980.* New York: R. R. Bowker, 1981, p. 391.

Lasser, J. K. "Lessons from the Paper Covers: Part II." *Saturday Review,* 33 (November 18, 1950), 26.

Lee, Billy C., and Charlotte Laughlin. "Alfred Hitchcock: Dell Paperbacks." *Paperback Quarterly,* 3 (Spring, 1980), 23-36.

Lewis, Dave. "Christ No, Hell Yes." *Collecting Paperbacks?,* Vol. 2, No. 4, pp. 6-7.

Lewis, Freeman. *Paper-Bound Books in America.* New York: The New York Public Library, 1952.

Lyles, Bill. "Agatha Christie in Dell Mapbacks." *Paperback Quarterly*, 3 (Fall, 1980), 26-38.

_____. "C. W. Grafton." *The Poisoned Pen*, 3 (December, 1980), 7-9.

_____. "Nero Wolfe in the Dell Mapbacks." *Paperback Quarterly*, 2 (Winter, 1979), 13-25.

Lyles, W. H. "Science-Fiction and Fantasy in the Dell Mapbacks." *Paperback Quarterly*, 5 (Winter, 1982), 40-49.

Lyles, William. "Dashiell Hammett in the Dell Mapbacks." *Paperback Quarterly*, 4 (Fall, 1981), 15-23.

Lyles, William H. *Dell Paperbacks, 1942 to Mid-1962: A Catalog-Index*. Westport, Conn.: Greenwood Press, 1983.

Madison, Charles A. *Book Publishing in America*. New York: McGraw-Hill, 1960.

Manguel, Alberto, and Gianni Guadalupi, eds. *The Dictionary of Imaginary Places*. New York: Macmillan, 1980.

Mott, Frank Luther. *Golden Multitudes: The Story of Best Sellers in the United States*. New York: Macmillan, 1947.

O'Brien, Geoffrey. *Hardboiled America: The Lurid Years of Paperbacks*. New York: Van Nostrand Reinhold, 1981.

The Paperback Collector's Newsletter. Edited by Louis Black. 1977-1979. Superseded by *Collecting Paperbacks?* (q.v.).

Paperback Quarterly. Edited by Billy C. Lee, 1710 Vincent Street, Brownwood, Tex. 76801. Published, 1978-present.

Peters, Jean. "Publishers' Imprints." In Peters, ed. *Collectible Books: Some New Paths*. New York: R. R. Bowker, 1979, pp. 198-224.

Petersen, Clarence. *The Bantam Story: Thirty Years of Paperback Publishing*. Second edition. New York: Bantam, 1975.

Post, J. B. *An Atlas of Fantasy*. Baltimore: The Mirage Press, 1973.

_____. Revised edition. New York: Ballantine, 1979.

Publishers Weekly. The following issues have material relating to the Dell paperbacks: May 19, 1945, pp. 1990-1993; January 14, 1950, p. 141; November 18, 1950, p. 2198; September 19, 1953, p. 1203; May 15, 1954, pp. 2084-2085; July 17, 1954, p. 206; January 15, 1955, p. 242; April 22, 1957, pp. 22-23; January 27, 1958, p. 212; July 18, 1960, p. 61; February 26, 1962, p. 29; August 3, 1964, pp. 62, 64-65; May 24, 1965, p. 34; October 18, 1965, pp. 19-22; April 4, 1966, p. 30; December 4, 1974, p. 51; August 4, 1975, pp. 37-38; January 9, 1978, p. 68; October 23, 1978, pp. 18, 20; March 11, 1983, p. 14.

Racine Journal-Times. December 16, 1971. Obituary on Lloyd Smith.

Raisz, Erwin. *General Cartography*. New York: McGraw-Hill, 1948.

Reed, Walt. *Great American Illustrators*. New York: Abbeville Press, 1979.

_____, ed. *The Illustrator in America 1900-1960's*. New York: Reinhold, 1966.

Reginald, R., and M. R. Burgess. *Cumulative Paperback Index 1939-1959*. Detroit: Gale Research Company, 1973.

Schick, Frank L. *The Paperbound Book in America*. New York: R. R. Bowker, 1958.

Schreuders, Piet. *Paperbacks, U.S.A.: A Graphic History, 1939-1959*. San Diego: Blue Dolphin, 1981. Translated by Josh Pachter. Originally published as *Paperbacks, U.S.A.: Een Grafische Geschiedenis, 1939-1959* (Amsterdam:

Loeb, 1981). Also published as *The Book of Paperbacks: A Visual History of the Paperback* (London: Virgin Books, 1981). French and Japanese editions forthcoming.

Smith, Roger H. *Paperback Parnassus.* Boulder, Colo.: Westview Press, 1976.

Söderman, Harry, and John J. O'Connell. *Modern Criminal Investigation.* New York: Funk & Wagnalls, 1935.

Steinberg, S. H. *Five Hundred Years of Printing.* Baltimore: Penguin, 1961.

"The Story of Dell Publishing Co., Inc." *Book Production Magazine,* 80 (November, 1964), 32-35.

Tebbel, John. *A History of Book Publishing in the United States.* vol. 4. *The Great Change, 1940-1980.* New York: R. R. Bowker, 1981.

U.S. Congress, House of Representatives. *Report of the Select Committee on Current Pornographic Materials.* House Report no. 2510. 82d Cong., 2d sess. Washington, D.C.: Government Printing Office, 1952.

Wakerman, Elyce. *Air Powered: The Art of the Airbrush.* New York: Random House, 1979.

Walker, Mort. *Backstage at the Strips.* New York: A & W Visual Company [1975?].

Western at War. Racine, Wis.: Western Printing & Lithographing, 1943.

The Western Breeze. March, 1929. Early house organ of Western Printing & Lithographing.

Western Printing & Lithographing, later Western Publishing. *The Westerner.* The following articles have material relating to the Dell paperbacks: "The Western Story," No. 1 (March, 1949), pp. 3-8; "Saturday and Sunday Painters," No. 11 (October, 1950), pp. 16-17; "Pokip Streamlines Material Flow," No. 13 (December, 1950), pp. 20-23; "Neither Snow nor Rain," No. 14 (January, 1951), p. 18; "Art Appreciation in Racine," No. 15 (February, 1951), pp. 14-15; Jeanette Case, "Meet the Artist," No. 16 (March, 1951), p. 20; "Let George Do It," No. 28 (March, 1952), p. 7; "The Art of Selling," No. 40 (March, 1953), pp. 2-7; "Westerner Wins Medal of Honor," No. 55 (June, 1954), pp. 12-13; Gerald Gregg, "This Is My Job," No. 78 (May, 1956), pp. 18-19; "Great Locomotive Chase," No. 82 (September, 1956), pp. 16-17; "Western in New York," No. 88 (March, 1957), pp. 3-6; "The Story of Western 1907-1962, Part III," No. 151 (June, 1962), pp. 2-7; "A Dell Affair with Western," 1 [New Series] (Fall, 1980), 10-11.

Western Publishing Company, Inc. fifty-fifth Annual Report 1962.

Index

Issue numbers for Dell books produced between 1942 and May, 1962, appear in parentheses. Most fictitious places (for example, Sudwich, Conn.) are not indexed, nor are fictitious characters unless, like Nero Wolfe, they are well-known characters. The abbreviations "fc" and "bc" refer, respectively, to artwork on the "front cover" and "back cover."

Aarons, Edward S., 25

Abbett, Robert, xvii, 43, 76-77

Abbey, Kieran, *Beyond the Dark* (#93), fc, 80; bc, 90, 97

abridgments, xvii, 9, 11, 24, 43

Accomplice, The (Matthew Head, #346), fc, 81; bc, 106, 107

Ace paperbacks, 28, 32

Across the River and Into the Trees (Ernest Hemingway, #D117), 27

actors and directors. *See* Autry, Gene; Davis, Bette; Flynn, Errol; Gable, Clark; Haskin, Byron; Hitchcock, Alfred; Monroe, Marilyn; Pal, George; Powers, Tom; Rogers, Ginger; Rogers, Roy; Thompson, Sydney

Adams, Cleve F., *The Crooking Finger* (#104), 13; fc, 60-61, 64

Adams, Dr. Clifford R., and Vance O. Packard, *How to Pick a Mate* (#224), 34; bc, 109

Adams, Samuel Hopkins, *The Harvey Girls* (#130), 34, 124; bc, 92, 108

advances and royalties, 7, 8, 11-12, 16, 35, 40, 49, 134 n.21

adventures, 119, 128

advertisements (Dell), 123

Affair of the Scarlet Crab, The (Clifford Knight, #75), bc, 110

Africa, map, 87, 88, 116

Age of Consent (Clem Yore, #622), 9, fc, 72; reissue (1965), 9

Agee, James, "The Morning Watch," 33

agents, literary. *See* Burger, Knox; Chapin, Victor; Congdon, Don; Curtis Brown Limited; Donovan, Arlene; Lenniger, August; Meredith, Scott; Wilkinson, Max

airbrushed covers, xvi, xix, 57, 58-66, 69, 70

Alaska, map, 88

Albatross paperbacks, 5

Albrand, Martha, 79, 111; *Wait for the Dawn* (#544), bc, 109

"Alfred Hitchcock Suspense Magazine," 44

Alias the Dead (George Harmon Coxe, #377), 124; fc, 81

All Detective, 4

All Western, 4

Allen, Hervey: *Anthony Adverse* (#281, 283, 285), 34, 35, bc, 70, 85, 87, 89; *Anthony Adverse in America* (#285), 122; *The Forest and the Fort* (#D110), 35

Alpha Books. *See* Dell Visual Books

Alphabet Hicks (Rex Stout, #146), 128; bc, 96, 109

Ambassador, The (Morris L. West), 51

Ambler, Eric, *A Coffin for Dimitrios*, 35

American Academy of Art, 57
American Caesar (William Manchester), 51
American Gun Mystery, The (Ellery Queen,
   #4), 9; bc, 106
American Heritage Dictionary, The, 51
American Heritage Publishing Company,
   The, 48
American Heritage Reader, The (#C101), 24
American News Co., 5, 12, 16, 26
Ames, Delano, 31, 111; *Murder Begins at
   Home* (#552), bc, 88
Ames, Louise Bates, and Frances L. Ilg,
   Child Behavior (#D180, LC120, LS107), 19
Anchor paperbacks, 49
Andromeda Strain, The (Michael Crichton),
   51
And So to Murder (Carter Dickson, #175),
   bc, 96
animals, in Dell character lists, 126
Anna Lucasta (Jean Francis Webb, #331),
   33; bc, 90
Anna Lucasta (motion picture), 33
Annapolis, Md., map, 92
anthologies, xvii, 8, 23, 32-33, 40, 42
Anthony Adverse (Hervey Allen, #281, 283,
   285), 34, 35; bc, 70, 85, 87, 89
Anthony Adverse in America (Hervey Allen,
   #285), 122
apartments, maps, 104-5, 114
Appointment with Death (Agatha Christie,
   #105), fc, 61, 64; bc, 110
Ard, William, *Deadly Beloved* (#991), 11
Arizona, map, 113
Armchair in Hell (Henry Kane, #316), fc,
   69; bc, 90
art. *See* airbrushed covers; art, cover; Art
   Deco; Art Department, Western Printing
   & Lithographing; back covers; maps,
   back-cover; photo covers; trompe l'oeil
   covers
art, cover, xvi, xvii, xviii, xix, xx, 3, 7,
   22-23, 25, 39, 43, 48, 50, 55, 56-118;
   accuracy, 80-82; airbrushed, xv, xix, 57,
   58-66, 69, 70; alterations, 67, 73; authors'
   reactions, 37, 79-80, 110-17; credit for,
   71; design, 57, 58-62, 70, 74-75, 76,
   84-85; dust jacket, 76; grisliness, 62, 69;
   layouts, 58, 61, 70; models for, xviii, 69,
   71, 72, 73, 79; 1942-1951, 56-57, 69-73,
   79-81; 1952-1962, 56, 74-82; after 1962,
   56, 82; original artwork, 59, 66, 75;
   origin of, 56-57, 58; payment for, 75;
   photo covers, 71, 80; prices on covers,

75; printing of covers, 75; production of
   color plates for covers, 75; rejected
   covers, 68; silkscreened covers, 75-76;
   trompe l'oeil covers, 58, 61, 62, 63, 65;
   typography on, 74, 75
Art Deco, 60
Art Department, Western Printing & Lith-
   ographing, 8, 22-23, 70, 74, 85, 99, 110.
   See also Creative Department, Western
   Printing & Lithographing
artists. *See* Abbett, Robert; Avati, James;
   Bama, James; Belew, Ruth; Bennett,
   Harry; Borack, Stanley; Botticelli,
   Sandro; Brooks, Walter; Brown, Rey-
   nold; Burns, Paul C.; Cassandre;
   Chwast, Seymour; Cissman, Jeanette;
   CoConis, Ted; Dali, Salvador; de Soto,
   Rafael; Des Vignes, Jean; Eggenhofer,
   Nick; Frederiksen, George A.; Gauguin,
   Paul; George, William; Gere, Byron;
   Giles, F. Kenwood; Glanzman, Louis;
   Glaser, Milton; Gould, Chester; Gregg,
   Bill; Gregg, Gerald; Hallam, Ben; Hoff-
   man, H. L.; Homer, Winslow; Hooks,
   Mitchell; Ingres, Jean; Jacobson,
   William George; Johnson, Ray; Kaiser,
   William; Kalin, Victor; Kaufman, Van;
   Kaz; Kissner, Robert; Lambert, Saul;
   Lemay, Harry; Lesser, Ronnie; McGinnis,
   Robert; McWilliams, Alden; Maguire,
   Robert; Meyers, Bob; Monet, Claude;
   Nast, Thomas; Parker, Al; Petty,
   George; Phillips, Barye; Powers,
   Richard; Price, Roy; Prout, George;
   Push-Pin Studios; Pyle, Howard; Rem-
   ington, Frederic; Renoir, Pierre-Auguste;
   Rockwell, Norman; Salbreiter, Bernard;
   Scudellari, Robert; Sherwan, Earl;
   Sherwan, Marguerite; Shoyer, William;
   Stanley, Robert; Teason, William;
   Texidor, Fernando; Vallely, H. E.;
   Vargas, Alberto; Whitcomb, Jon; Whit-
   more, Coby; Wood, Grant; Wyeth,
   Andrew; Yates, Bill; Young, Chic
art schools. *See* American Academy of
   Art; Chaite Studios; Harry Wilson
   Studios; Layton School of Art
Ash, Irene, trans., *Bonjour Tristesse*
   (Françoise Sagan) (#D166), 24
Asia, map, 87
Assassins Have Starry Eyes (Donald Hamil-
   ton), 25
Assignment: Murder (Donald Hamilton,

#A123), 25; fc, 113

Assignment in Guiana (George Harmon Coxe, #321), 31; bc, 96

Atwood, Margaret, *Bodily Harm*, xxii

Austen, Jane, 32

Australia, maps, 86, 87

Australia, Original Novels paperbacks, 25

Autry, Gene, 32; ed., *Gun Smoke Yarns* (#217), fc, 69, 71

Avati, James, 74

Avon paperbacks, 3, 13, 16, 17, 28, 74, 84, 119

Bach, Richard: *A Gift of Wings*, 49; *Jonathan Livingston Seagull*, 49, 51

Bachmann, Lawrence, and Hannah Lees, *Death in the Doll's House* (#122), bc, 104

Bachorz, Edwin, xv, 12, 13

back covers: maps, xv, xviii, xx, 8, 9, 74, 83-118; other than maps, 85, 100, 104, 108-9

Backwoods Woman (Jack Boone, #557), bc, 100, 108

Bad for Business (Rex Stout, #299), 30, fc, 62, 65, bc, 110; Century edition, 110

Bad Seed, The (William March, #847, F180), 19

Baited Blonde, The (Robinson MacLean, #508), bc, 88

Baldwin, Faith, 31, 69; *Enchanted Oasis* (#255), bc, 88; *The Heart Remembers* (#288), bc, 90; *Honor Bound* (#116), fc, 69; *The Moon's Our Home* (#368), 31, bc, 88; *Rich Girl, Poor Girl* (#196), 31; *Self-Made Woman* (#163), fc, 69, bc, 90; *Skyscraper* (#236), 124; *Week-End Marriage* (#73), bc, 100, 109

Baldwin, James, 33; *Nobody Knows My Name*, 49

Ballantine paperbacks, 28, 32, 77

Ballyhoo, 4

Bama, James, 71

Banbury Bog (Phoebe Atwood Taylor, #251), 128

Bandit Trail, The (William MacLeod Raine, #424), bc, 86

banners, on back-cover maps, 110

Bantam Books (New York), xv, 6, 9, 13, 17, 28, 76, 84, 119, 131; "World's Great Novels of Detection," 84

Bantam Publications (Los Angeles), 6

Barker, S. Omar, 111; " 'They've Shot Jug Murphy,' " 111

Barnard, Allan, xv, xviii, 9, 20-21, 27, 35, 39, 42, 43, 45, 49, 72, 84; ed., *Cleopatra's Nights* (#414), 9, bc, 87; ed., *The Harlot Killer* (#797), 9

Barnard, Laurel, xvii, 42

Baron, Richard, 53, 54

Barta, J. J., xv, 7-8, 11, 16, 41

Bar the Doors (Alfred Hitchcock, ed., #143), fc, 62

Bart House paperbacks, 16

baseball annuals, xvii, 43-44

Bashful Billionaire (Albert G. Gerber), 50

Bat, The (Mary Roberts Rinehart, #652), fc, 66, 75-76

Bats Fly at Dusk (A. A. Fair, #254), fc, 62, 81

Baum, Vicki, *Once in Vienna* (#524), 120; bc, 92

Bax, Roger (pseud. of Paul Winterton), *Two If by Sea* (#634), bc, 111

Beam Ends (Errol Flynn, #195), bc, 87

Beatles, 50

Beatles in Help!, The (Al Hine), 50

Becker, Stephen, xv, 23-24

Belew, Ruth, xv, 8, 84-85, 87, 94, 95, 97, 98, 99, 100, 104, 105, 110, 117

Belgium, collection marabout, 25

Bell, William, xvii, 5

Bellow, Saul, 33

Benefit Performance (Richard Sale, #252), bc, 91

Bengal Fire (Lawrence G. Blochman, #311), bc, 92

Benjamin Blake (Edison Marshall, #431), 11

Bennett, George, ed., *Great Tales of Action and Adventure*, 47

Bennett, Harry, 71, 77

Bennetts, Leslie, 36

Benson, O. G., 36-37, 41; *Cain's Woman* (#A200), 36-37

Berger, Thomas, 49

Berkley paperbacks, 77

Berlin, map, 92

Bermuda, map, 88

bestsellers, 34-35, 50-51

Beulah Land (Lonnie Coleman), 51

Beyond the Dark (Kieran Abbey, #93), fc, 80; bc, 90, 97

Bezucha, Robert, 57

Big Country, The (Donald Hamilton, #B115), bc, 113

Biggers, Earl Derr, *Keeper of the Keys* (#47), 11

Big Little Books, 59

Bird, Brandon (pseud. of George and Kay Evans), *Death in Four Colors* (#531), 124; fc, 80

Birthday Murder, The (Lange Lewis, #214), bc, 117

Birth of Venus, The (Botticelli painting), 81

Bitter Ending (Alexander Irving, #289), bc, 107

Black, Don, xvii, 44

Blackbirder, The (Dorothy B. Hughes, #149), fc, 69; bc, 104, 114

Black Curtain, The (Cornell Woolrich, #208), 31

Blasco Ibáñez, Vicente, *Blood and Sand* (#500), bc, 89, 108

Blind Man's Bluff (Baynard Kendrick, #230), fc, 81; bc, 106

Blochman, Lawrence G.: *Bengal Fire* (#311), bc, 92; *Blow-Down* (#156), 128, fc, 58; *Bombay Mail* (#488), bc, 88, 107; *Midnight Sailing* (#43), bc, 107; *See You at the Morgue* (#7), bc, 99, 103, 104; *Wives to Burn* (#134), bc, 88

Blondie and Dagwood's Footlight Folly (Chic Young), 32

Blood and Sand (Vicente Blasco Ibáñez, #500), bc, 89, 108

Blood Money (Dashiell Hammet, #53, 486), 139 n.16; bc, 91

Blood on Biscayne Bay (Brett Halliday, #268), bc, 91; (#D342), fc, 66, 78

Blood on the Black Market (Brett Halliday, #64), fc, 70; bc, 108

Blood on the Stars (Brett Halliday, #385), 27; fc, 72

Blow-Down (Lawrence G. Blochman, #156), 128; fc, 58

Blue City (Kenneth Millar, #363), bc, 93

Blume, Judy, 46

blurbs: advance, on Dell First Editions, xi; back-cover, 108; front-cover, xi, xix, 11, 21, 23-24, 120, 122; head-of-title, 83, 129; inside, 39, 127, 130; spine, 120

Bodily Harm (Margaret Atwood), xxii

Body Missed the Boat, The (Jack Iams, #274), bc, 116

Body Snatchers, The (Jack Finney, Dell First Edition #42), fc, 40

Body Snatchers, The (motion picture). See *Invasion of the Body Snatchers*

Bogner, Norman, *Seventh Avenue*, 120

Bokabare, Madagascar, map, 92

Bold Rider (Luke Short, #A134), 120

Boltar, Russell (pseud. of Dr. Bernard L. Cinberg), 49; *The Operation* (#F171), 122. See also Cinberg, Dr. Bernard L.

Bombay Mail (Lawrence G. Blochman, #488), bc, 88, 107

Bond, Michael, "Paddington Bear" series, 46

Bonjour Tristesse (Françoise Sagan, #D166), 19, 24, 26, 35

Bonn, Thomas L., xxi

Bonnell, James Francis, *Death over Sunday* (#19), 127; bc, 103

Bonner, Dol, in Rex Stout's mysteries, 30

book collecting, xxi

Book of Etiquette, A (Virginia Sidney Hale), 4

bookracks (Dell), 17, 26, 131

"Books Are Weapons" blurbs, 130

Boomerang Clue, The (Agatha Christie, #46), fc, 62, bc, 96; (#664), fc, 81-82, bc, 96

Boone, Jack, *Backwoods Woman* (#557), bc, 100, 108

Borack, Stanley, 39

Border Lord, The (Jan Westcott, #439), bc, 111

Borzoi Books, xxi

Boston, map, 92

Botticelli, Sandro, *The Birth of Venus* (painting), 81

Boucher, Anthony, 37; *The Case of the Seven Sneezes* (#334), 124, 127, 129, fc, 80

Bounty Lands, The (William Donohue Ellis, #F71), 24

Bower, B. M., *Pirates of the Range* (#466), fc, 72; bc, 109

Boyd, Eunice Mays, *Murder Wears Mukluks* (#259), 129; bc, 109

Bradbury, Ray, 111; "The Million Year Picnic," 88, 111

Brad Dolan's Miami Manhunt (William Fuller, #A158), 26-27

Brand, Max: *Calling Doctor Kildare*, 110; *Young Doctor Kildare* (#329), bc, 110

Brandy for a Hero (William O'Farrell, #306), bc, 90

Brautigan, Richard, 49

Bravados, The (motion picture), 22

Breach of Faith (Theodore H. White), 50

Bread Upon the Waters (Irwin Shaw), 51

Brehm, Lawrence, 57

Brock, Stuart, *Just Around the Coroner* (#337), bc, 106, 117

Broken Lance, Kans., map, 92

Broken Vase, The (Rex Stout, #115), fc, 62

Brooks, Walter, xv, xvii, 18, 23, 45, 66, 73, 74-76, 77-78, 78-79, 85, 101, 118, 120, 122, 127, 129, 130

Brothers, Dr. Joyce, 48

Brothers Karamazov, The (Fyodor Dostoyevsky, #F55), 20

Brown, Fredric, *Madball* (Dell First Edition #2E), 41

Brown, Reynold, 71

Buckaroo's Code (Wayne D. Overholser, #372), 126; bc, 114

Budapest, map, 92

Burdick, Eugene, and Harvey Wheeler, *Fail-Safe*, 50

Burger, Knox, xv, xvii, 6, 7, 21-22, 27, 33, 35, 39-40, 40-41, 45, 76

Burke, Richard: *Chinese Red* (#260), 83, bc, 102, 107-8, 117; *The Frightened Pigeon* (#204), fc, 80

Burns, Paul C., 71

Burns, Robert, 43

Burroughs, Edgar Rice: *Cave Girl* (#320), bc, 88; *Tarzan and the Lost Empire* (#536), 126, bc, 93

Burt, Katharine Newlin: *Lady in the Tower* (#191), 128

Butler, Gerald: *Kiss the Blood Off My Hands* (#197), bc, 105, 117

Cabinda Affair, The (Matthew Head, #390), bc, 88

Cactus Cavalier (Norman A. Fox, #406), bc, 94

Cain, James M., 39; ''The Girl in the Storm,'' 39

Cain's Woman (O. G. Benson, #A200), 36-37

Calcutta, map, 92

California, 104; map, 88

Callahan, William F., Jr., xvii, 19, 54

Calling Doctor Kildare (Max Brand), 110

Cambridge, Md., Western Printing & Lithographing plant, 26

Camera Clue, The (George Harmon Coxe, #453), bc, 105

Camille (Alexandre Dumas *fils*), 62

Canada, maps, 87, 89

Canaday, John, 31, 81, 85, 111; *What Is Art?*, 60. *See also* Head, Matthew

Canadian editions (Dell), 16, 26

Canadian offices, Dell Publishing Company, 16

Candidate for Love (Maysie Greig, #239), fc, 62; bc, 104, 117

Candlelight Romances, 48, 50

Captive of the Sahara, The (E. M. Hull, #402), bc, 93

Cards on the Table (Agatha Christie), 29

Career (motion picture), 34

Career (Victor Chapin, #B148), 25, 34; as *En Lettres de Feu*, 25

Care of Your Child, The (Bela Schick and William Rosenson, #340), 35

Carey, Helen A., and Douglas Stapleton, *The Corpse Is Indignant*, 124

Caribbean, maps, 89, 116

Carr, John Dickson, 29, 30; *The Case of the Constant Suicides* (#91), bc, 96; *Death-Watch* (#564), 30, bc, 92; *To Wake the Dead* (#635), fc, 81. *See also* Dickson, Carter

Carroll, Lewis, *Jabberwocky and Other Nonsense*, 47

cartoon books (Dell), 12, 131

cartoons, back-cover, 109

Case of Jennie Brice, The (Mary Roberts Rinehart, #40), fc, 69

Case of the Constant Suicides, The (John Dickson Carr, #91), bc, 96

Case of the Seven Sneezes, The (Anthony Boucher, #334), 124, 127, 129; fc, 80

Casey, Flash, in George Harmon Coxe's mysteries, 30

Cassandre (Adolphe Jean-Marie Mouron), 60

Castle in the Swamp (Edison Marshall, #487), bc, 88

castles, maps, 96

Catch-22 (Joseph Heller), 51

''Catechetical Guild Society'' books, 39

Cather, Willa, *Death Comes for the Archbishop*, 114

Cat Saw Murder, The (D. B. Olsen, #35), bc, 106

Cave Girl (Edgar Rice Burroughs, #320), bc, 88

CBS, 119

Celeste the Gold Coast Virgin (Rosamond Marshall, #382), 34; bc, 91
censorship, xvi, 9, 13, 27, 68, 73
Centerville, Ky., map, 92
Central City, Colo., map, 92
Central Park (New York City), map, 96-97
central projection, 103
Century books, 110
Cerf, Bennett, 42
Certain Smile, A (Françoise Sagan, #D206), 19
Chaite Studios, 78
Chapel books, 38
ChapelBooks, 38
Chapin, Victor, 34; *Career* (#B148), 25, 34; as *En Lettres de Feu*, 25
chapter titles, 119, 130
character lists, 83, 119, 124-27
Charleston, S.C., map, 92
Charlotte Amalie, map, 116
charts, back-cover, 109
Chavez, Judy, 51; and Jack Vitek, *Defector's Mistress*, 51
Chesapeake Bay, Md., map, 112-13
Chicago, map, 94
Chicago Confidential (Jack Lait and Lee Mortimer, #D101), 34
Chicago Manual of Style, 9
Child Behavior (Frances L. Ilg and Louise Bates Ames, #D180, LC120, LS107), 19
"Child of Compassion" (A. G. Cronin), 39
Children's Hospital Medical Center of Boston, 48
Chinese Red (Richard Burke, #260), 83; bc, 102, 107-8, 117
Christie, Agatha, 9, 29, 78, 83; *Appointment with Death* (#105), fc, 61, 64, bc, 110; *The Boomerang Clue* (#46), fc, 62, bc, 96; (#664), fc, 81-82, bc, 96; *Cards on the Table*, 29; *The Labors of Hercules* (#491), fc, 72; *The Man in the Brown Suit* (#319), bc, 88; *The Murder at the Vicarage* (#226), 128; *Murder in Mesopotamia*, 83, 108; *Murder on the Links* (#454), bc, 93; *N or M?* (#187), 128; *The Patriotic Murders*, 35; *Sad Cypress* (#172, 529), 34; *The Secret of Chimneys* (#199), bc, 95. Characters: Hercule Poirot, 29, 72; Miss Marple, 29
Chute, B. J., *Greenwillow* (#D385), 37
Chwast, Seymour, 68, 78
Cinberg, Dr. Bernard L., 49; *For Women*

Only, 49. *See also* Boltar, Russell
Circular Staircase, The (Mary Roberts Rinehart), 35; (#585), bc, 117
circulation of Dell books, 16, 20
Cissman, Jeanette, xvii, 23, 75
City of Love (Daniel Talbot, ed., Dell First Edition #45), 33
Claiborne, Ross, xvii, 43, 46, 47-48, 49, 55
Clavell, James: *Noble House*, 51; *Shōgun*, 51; *Tai-Pan*, 51
Cleaver, Eldridge, *Soul on Ice*, 49
Cleopatra, 87
Cleopatra's Nights (Allan Barnard, ed., #414), 9; bc, 87
Cliff Notes, 48
Clover Books. *See* Seal Books
Clue of the Judas Tree, The (Leslie Ford, #61), 124; bc, 94
Coates, Robert, *Wisteria Cottage* (#371), 27
CoConis, Ted, 79
Code of the Woosters, The (P. G. Wodehouse, #393), bc, 96
Coffin for Dimitrios, A (Eric Ambler), 35
Cold Steal (Alice Tilton, #142), fc, 61, 65
Coleman, Lonnie, *Beulah Land*, 51
collecting, xxi; collecting books, xxi
collection marabout paperbacks (Belgium), 25
collections of Dell books, 143
Collier's, 22, 39, 41
Colonial Press, 52
color plates for covers, 75
Columbia-Viking Desk Encyclopedia, 50
Columbus, Ohio, map, 92
Comes the Blind Fury (John Saul), 51
comic books: Dell, 5, 13, 15, 16, 18, 19, 32, 46, 74; Western Publishing, 46
"comic" novels (Dell), 32, 44
Commercial Sales Division, Western Printing & Lithographing, 18, 21
Communists, 25
Congdon, Don, 37, 40; ed., *Stories for the Dead of Night* (#B107), 23
Congo Venus, The (Matthew Head, #605), fc, 72, 81; bc, 85
Continental Op, The (Dashiell Hammett, #129), 127, 128; fc, 69; bc, 90-91, 97
contracts (Dell), 8, 12, 20
Cool, Bertha, in A. A. Fair's mysteries, 30
Cool, Pat, 52
Cooper, Courtney Ryley, *The Pioneers* (#290), bc, 86

copy-editing, 8, 9, 25-26
copyright page, 129
Corbin, Glenn, *Trouble on Big Cat*: Dell
    First Edition #25, 25; Star Western, 25;
    Viking #235, 25
Cores, Lucy, *Painted for the Kill* (#87), bc,
    106-7
Corpse Came Calling, The (Brett Halliday,
    #168), 124, 126; fc, 69; bc, 105
Corpse in the Corner Saloon, The (Hampton
    Stone, #464), bc, 101, 105, 111-12
Corpse Is Indignant, The (Douglas Stapleton
    and Helen A. Carey), 124
Corrigan, Robert W., 47
cost of producing Dell paperbacks, 12,
    134 n.24
Cotswolds, the (England), map, 88-89
Counterfeit Wife (Brett Halliday, #280), 129
country estates, maps, 94-95, 98
Count Your Calories, 48
Couzens, Dorothy L., 24
cover art. *See* art, cover
covers, laminated, 130
Coxe, George Harmon, 29, 30-31, 110-11;
    Alias the Dead (#377), 124, fc, 81; *Assign-
    ment in Guiana* (#321), 31, bc, 96; *The
    Camera Clue* (#453), bc, 105; *Four
    Frightened Women* (#5), bc, 94, 103; *The
    Glass Triangle* (#81), fc, 80; *The Groom
    Lay Dead* (#502), 31; *The Lady Is Afraid*
    (#147), 124; *Mrs. Murdock Takes a Case*
    (#202), bc, 105; *Murder with Pictures*
    (#441), 126, fc, 72, bc, 92, 105; *Murder
    for the Asking* (#58), 125; *Murder for Two*
    (#276), bc, 110. Characters: Flash Casey,
    30; Kent Murdock, 30, 72, 105
Creasey, John, *So Young, So Cold, So Fair*
    (#985), fc, 78
Creative Center, Western Printing &
    Lithographing, 85
Creative Department, Western Printing &
    Lithographing, 57, 62, 63. *See also* Art
    Department, Western Printing & Litho-
    graphing
Creeping Siamese, The (Dashiell Hammett,
    #538), fc, 72; bc, 91
Crichton, Michael, *The Andromeda Strain*,
    51
Crime Hound (Mary Semple Scott, #34), bc,
    85
crime sketches, 83-84; in hard-cover
    books, 83, 85-86, 88, 95, 96, 105, 106,

111. *See also* maps, back-cover, indi-
    vidual locations
Crimson Feather, The (Sara Elizabeth
    Mason, #207), bc, 101, 104, 110, 113
Crockett, Lucy Herndon, *The Magnificent
    Bastards* (#D145, F95), 19, 26
Cronin, A. G., "Child of Compassion," 39
Crooking Finger, The (Cleve F. Adams,
    #104), 13; fc, 60-61, 64
Crossen, Kendell Foster, *Year of Consent*
    (Dell First Edition #32), fc, 40
Crimson Feather, The (Sara Elizabeth
    Mason, #207), bc, 101, 104, 110, 113
Crockett, Lucy Herndon, *The Magnificent
    Bastards* (#D145, F95), 19, 26
Cronin, A. G., "Child of Compassion," 39
Crooking Finger, The (Cleve F. Adams,
    #104), 13; fc, 60-61, 64
Crossen, Kendell Foster, *Year of Consent*
    (Dell First Edition #32), fc, 40
Cross-Eyed Bear Murders, The (Dorothy
    B. Hughes, #48), bc, 114
Crosstown (John Held, Jr., #477), 126; bc,
    87
crossword puzzle books, 119
Crows Can't Count (A. A. Fair, #472), 131;
    bc, 87
Cry for the Strangers (John Saul), 51
Cue for Murder (Helen McCloy, #212), fc,
    80; bc, 107
Cummings, J. Hoyt, 40
Cunningham, A. B., *The Death of a Worldly
    Woman* (#365), bc, 105
Cunningham, Eugene, 21
Cunningham, John, *Warhorse* (#D177), 40
Cupid's Diary, 4
Curtains for the Editor (Thomas Polsky,
    #82), fc, 62; bc, 106
Curtis, Charles P., Jr., and Ferris Greenslet,
    eds., *The Practical Cogitator*, 50
Curtis Brown Limited, 11
Cushman, Dan, 32
Cuthbert, Clifton, *The Robbed Heart* (#512),
    fc, 72; bc, 90

Dali, Salvador, 60, 81
Dance of Death (Helen McCloy, #33), fc,
    80; bc, 99, 104
Dangerous Ground (Francis Sill Wickware,
    #248), bc, 104, 109, 110
Daniels, Harold: *In His Blood* (Dell First
    Edition #73), 25, 40; as *Jusqu'au cou*, 25

Dannay, Frederic, 110-11. *See also* Queen, Ellery

Danse Macabre (Stephen King), xxii

Dark Passage (David Goodis, #221), 31; bc, 105

Dark Passage (motion picture), 105

Date with Darkness (Donald Hamilton, #375), 25; fc, 72; bc, 112-13

Date with Death (Leslie Ford, #547), bc, 92

Davis, Bette, 31

Dead Can Tell, The (Helen Reilly, #17), bc, 96, 99, 103

Deadeye Dick (Kurt Vonnegut, Jr.), 49

Deadly Beloved (William Ard, #991), 11

Deadly Truth, The (Helen McCloy, #107), fc, 80

Dead Man's Gift (Zelda Popkin, #190), 84, 127; bc, 105-6

Dead Sure (Stewart Sterling, #420), fc, 71

Dead Wrong (Stewart Sterling, #314), bc, 106

Dead Yellow Women (Dashiell Hammett, #308), fc, 69; bc, 91

Death Comes for the Archbishop (Willa Cather), 114

Death Draws the Line (Jack Iams, #457), bc, 90, 116

Death Has Deep Roots (Michael Gilbert, #744), fc, 80

Death in Five Boxes (Carter Dickson, #108), 127

Death in Four Colors (Brandon Bird, #531), 124; fc, 80

Death in the Back Seat (Dorothy Cameron Disney, #76), fc, 70

Death in the Doll's House (Hannah Lees and Lawrence Bachmann, #122), bc, 104

Death in the Library (Philip Ketchum, #1), 3

Death Knell (Baynard Kendrick, #273), fc, 69; bc, 105

Death of a Tall Man (Frances and Richard Lockridge, #322), 126

Death of a Worldly Woman, The (A. B. Cunningham, #365), bc, 105

Death over Sunday (James Francis Bonnell, #19), 127; bc, 103

Death-Watch (John Dickson Carr, #564), 30; bc, 92

Death Wears a White Gardenia (Zelda Popkin, #13), fc, 62; bc, 106

de Camp, L. Sprague, 80; *Rogue Queen* (#600), fc, 80

Deep Throat (D. M. Perkins), 50

Defector's Mistress (Judy Chavez and Jack Vitek), 51

De Graff, Robert, 5

Delacorte, George T., Jr., xv, 3-4, 4-5, 19, 39, 41, 42, 54, 79, 119, 140 n.38

Delacorte Press, 48, 49, 54; "Books for Younger Readers," 49; "Delacorte Press—Eleanor Friede Books," 49, 55; "A Seymour Lawrence Book—Delacorte Press," 49, 55

Dell Books. *See* Dell reprints

Dell Crossword Dictionary: Kathleen Rafferty (#434), 34; later edition, 51

Dell Distributing, Inc., 26

Dell employees and consultants. *See* Barnard, Allan; Callahan, William F., Jr.; Claiborne, Ross; Cool, Pat; Corrigan, Robert W.; Delacorte, George T., Jr.; Donovan, Arlene; Dowdey, Clifford; Erickson, Rolf; Fine, Donald I.; Friede, Eleanor; Grosse, William R.; Guzzardi, Peter; Holshue, Galen; Hoopes, Ned E.; Huett, Richard; Jacobson, Scott; Johnson, Edgar; Lawrence, Merloyd Ludington; Lawrence, Seymour; Lawson, Art; Lilly, Paul; McLaughlin, James R.; Mersand, Joseph; Meyer, Helen; Mitchell, Walter B. J., Jr.; Myers, David; Oehler, Milton; Reasoner, Charles; Saxon, Charles; Scudellari, Robert; Sharpe, Elizabeth; Smith, Robin; Storch, Otto; Swanberg, W. A.; Texidor, Fernando; Tobey, Carl; Van Zwienen, John; Vilirgas, Vera V.; Walker, Mort; Weiss, M. Jerome; Williams, Richard L.; Yates, Bill

Dell Encyclopedia of Dogs, The, 48

Dell First Editions, 6, 18, 19, 20, 21-22, 36-37, 39-42, 46; advance blurbs on covers, xi; advances and royalties, 40; authors, 22, 40, 41-42; editing, 22, 36, 37, 41; galley proofs, 41; genres, 39-40; hard-cover reissues, 41-42; manuscript sources, 22, 40; motion-picture tie-ins, 22, 40; mysteries, 36-37, 41; numbering system, xxiii; prices, 27, 40; printing dates, 40-41; print runs, 22, 40; royalties and advances, 40; sales, 22, 40; science-fiction, 39-40; simultaneous publication in hard cover, 40

Dell Great Mystery Library, 21, 38, 78

Dell International, Inc., 26

Dell paperbacks: abridgments, xvii, 9, 11, 24; advances and royalties, 7, 8, 11-12, 16, 35, 40, 49, 134 n.21; adventures, 119, 128; advertisements, 123; Alpha Books (see Dell Visual Books); anthologies, xvii, 8, 23, 32-33, 40, 42; art, cover, xv, xvi, xvii, xviii, xix, xx, 3, 7, 22-23, 25, 37, 39, 43, 48, 50, 55, 56-118; authors' name changes, 24; back-cover blurbs, 108; back-cover cartoons, 109; back-cover charts, 109; back-cover illustrations, 85, 100, 104, 108-9; back-cover maps, xv, xviii, xx, 8, 9, 74, 83-118; banners on back-cover maps, 110; bestsellers, 34-35, 50-51; bookracks, 17, 26, 131; "Books Are Weapons" blurbs, 130; Canadian editions, 16, 26; Candlelight Romances, 48, 50; cartoon books, 12, 131; censorship, xvi, 9, 13, 27, 68, 73; Chapel Books, 38; chapter titles, 119, 130; character lists, 83, 119, 124-27; circulation, 16, 20; Clover Books (see Seal Books); collection at Library of Congress, 143; collections, 143; color plates for covers, 75; "comic" novels, 32, 44; contracts, 8, 12, 20; copy-editing, 8, 9, 25-26; copyright page, 129; cost of producing, 12, 134 n.24; cover art (see art, cover); cover blurbs, xi, xix, 11, 21, 23-24, 108, 120, 122; crossword puzzle books, 119; Dell Visual Books, xvii, xviii, 43; Delta Books, 48-49; digest-sized books, 43-44; distribution, 16, 26, 52; double-columned text, 130; edge-staining, 10, 24; editing, 9, 22, 36, 37, 41; endpapers, 39, 74, 83, 121, 130; erotica, 9, 27, 51-52, 72, 78, 80, 81, 120; "Every Child's First Color and Learn Book Series," 46; fantasy and science-fiction, xix, 8, 28, 32, 50, 84, 93, 94, 98, 131; first editions, xi, xxiii, 6, 18, 19, 20, 21-22, 27, 36-37, 39-42, 46; foreign editions, 25; 4-digit reissues, 13, 85; front-cover blurbs, xi, xix, 11, 21, 23-24, 120, 122; galley proofs, xv, 7, 12; genre fiction, 28-32, 49-50 (see also individual genres); Gothic mysteries, 29, 69, 72; Great Mystery Library, 21, 38, 78; Harlin Quist books, 47; head-of-title blurbs, 83, 129; historical fiction, 87, 91; historical romances, 119, 121; Home

Activity Series, 46; horror fiction, 50; humor books, xvi, xvii, xviii, 7, 9, 12, 109; IBM numbers, xxi, xxiii-xxiv, 53; IBM numbers on inside front covers, 75; inside blurbs, 39, 127, 130; interior maps, 85; ISBN numbers, xxiii, 53; issue numbers on covers, xxiii-xxiv, 27, 130-31; laminated covers, 130; Laurel Editions, xvii, xviii, xxiii, 18, 19, 20, 26, 32, 40, 42-43, 46, 47-48, 77, 78, 118, 120; Laurel-Leaf Library, 47, 50; lawsuits, 26, 35-36; lettering, xvi, 57, 60, 61, 62, 63, 70; literature, 32-33; logos, xvi, 62, 74, 106, 119-20, 121, 130; "mapbacks," xi, xx, 9, 83-118; markets, 20, 36, 46, 47, 48, 49, 52, 54; Mayflower Books (Laurel-Leaf Library), 47; motion-picture tie-ins, 19, 22, 26, 33-34, 40, 71; "Murder Ink." mysteries, 49-50, 118; mysteries, 8, 21, 24, 28, 29-31, 36-37, 49-50, 60, 83-84, 86, 89-90, 90-92, 93, 94-95, 99, 103, 111-14, 115, 116-17, 119, 121, 124-25, 126, 127-29, 130, 135 n.2 (Chap. 2); after 1962, 45-55; non-fiction, 19, 20, 21, 22, 28, 32-33, 49, 50, 130; Nova-Dell books, 54; numbering system, xxi, xxiii-xxiv, 27, 53; origin, 5, 6; page proofs, 12; paging, 7; photo covers, 71, 80; prices, xxiii, 5, 27, 38, 39, 50, 131; printing, 7, 13-16, 26, 52-53, 129; printing of covers, 75; print runs, 13, 19, 26, 42, 51; production cost, 12, 134 n.24; promotional devices, 26, 38, 52; proof-reading, xviii, 7, 12; proofs, xv, 7, 12; puzzle books, 119; reissues, 4-digit, 13, 85; rejected titles, 9; reprints, xv-xviii, 18-20, 38, 49-50; returns by dealers, 75; romances, 8, 28, 31, 47, 50, 62, 65, 69, 84, 86, 89, 90, 92, 95, 119, 121, 128; royalties and advances, 7, 8, 11-12, 16, 35, 40, 49, 134 n.21; sales, 16-17, 19, 20, 21, 26, 34-35, 42, 48, 50; "Scene of the Crime" mysteries, 49-50, 118; science-fiction and fantasy, xix, 8, 28, 32, 50, 84, 93, 94, 98, 131; Seal Books, 46-47; series, xxiii; sex on covers, 27, 78, 80, 81, 120; sexually oriented titles, 9, 51, 52; sizes, 26; Spanish-language, 54; Special Student Editions, xxiii, 43; spine blurbs, 120; Sunrise Semester Library, xviii, 43; "tantalizer-pages," 119, 127; 10¢ series, 9, 38-39, 72; title changes, 24-25; title-pages, 83, 119, 122, 129; "Told-in-Pictures" series, xxiii, 44; trompe l'oeil covers, 58, 61, 62, 63, 65; "Twilight" series, 50; typesetting, xv, 7, 8, 12-13, 41, 129; typography, xviii, 21, 130; typography on covers, 74, 75; unnumbered books, xxiii, 32; Visual Books, xvii, xxiii, 43; westerns, xvii, xviii, 8, 21, 24-25, 28, 31-32, 50, 66, 69, 71, 78, 84, 86, 87, 89, 94, 95, 114-15, 119, 121, 131; Yearling Books, 46, 120

Dell Paperbacks, 1942 to Mid-1962 (William H. Lyles), xi, xxiii

Dell Previews, 26

Dell Publishing Company, 3-5, 129; acquisition of new lines, 53-54; and The American Heritage Publishing Company, 48; baseball annuals, xvii, 43-44; Canadian offices, 16; collection, 143; comic books, 5, 13, 15, 16, 18, 19, 32, 46, 74; Dial Press, 53; dismissals in 1983, 55; Ivy Books, 48; magazines and pulps, xvii, 4, 5, 43-44, 119; *Major League Baseball*, xvii, 43-44; Mayflower Books, Ltd., 54; New York City offices, 58; Noble and Noble, Publishers, Inc., 54; numbers on magazines, 4; offices, frontis., 4, 5, 58; origin, 3-5; Pine Brook, N.J., distribution center, 52; prices of books, 49; printers of books, 52-53; "Publications for Parents," 48; pulps and magazines, xvii, 4, 5, 43-44, 119; Radcliffe Biography Series, 48; relationship with Western Printing & Lithographing, xxi, 3, 5-27, 39, 45, 46, 74; sale of, to Doubleday, 54; sales, 5; Sales Department, 68, 74, 75, 76, 130; Spot Notes, 48; and Vineyard Books, 48; Yearling Books, 46, 120

Dell Purse Books, 48

Dell reprints, xv-xviii, 18-20, 38, 49-50. *See also* Dell paperbacks

Dell Seal Books, 46-47

Dell 10¢ series, 9, 38-39, 72; format, 39; titles planned but not published, 39

Dell Visual Books, xvii, xxiii, 43

Dell Yearling Books, 46, 120

del Rey, Lester, 84

Delta Books, 48-49

De Mille, Cecil B., 33

Demon Caravan, The (Georges Surdez, #501), fc, 72

Denver, Colo., map, 92

De Soto, Hernando, 81

de Soto, Rafael, 81

Desperate Angel (Helen Topping Miller, #462), bc, 104

Des Vignes, Jean, 71

Detroit News, The, 44

Devil in the Bush, The (Matthew Head, #158), bc, 85, 111

Devil's Stronghold, The (Leslie Ford, #395), bc, 103

Dewey, Thomas B., *Go, Honeylou* (#B215), fc, 77

diagrams, back-cover. *See* maps, back-cover

Dial Press, 53; Dial Books for Young Readers, 54

Dickens, Charles, 47

Dickson, Carter: *And So to Murder* (#175), bc, 96; *Death in Five Boxes* (#108), 127; *A Graveyard to Let* (#543), 30; *He Wouldn't Kill Patience* (#370), 126, bc, 96; *Scotland Yard: The Department of Queer Complaints* (#65), 127, bc, 92, 97, 117; *The Unicorn Murders* (#16), bc, 85. *See also* Carr, John Dickson

Dick Tracy and the Woo-Woo Sisters (Chester Gould), 32

Dietrich, Robert (pseud. of E. Howard Hunt), 41

digest-sized books, 43-44

Dinner at Antoine's (Frances Parkinson Keyes), 35

directors. *See* actors and directors

Disney, Dorothy Cameron: *Death in the Back Seat* (#76), fc, 70; *The Golden Swan Murder* (#15), 129, bc, 104; *Strawstack Murders* (#62), bc, 110

Disney, Walt, 5, 22, 70

Di Stefano, Anne, xvii, 19

distribution (Dell), 16, 26, 52

Ditis, Frédéric, xvii, 43

Dividend on Death (Brett Halliday, #617), fc, 72; bc, 109

Doctor Died at Dusk, The (Geoffrey Homes, #14), bc, 93

Doctor Hudson's Secret Journal (Lloyd C. Douglas, #304), 35

Doctorow, E. L., 54; *Ragtime*, 54

Dodge, David: *It Ain't Hay* (#270), fc, 69; *The Long Escape* (#405), 129; *The Red Tassel* (#565), fc, 73

Do Not Disturb (Helen McCloy, #261), bc, 106

Do Not Murder Before Christmas (Jack

Iams, #514), 130; bc, 116

Donovan, Arlene, xvii, 22, 40, 46

Dostoyevsky, Fyodor, *The Brothers Karamazov* (#F55), 20

double-columned text, 130

Doubleday & Co., xvi, 22, 54, 55

Double for Death (Rex Stout, #9), bc, 94

Double or Quits (A. A. Fair, #D361), fc, 78

Double Treasure (Clarence Budington Kelland, #335), fc, 71-72; bc, 92

Douglas, Lloyd C.: *Doctor Hudson's Secret Journal* (#304), 35; *Invitation to Live* (#380), 35

Dowdey, Clifford, xvii, 4

Down (Walt Grove, Dell First Edition #1E), 22

Doyle, Sir Arthur Conan, 144

Draw or Drag (Wayne D. Overholser, #556), bc, 114

Dreadful Hollow (Irina Karlova, #125), 127; fc, 58, 63; bc, 94

Dresser, Davis, 30. *See also* Halliday, Brett

Droemer (publisher), 43

Dr. Parrish, Resident (Sydney Thompson, #215), bc, 95

DuBouillon, A., trans., *Jusqu'au cou* (Harold Daniels, *In His Blood*), 25

Dumas *fils*, Alexandre, *Camille*, 62

Dunleavy, Peggy, xvii, 21

Durnham, Marilyn, *The Man Who Loved Cat Dancing*, 51

Dutchess county, N.Y., map, 89

Dutton, E. P., 54

Dystel, Oscar, 55

Eberhart, Mignon G., 29-30, 83, 111; *Hunt with the Hounds* (#546), bc, 88; *Speak No Evil* (#25), 30; *With This Ring* (#83), 125, fc, 69, bc, 95, 98

Economist (London), 111

Edge of Panic (Henry Kane, #535), 29

edge-staining of paperbacks, 10, 24

editing of Dell books, 9, 22, 36, 37, 41

Edmonds, Walter D., *The Wedding Journey* (Dell 10¢ series #6), 38

Eggenhofer, Nick, 78

Eiffel Tower, 81

Eiger, Richard, 75

Eighth Circle, The (Stanley Ellin, #D311), fc, 78

Eisenhower Was My Boss (Kay Summersby, #286), 34; bc, 87

Electronic Perfect Binders, 52

Ellin, Stanley: *The Eighth Circle* (#D311), fc, 78; *Quiet Horror* (#D325), fc, 68

Ellis, William Donohue, 24; *The Bounty Lands* (#F71), 24

Ellison, Ralph, 41

Elmer Gantry (Sinclair Lewis, #S10), 26

El Paso, Tex., map, 92

Emerick, Lucille, *The Web of Evil* (#479), fc, 72

Enchanted Oasis (Faith Baldwin, #255), bc, 88

Endore, Guy, *The Werewolf of Paris*, 27

endpapers, 39, 74, 83, 121, 130

Engel, Leonard, ed., *New Worlds of Modern Science* (#B102), 20

England, maps, 87, 88-89

En Lettres de Feu (trans. of Victor Chapin, *Career*), 25

Erickson, Rolf, xvii, 46, 75

Ermine, Will, *Outlaw on Horseback* (#284), bc, 86

erotica, 9, 27, 51-52, 72, 78, 80, 81, 120

Erskine, Albert, and Robert Penn Warren, eds., *Short Story Masterpieces* (Dell First Edition #F16), 20, 33, 42; *Six Centuries of Great Poetry* (Dell First Edition #FE69), 20, 33

Esquire, 77

Esso road and city maps, 85

Estonia, map, 111

Europe, maps, 87, 111

Evans, George, 80. *See also* Bird, Brandon

Evans, Kay. *See* Bird, Brandon

"Every Child's First Color and Learn Book Series," 46

eye, as symbol, 119

Fact Detective Mysteries (W. A. Swanberg, ed., #332), bc, 87

Fail-Safe (Eugene Burdick and Harvey Wheeler), 50

Fair, A. A. (pseud. of Erle Stanley Gardner), 29, 30, 130; *Bats Fly at Dusk* (#254), fc, 62, 81; *Crows Can't Count* (#472), 131, bc, 87; *Double or Quits* (#D361), fc, 78; *Fools Die on Friday* (#542, 1542), fc, 67, 73; *Gold Comes in Bricks* (#84), fc, 69; *Spill the Jackpot* (#109), 34, fc, 81; *Turn on the Heat* (#59), bc, 105; (#59, 620), 34. Characters: Bertha Cool, 30; Donald Lam, 30, 73, 87

Fallen Sparrow, The (Dorothy B. Hughes, #31), bc, 114

Fall Roundup, The (Harry E. Maule, ed.), 24-25

fantasy and science-fiction, xix, 8, 28, 32, 39-40, 50, 84, 93, 94, 98, 131

Farjeon, Jefferson, *Greenmask* (#111), 127

Farmhouse, The (Helen Reilly, #397), bc, 89

Fawcett Publishing Company, 25; Gold Medal paperbacks, 28, 36, 39, 40

Fear and Trembling (Alfred Hitchcock, ed., #264), fc, 61

Federal Agent, 4

Federal Trade Commission, 11

Feffer and Simmons (publisher), 54

Feltrinelli (publisher), 43

Ferrone, John, xvii, 21, 42

Fiery Trial, The (Carl Sandburg, #F77), fc, 79

Fine, Donald I., xvii-xviii, 22, 41, 45, 49

Finney, Jack, *The Body Snatchers* (Dell First Edition #42), fc, 40

Fire Will Freeze (Margaret Millar, #157), bc, 104

First Editions. *See* Dell First Editions

First Men in the Moon, The (H. G. Wells, #201), 8, 34; fc, 71; bc, 88

Fischer, Bruno, *The Hornets' Nest* (#79), 127; bc, 103

Fisher, Richard, xviii, 20, 43

Xit to Kill (Brett Halliday, #D314), 30

Five Novels Monthly, 4

Flynn, Errol: *Beam Ends* (#195), bc, 87; *Showdown* (#351), bc, 86

Flynn, T. T.: *The Man from Laramie* (Dell First Edition #14), 22; *Ridin' High* (#B209), fc, 73

"Fly Paper" (Dashiell Hammett), 90-91

Foldes, Yolanda, *Golden Earrings* (#216), 124; fc, 81; bc, 87

Fools Die on Friday (A. A. Fair, #542, 1542), fc, 67, 73

Footner, Hulbert, *The Murder That Had Everything* (#74), bc, 103

Footprints on the Ceiling, The (Clayton Rawson, #121), 124; bc, 88

Forbes, Gordon, *Too Near the Sun* (Dell First Edition #D56), 40

Ford, Leslie, 29, 30, 111; *The Clue of the Judas Tree* (#61), 124, bc, 94; *Date with Death* (#547), bc, 92; *The Devil's Stronghold* (#395), bc, 103; (as David Frome), *The Hammersmith Murders* (#36), 30; *Honolulu Story*, 27; *Ill Met by Moonlight*

(#6), fc, 62, 66, bc, 86, 92; *Murder with Southern Hospitality* (#505), 27; *The Philadelphia Murder Story* (#354), 127, bc, 92; *The Woman in Black* (#447), 125

foreign editions of Dell paperbacks, 25

Forest and the Fort, The (Hervey Allen, #D110), 35

Forester, C. S., *Plain Murder* (Dell First Edition #30), 40

Forlorn Island (Edison Marshall, #364), bc, 88

Fortier, Yolande, xviii, 21

For Women Only (Dr. Bernard L. Cinberg), 49

Foto, 4

4-digit reissues (Dell), 13, 85

Four Frightened Women (George Harmon Coxe, #5), bc, 94, 103

Fox, James M., 31, 111; *The Gentle Hangman* (#526), bc, 91; *The Inconvenient Bride* (#463), fc, 72; *The Lady Regrets* (#338), 126, fc, 77, bc, 91. Character: John Marshall, 72

Fox, Norman A., 21, 32; *Cactus Cavalier* (#406), bc, 94; *The Longhorn Legion* (10¢ series #12), 38-39

Framed in Blood (Brett Halliday, #578), bc, 109

France, Presses de la Cité, 25

Francis (David Stern, #507), bc, 109

Frank, Gerold, *Judy*, 51

Franken, Rose, *Young Claudia* (#528), fc, 81

Frederiksen, George A., xvi, 56-57, 58, 63, 119

Frey, Don, xviii, 23

Friede, Eleanor, 49, 55

Frightened Pigeon, The (Richard Burke, #204), fc, 80

Frightened Stiff, The (Kelley Roos, #56), bc, 105

Frome, David, *The Hammersmith Murders* (#36), 30. *See also* Ford, Leslie

Fuller, William, *Brad Dolan's Miami Manhunt* (#A158), 26-27

Funny Side Up (#607), 9

Gable, Clark, 22, 42

Gable's Secret Marriage, 39

Gaines, Audrey, *While the Wind Howled* (#51), bc, 96

galley proofs, xv, 7, 12, 41

Gallimard (publisher), 43

Gardner, Erle Stanley. *See* Fair, A. A.

Garve, Andrew (pseud. of Paul Winterton),
  No Mask for Murder (#571), bc, 111
Gathings Committee on Current Porno-
  graphic Materials (U.S. Congress), 27
Gauguin, Paul, 60
Gault, Claire and Frank, *Pelé*, 47
Gault, William Campbell, 24
Gaunt Woman, The (Edmund Gilligan,
  #312), bc, 88, 89
Gelb, Don, 78
Geller, John, xviii, 5
Gemeentemuseum, The Hague, xxii
General Mills, 54
Generation Rap (Gene Stafford, ed.), 50
genre fiction, 28-32, 39-40, 49-50. *See also*
  individual genres
Gentle Hangman, The (James M. Fox,
  #526), bc, 91
George, William, 76
Gerber, Albert G., *Bashful Billionaire*, 50
Gere, Byron, xviii, 70, 85
Gesell Institute, 19
Gift of Wings, A (Richard Bach), 49
Gilbert, Michael, *Death Has Deep Roots*
  (#744), fc, 80
Giles, F. Kenwood, 71
Gilligan, Edmund, *The Gaunt Woman*
  (#312), bc, 88, 89
Girl from "Peyton Place," The (George
  Metalious and June O'Shea), 35-36
Girl from Storyville, The (Frank Yerby), 50
"Girl in the Storm, The" (James M. Cain),
  39
Girl Meets Body (Jack Iams, #384), bc, 116
Girl on the Best-Seller List, The (Vin
  Packer), 36
"Girl with Silver Eyes, The" (Dashiell
  Hammett), 39
Glanzman, Louis, 71
Glaser, Milton, 78
Glass Mask, The (Lenore Glen Offord,
  #198), bc, 104
Glass Triangle, The (George Harmon Coxe,
  #81), fc, 80
Globe Mini Mags, 48
Go, Honeylou (Thomas B. Dewey, #B215),
  fc, 77
Goblin Market, The (Helen McCloy, #295),
  bc, 88
Godey, John, *The Taking of Pelham One
  Two Three*, 51
Go Down to Glory (Richard Warren Hatch,
  #D114), fc, 76

Gold Comes in Bricks (A. A. Fair, #84), fc,
  69
Golden Eagle, The (John Jennings, #D267),
  fc, 81
Golden Earrings (Yolanda Foldes, #216),
  124; fc, 81; bc, 87
Golden Press, 8, 12, 43, 46
Golden Swan Murder, The (Dorothy
  Cameron Disney, #15), 129; bc, 104
Goldman, William, *Magic*, 51
Gold Medal paperbacks, 28, 36, 39, 40
Goldthwaite, Eaton K., 111; *Root of Evil*
  (#442), bc, 111; *Scarecrow* (#193), bc, 92
Goodis, David, 29, 31; *Dark Passage*
  (#221), 31, bc, 105
Goodman Publications, 22
Gothic mysteries, 29, 69, 72
Gould, Chester, *Dick Tracy and the Woo-
  Woo Sisters*, 32
Gould, Lois, *Such Good Friends*, 51
Grafton, C. W., 112; *The Rat Began to
  Gnaw the Rope* (#180), 104, 109, bc, 112;
  The Rope Began to Hang the Butcher
  (#232), 129, bc, 112
Grahame, Kenneth, 46
Grand Banks, Canada, map, 89
Graphic paperbacks, 16
Graveyard to Let, A (Carter Dickson, #543),
  30
Great Black Kanba (Constance and
  Gwenyth Little, #181), fc, 69; bc, 86
Great Britain, map, 87
Great Britain, paperback publishers, 25, 54
Great English Short Stories (Christopher
  Isherwood, ed., #LC102), 20
Great Locomotive Chase, The (motion pic-
  ture), 22
Great Mistake, The (Mary Roberts Rine-
  hart, #297), bc, 110
Great Mystery Library (Dell), 21, 38, 78
Great Smith (Edison Marshall, #D102), 34
Great Tales of Action and Adventure (George
  Bennett, ed.), 47
Green, Alan, *What a Body!* (#483), bc, 100,
  109
Greene, David H., xviii, 43
Greenmask (Jefferson Farjeon, #111), 127
Greenslet, Ferris, and Charles P. Curtis,
  Jr., eds., *The Practical Cogitator*, 50
Greenwillow (B. J. Chute, #D385), 37
Gregg, Bill, 71
Gregg, Gerald, xvi, 50, 56-57, 58-66, 69-70,
  71, 74, 82, 85

Gregg, Nell, 59

Greig, Maysie: *Candidate for Love* (#239), fc, 62, bc, 104, 117; *Satin Straps* (#309), bc, 92; *Yours Ever* (#446), bc, 88

Grey, Zane, 43

Groom Lay Dead, The (George Harmon Coxe, #502), 31

Gross, George, 24, 79-80

Grosse, William R., 51

Grosset & Dunlap, 47

Grove, Walt, *Down* (Dell First Edition #1E), 22

Grove Press, 49, 54

Gruber, Frank, 4

Guild Family Readers, 39

Guinness Book of World Records, The, 51

Gunn, James E., xvi, 9; ed., *Funny Side Up* (#607), 9

Gun Smoke Yarns (Gene Autry, ed., #217), fc, 71

Guy de Maupassant (Francis Steegmuller, ed., #LC135), 25; World #C949, 25

Guzzardi, Peter, 118

"Had-I-But-Known" mysteries, 29-30

Haggard, H. Rider: *King Solomon's Mines* (#433), 33, 34, 35, bc, 93; *She* (#339), fc, 80, bc, 93, 117

Haldeman-Julius Publications, 6

Hale, Christopher, *Midsummer Nightmare* (#150), bc, 94-95

Hale, Virginia Sidney, *A Book of Etiquette*, 4

Half Angel (Fanny Heaslip Lea, #118), fc, 61, 64

Hallam, Ben, xviii, 63, 70

Halliday, Brett, xviii, 29, 30, 31, 72, 79; *Blood on Biscayne Bay* (#268), bc, 91, (#D342), fc, 66, 78; *Blood on the Black Market* (#64), fc, 70, bc, 108; *Blood on the Stars* (#385), 27, fc, 72; *The Corpse Came Calling* (#168), 124, 126, fc, 69, bc, 105; *Counterfeit Wife* (#280), 129; *Dividend on Death* (#617), fc, 72, bc, 109; *Fit to Kill* (#D314), 30; *Framed in Blood* (#578), bc, 109; *Marked for Murder* (#222), bc, 91; *Michael Shayne's Long Chance* (#112), 127; *Murder and the Married Virgin* (#128, 323), 34; *Murder Is My Business* (#184), 127, 128; *Murder Takes No Holiday* (#D379), 30; *Murder Wears a Mummer's Mask* (#78, 388), 34, 128, bc,

93; *The Private Practice of Michael Shayne* (#23, 429), 34, bc, 91; *Target: Mike Shayne* (#D355), 30; *A Taste of Violence* (#426), bc, 92; *This Is It, Michael Shayne* (#533), bc, 108; *When Dorinda Dances* (#D359), fc, 78. Character: Michael Shayne, 30, 72, 79, 80, 91, 105, 108, 129. Pseud. of Davis Dresser, 30; pseud. of Robert Terrall, 30

Halo for Nobody, A (Henry Kane, #231), 29, 128

Hamilton, Donald, 25, 79-80, 112-13; *Assassins Have Starry Eyes*, 25; *Assignment: Murder* (#A123), 25, fc, 113; *The Big Country* (#B115), bc, 113; *Date with Darkness* (#375), 25, fc, 72, bc, 112-13; *Mad River* (Dell First Edition #91), fc, 79-80, bc, 113; *The Man from Santa Clara* (#B170), 25; *Murder Twice Told* (#577), 39, fc, 72, bc, 112; *Red Sector*, 25; *The Steel Mirror* (#473), fc, 81, bc, 112; *The Two-Shoot Gun*, 25

Hamilton, Bermuda, maps, 88, 92

Hammersmith Murders, The (David Frome, #36), 30

Hammett, Dashiell, xix, 29, 84, 85, 90-91; *Blood Money* (#53, 486), 139 n.16, bc, 91; *The Continental Op* (#129), 127, 128, fc, 69, bc, 90-91, 97; *The Creeping Siamese* (#538), fc, 72, bc, 91; *Dead Yellow Women* (#308), fc, 69, bc, 91; "Fly Paper," 90-91; "The Girl with Silver Eyes," 39; *Hammett Homicides* (#223), 39, fc, 69, bc, 91; *A Man Called Spade* (#90, 411, 452), 34, (#411), fc, 72; *A Man Called Thin*, 139 n.15; *Nightmare Town* (#379), bc, 91; *Return of the Continental Op* (#154), 128, bc, 91; *Woman in the Dark*, 139 n.15. Character: Sam Spade, 72

Hammett Homicides (Dashiell Hammett, #223), 39; fc, 69; bc, 91

Hamming-Whitman (publisher), 5

Hand in the Glove, The (Rex Stout, #177), 30; bc, 95

Happy Hooker, The (Xaviera Hollander), 50, 51

hard-boiled mysteries, 29

Harlem (New York City), map, 90

Harlequin Romances, 31, 48

Harlin Quist books, 47

Harlot Killer, The (Allan Barnard, ed., #797), 9

Harlow (Irving Shulman), 51
Harper & Row, ChapelBooks, 38
Harrison, Jim, 49
Harry Wilson Studios, 57
Harvey Girls, The (Samuel Hopkins Adams, #130), 34, 124; bc, 92, 108
H as in Hunted (Lawrence Treat, #218), bc, 115
Haskin, Byron, 96
Hatch, Richard Warren, *Go Down to Glory* (#D114), fc, 76
Hatfield-McCoy country, map, 86
Haunted Lady (Mary Roberts Rinehart, #361), bc, 104
Hawkins, James E., xvi, 7, 8-9, 13, 25-26, 27, 85
Hawkins, Virginia, xviii, 26
Hawthorne, Nathaniel, 32
Haycox, Ernest, 32
Head, Matthew (pseud. of John Canaday), 29, 31; *The Accomplice* (#346), fc, 81, bc, 106, 107; *The Cabinda Affair* (#390), bc, 88; *The Congo Venus* (#605), fc, 72, 81, bc, 85; *The Devil in the Bush* (#158), bc, 85, 111; *The Smell of Money* (#219), bc, 85, 95, 111. *See also* Canaday, John
Headless Lady, The (Clayton Rawson, #176), bc, 96
Head-of-Title blurbs, 83, 129
Hearst Company, 16
Heart Remembers, The (Faith Baldwin, #288), bc, 90
Heberden, M. V., *They Can't All Be Guilty* (#401), bc, 93
Heilman, Harry, 44
Heinlein, Robert, *Universe* (10¢ series #36), 9
Held, John, Jr., *Crosstown* (#477), 126; bc, 87
Hell, map, 93, 98
Hell Cat (Idabel Williams, #521), bc, 90
Heller, Joseph, *Catch-22*, 51
Help! (motion picture), 50
Hemingway, Ernest, *Across the River and Into the Trees* (#D117), 27
Hentoff, Nat, *Jazz Country*, 47
He Wouldn't Kill Patience (Carter Dickson, #370), 126; bc, 96
Hilton, Francis W., *Skyline Riders* (#250), 126; fc, 66, 71
Hinds, Ruby, xviii, 69
Hine, Al, *The Beatles in Help!*, 50

Hinton, S. E., *The Outsiders*, 47
historical fiction, 87, 91
historical romances, 119, 121
Hitchcock, Alfred, 8, 32, 33, 61, 90; "Alfred Hitchcock Suspense Magazine," 44; ed., *Bar the Doors* (#143), fc, 62; ed., *Fear and Trembling* (#264), fc, 61; ed., *Hold Your Breath* (#206), fc, 71; ed., *Suspense Stories* (#92), bc, 95-96, 98
Hite, Shere, xx, 79; *The Hite Report*, xx, 79
Hite Report, The (Shere Hite), xx, 79
Hoffman, H. L., 82
Holding, Elisabeth Sanxay: *The Innocent Mrs. Duff* (#194), 128; *Murder Is a Kill-Joy* (#103), 124, 125, fc, 80
Hold Your Breath (Alfred Hitchcock, ed., #206), fc, 71
Holiday Homicide (Rufus King, #22), 125; bc, 96, 98, 107
Hollander, Xaviera, 52; *The Happy Hooker*, 50, 51; *Xaviera*, 51
Holshue, Galen, xviii, 16
Home Activity Series, 46
Homer, Winslow, 59
Homes, Geoffrey: *The Doctor Died at Dusk* (#14), bc, 93; *The Man Who Didn't Exist* (#41), 125, bc, 104, 117
Honolulu Story (Leslie Ford), 27
Honor Bound (Faith Baldwin, #116), fc, 69
Hooks, Mitchell, xviii, 76, 78
Hoopes, Ned E., 47
Hornets' Nest, The (Bruno Fischer, #79), 127; bc, 103
horror fiction, 50
hotels, maps, 106, 117
House of Darkness (Allan MacKinnon, #237), fc, 69; bc, 84, 86, 97
House of Numbers, The (motion picture), 22
houses, maps, 103-4, 112, 113, 114
How to Pick a Mate (Dr. Clifford R. Adams and Vance O. Packard, #224), 34; bc, 109
Huett, Richard, 43, 47, 49
Hughes, Dorothy B., 29, 31, 114; *The Blackbirder* (#149), fc, 69, bc, 104, 114; *The Cross-Eyed Bear Murders* (#48), bc, 114; *The Fallen Sparrow* (#31), bc, 114; *Ride the Pink Horse* (#210), 130, bc, 114; *The So Blue Marble* (#100), bc, 114
Hughes, Howard, 50
Hull, E. M.: *The Captive of the Sahara* (#402), bc, 93; *The Sheik* (#174), 34, 35, bc, 88

Human Beast, The (Emile Zola, #608), 34
humor books, xvi, xvii, xviii, 7, 9, 12, 109
Hunt, E. Howard, 41
Hunt, Peter, *Murders at Scandal House*
  (#42), bc, 85, 94
Hunter, Sam: *Modern American Painting
  and Sculpture* (#LY102), 20; *Modern
  French Painting* (Dell First Edition
  #FE98), 20
Hunt with the Hounds (Mignon G. Eber-
  hart, #546), bc, 88

Iams, Jack, xx, 116-17, 130; *The Body
  Missed the Boat* (#274), bc, 116; *Death
  Draws the Line* (#457), bc, 90, 116; *Do
  Not Murder Before Christmas* (#514), 130,
  bc, 116; *Girl Meets Body* (#384), bc, 116;
  Love—and the Countess to Boot (#139),
  bc, 116; *What Rhymes with Murder?*
  (#631), bc, 101, 116-17
Ibañez, Vicente Blasco. *See* Blasco Ibañez,
  Vicente
I Confess, 4
IBM numbers: inside Dell front covers,
  75; of Dell paperbacks, xxi, xxiii-xxiv, 53
If a Body (George Worthing Yates, #159),
  bc, 85-86, 86-87, 89
Ilg, Frances L., and Louise Bates Ames,
  Child Behavior (#D180, LC120, LS107),
  19
Ill Met by Moonlight (Leslie Ford, #6), fc,
  62, 66; bc, 86, 92
illustrations. *See* art, cover
Ilton, Paul, and MacLennan Roberts,
  Moses and the Ten Commandments
  (#B105), 33
Inconvenient Bride, The (James M. Fox,
  #463), fc, 72
India, map, 88
Information Center Service, Small Books
  Program (U.S. Information Agency), 43
Ingres, Jean, 59
In His Blood (Harold Daniels, Dell First
  Edition #73), 25, 40; as *Jusqu'au cou,* 25
Innocent Bystander (Craig Rice, #461), bc, 96
Innocent Mrs. Duff, The (Elisabeth Sanxay
  Holding, #194), 128
Intimate Sex Lives of Famous People, The
  (Irving Wallace et al.), 120
Invasion from Mars (Orson Welles, ed.,
  #305), 8, 32; bc, 88, 111
Invasion of the Body Snatchers (motion
  picture), 22

Invisible Man, The (H. G. Wells, #269), 8;
  bc, 88
Invitation to Live (Lloyd C. Douglas, #380),
  35
Iping, Sussex (England), map, 88
Irish, William, 38. *See also* Woolrich,
  Cornell
Iron Gates, The (Margaret Millar, #209),
  bc, 96
Iron Spiders Murders, The (Baynard H.
  Kendrick, #50), 127; bc, 88
Irving, Alexander, *Bitter Ending* (#289), bc,
  107
ISBN numbers, xxiii, 53
Isherwood, Christopher, ed., *Great English
  Short Stories* (#LC102), 20
islands, maps, 87-88, 111
isometric projection, 103
issue numbers on Dell paperback covers,
  xxiii-xxiv, 27, 130-31
It Ain't Hay (David Dodge, #270), fc, 69
Ivy Books, 48
I Was a Nazi Flier (Gottfried Leske, #21),
  34; bc, 109

"J.," *The Sensuous Woman,* 51
Jabberwocky and Other Nonsense (Lewis
  Carroll), 47
Jackson, Charles, *The Sunnier Side* (#504),
  bc, 93
Jacobson, Scott, 52
Jacobson, William George, 71
Jaffe, Marc, xviii, 45
Janney, Russell, *The Miracle of the Bells*
  (#474), 35; bc, 88, 93
Jazz Country (Nat Hentoff), 47
Jenkins, Dan, *Semi-Tough,* 51
Jennings, John, *The Golden Eagle* (#D267),
  fc, 81
Jessup, Richard, 41
Jet Set, The (Burton Wohl), 49
Jim the Conqueror (Peter B. Kyne, #294),
  bc, 95
Johnson, Edgar, 47
Johnson, Ray, 71
Johnston, George, *Queen of the Flat-Tops*
  (#37), 34; bc, 86
Jokes, Gags and Wisecracks (Ted Shane,
  ed., #152), fc, 61, 65
Jonathan Livingston Seagull (Richard Bach),
  49, 51
Jones, James, 39
Juarez, Mexico, map, 92

Judas, Incorporated (Kurt Steel, #244), 124; fc, 62

Judy (Gerold Frank), 51

Juliet Dies Twice (Lange Lewis, #68), fc, 61; bc, 107

Jungle Hunting Thrills (Edison Marshall, #468), fc, 81; bc, 87

Jusqu'au cou, trans. A. DuBouillon (Harold Daniels, *In His Blood*), 25

Just Around the Coroner (Stuart Brock, #337), bc, 106, 117

Kaiser, William, 63

Kaiser Aluminum, 40

Kalin, Victor, xviii, 39, 71, 77

Kane, Frank, 41

Kane, Henry, 29, 89; *Armchair in Hell* (#316), fc, 69, bc, 90; *Edge of Panic* (#355), 29; *A Halo for Nobody* (#231), 29, 128; *Report for a Corpse* (#330), bc, 109; "Suicide Is Scandalous," 109; *Until You Are Dead* (#580), bc, 93

Kane, Irene, and Mary McGee Williams, *On Becoming a Woman* (#A179, B200), 36

Kansas City, Mo., 81

Kapilow, Mildred, xviii, 21

Karan, Lisa, 79

Karlova, Irina, *Dreadful Hollow* (#125), 127; fc, 58, 63; bc, 94

Kaufman, Lenard, *Tender Mercy* (#444), bc, 108

Kaufman, Van, 71

Kaz, *Nellie's Bedfellows* (#A209), 131

Keeper of the Keys (Earl Derr Biggers, #47), 11

Kelland, Clarence Budington, *Double Treasure* (#335), fc, 71-72; bc, 92

Kendrick, Baynard [H.], 29, 31, 39; *Blind Man's Bluff* (#230), fc, 81, bc, 106; *Death Knell* (#273), fc, 69, bc, 105; *The Iron Spiders Murders* (#50), 127, bc, 88; *The Last Express* (#95), 127; *Odor of Violets* (#162), 128, fc, 62, 69, bc, 104; *Out of Control* (#376), fc, 71; *The Whistling Hangman* (#113), bc, 105. Character: Duncan Maclain, 31, 39, 81

Kentucky, map, 86

Kerouac, Jack, *On the Road*, 9

Kersh, Gerald, *Night and the City* (#374), bc, 92

Ketchum, Philip, *Death in the Library* (#1), 3

Keyes, Frances Parkinson, *Dinner at Antoine's*, 35

keyhole, as symbol and logo, 119-20

Kind Are Her Answers (Mary Renault, #189), bc, 115

King, Rufus, *Holiday Homicide* (#22), 125; bc, 96, 98, 107

King, Stephen, *Dance Macabre*, xxii

King and Four Queens, The (motion picture), 22

King Solomon's Mines (motion picture), 33

King Solomon's Mines (H. Rider Haggard and Jean Francis Webb, #433), 33, 34, 35; bc, 93

Kissner, Robert, xviii, 85

Kiss the Blood Off My Hands (Gerald Butler, #197), bc, 105, 117

K. K. Comics, 18

Klempner, John, *Letter to Five Wives* (#554), 35

Knibbs, H. H., *The Ridin' Kid from Powder River* (#399), 11

Knight, Clifford, *The Affair of the Scarlet Crab* (#75), bc, 110

Knight, Ruth Adams, *Women Must Weep* (#482), bc, 85

Knopf, Alfred A., xxi

Kroll, Harry Harrison, *Their Ancient Grudge* (#435), 120, 130; bc, 86

Kuhn, Paul, xviii, 22

Ku Klux Klan, 34

Kummer, Frederic Arnold, *Ladies in Hades* (#415), bc, 93, 98

Kundu (Morris L. West, #A116), 41

Kyne, Peter B., *Jim the Conqueror* (#294), bc, 95

Labors of Hercules, The (Agatha Christie, #491), fc, 72

Ladies in Hades (Frederic Arnold Kummer, #415), bc, 93, 98

Lady in the Tower (Katharine Newlin Burt, #191), 128

Lady Is Afraid, The (George Harmon Coxe, #147), 124

Lady Regrets, The (James M. Fox, #338), 126; fc, 77; bc, 91

Lait, Jack, and Lee Mortimer, *Chicago Confidential* (#D101), 34; *New York: Confidential!* (#400, 440, 534), 34, bc, 90; *Washington Confidential* (#D108), 34, 35

Lam, Donald, in A. A. Fair's mysteries, 30, 73, 87

Lambert, Saul, 77

lamination of covers, 130
Lamm, Joan, xviii, 21
Lamy, Archbishop, 114
Lane, Allen, 5
Larrimore, Lida, 31; *Robin Hill* (#119), 31, bc, 95
Last Enemy, The (Berton Roueché, Dell First Edition #D90), 42; fc, 76
Last Express, The (Baynard Kendrick, #95), 127
Las Vegas, Nev., map, 92
Laurel Editions, xvii, 18, 19, 20, 40, 42-43, 47-48, 120; Laurel Classical series, 47; Laurel Dickens, 47; Laurel Hawthorne, 32; Laurel Jane Austen, 32; Laurel Language Library, 47; Laurel Poetry Series, xviii, 32, 42-43, 47, 48, 78, 118; Laurel Readers, 77; Laurel Shakespeare, 26, 47, 48, 118; numbering systems, xxiii; origin, xvii, 42; prices, xxiii; print runs, 42; sales, 42, 48; short stories series, 47, 48; *20,000 Years of World Painting* series, 47
Laurel-Leaf Library, 47, 50; Mayflower Books, 47; "Young Love" series, 47
Lawrence, Merloyd Ludington, 48
Lawrence, Seymour, 49, 55
Lawson, Art, xviii, 4
Lawson, Robert, 46
lawsuits, 26, 35-36
Layton School of Art, 57
Lea, Fanny Heaslip, *Half Angel* (#118), fc, 61, 64
Leaning Tower and Other Stories, The (Katherine Anne Porter), 48-49
Leave Cancelled (Nicholas Monsarrat, #327), fc, 79; bc, 109
Leave It to Psmith (P. G. Wodehouse, #357), bc, 96, 103
Le Carré, John, *The Looking Glass War*, 51
Lees, Hannah, and Lawrence Bachmann, *Death in the Doll's House* (#122), bc, 104
"Leiningen versus the Ants" (Carl Stephenson), 95-96, 98
Lemay, Harry, 75
Lenniger, August, 40
Lenski, Lois, 46
Leonard, Elmore, 21, 41
Leone, Leonard, 76
Leroux, Gaston, *The Phantom of the Opera* (#24), 34; bc, 106
Leske, Gottfried, *I Was a Nazi Flier* (#21),

34; bc, 109
Lesser, Ronnie, 79
lettering on Dell paperbacks, xvi, 57, 60, 61, 62, 63, 70
Letter to Five Wives (John Klempner, #554), 35
Levin, Ira, *Rosemary's Baby*, 51
Lewis, Lange: *The Birthday Murder* (#214), bc, 117; *Juliet Dies Twice* (#68), fc, 61, bc, 107
Lewis, Sinclair, *Elmer Gantry* (#S10), 26, 71
Liberty Street wing, Western Printing & Lithographing (Racine), 8, 59, 62
Library of Congress, xxii, 9, 143
Life, 4
Lilly, Paul, 19
Lion paperbacks, 16
literature in Dell lines, 32-33
lithography, 58, 59
Little, Constance and Gwenyth, *Great Black Kanba* (#181), fc, 69; bc, 86
Little Blue Books, 6
Little Women (Jean Francis Webb, #296), 33-34, 34-35, 124; bc, 108
Little Women (motion picture), 33-34, 108, 124
Livermore and Knight, 52
Locke, June, xviii, 71
Locke, V., 71
Lockridge, Frances and Richard, 29, 31; *Death of a Tall Man* (#322), 126; *Murder within Murder* (#229), bc, 90
Lockridge, Ross, Jr., *Raintree County* (#F58), 19, 35
logos, xvi, 62, 74, 106, 119-20, 121, 130
London, maps, 91-92, 97
Lone Wolf, The (Louis Joseph Vance, #10), bc, 93
Long Escape, The (David Dodge, #405), 129
Longhorn Legion, The (Norman A. Fox, 10¢ series #12), 38-39
Long Rifle, The (Stewart Edward White, #D147), 24; fc, 78
Looking Glass War, The (John Le Carré), 51
Lorilard, P., Co., 43
Los Angeles: branch, Western Printing & Lithography, 6; maps, 91
Love—and the Countess to Boot (Jack Iams, #139), bc, 116
Lowe, Sam, 58
Luce, Henry, 4
Lyles, William H., *Dell Paperbacks, 1942 to Mid-1962*, xi, xxiii

"M.," *The Sensuous Man*, 51

Mabon, John Scott, xviii, 18

McCloy, Helen: *Cue for Murder* (#212), fc, 80, bc, 107; *Dance of Death* (#33), fc, 80, bc, 99, 104; *The Deadly Truth* (#107), fc, 80; *Do Not Disturb* (#261), bc, 106; *The Goblin Market* (#295), bc, 88; *She Walks Alone* (#430), bc, 89, 107; *Through a Glass, Darkly* (#519), bc, 104; *Who's Calling?* (#151), fc, 62, bc, 110

MacCormac, John, *This Time for Keeps* (#32), 34; bc, 109

McCoy-Hatfield country, map, 86

McCulley, Johnston, *The Mark of Zorro* (#553), fc, 72

MacDonald, John D., 40, 42

McGerr, Pat: *Pick Your Victim* (#307), bc, 106; *The Seven Deadly Sisters* (#412), bc, 108

McGinnis, Ferne, 79

McGinnis, Robert, xx, 36, 66, 75, 78-79, 82

McGivern, Judge Owen, 36

McKimmey, James, 37; *The Perfect Victim* (#A159), 42; *Winner Take All* (#A185), 37

MacKinnon, Allan, *House of Darkness* (#237), fc, 69; bc, 84, 86, 97

Maclain, Duncan, in Baynard Kendrick's mysteries, 31, 39, 81

McLaughlin, James R., 55

MacLean, Robinson, *The Baited Blonde* (#508), bc, 88

Macmillan, 49

MacNichol, Ralph, xvi, 13, 27

McWilliams, Alden, 71

Madball (Fredric Brown, Dell First Edition #2E), 41

Made up to Kill (Kelley Roos, #106), 124

Mad River (Donald Hamilton, Dell First Edition #91), fc, 79-80; bc, 113

magazines. See "Alfred Hitchcock Suspense Magazine"; *All Detective*; *All Western*; *Ballyhoo*; *Collier's*; *Cupid's Diary*; *Esquire*; *Federal Agent*; *Five Novels Monthly*; *Foto*; *I Confess*; *Life*; *New Yorker*; *Playboy*; *Publishers Weekly*; *Saturday Review of Literature*; *Western, The*; *Whisper*; *Yank*; *Zane Grey's Western Magazine*

magazines and pulps (Dell), xvii, 4, 5, 43-44, 119

Magic (William Goldman), 51

Magnificent Bastards, The (Lucy Herndon Crockett, #D145, F95), 19, 26

Maguire, Robert, 77

Major League Baseball, xvii, 43-44

Malraux, André, 82

Man Called Spade, A (Dashiell Hammett, #90, 411, 452), 34; (#411), fc, 72

Man Called Thin, A (Dashiell Hammett), 139 n.15

Manchester, William, *American Caesar*, 51

Man from Laramie, The (motion picture), 22

Man from Laramie, The (T. T. Flynn, Dell First Edition #14), 22

Man from Santa Clara, The (Donald Hamilton, #B170), 25

Manhattan (New York City), maps, 89-90, 93, 96-97, 98-99, 106, 116

Manhunt West (Walker A. Tompkins, #551), 32

Man in Lower Ten, The (Mary Roberts Rinehart, #124), bc, 107

Man in the Brown Suit, The (Agatha Christie, #319), bc, 88

Mannes, Marya, *Message from a Stranger* (#515), bc, 109

manuscript sources, 22, 40

Man Who Didn't Exist, The (Geoffrey Homes, #41), 125: bc, 104, 117

Man Who Loved Cat Dancing, The (Marilyn Durnham), 51

"mapbacks," xi, xx, 9, 83-118

maps, back-cover, xv, xviii, xx, 8, 9, 74, 83-118; banners, 110; colors corresponding to authors' descriptions, 104, 105, 109-10. See also crime sketches

maps, interior, 85

maps of areas. See crime sketches; individual locations

March, William, *The Bad Seed* (#847, F180), 19

Margolies, Pete, xviii, 21, 40

marijuana, 69

Marine, Edmund, xviii, 74

Marked for Murder (Brett Halliday, #222), bc, 91

markets, 20, 36, 46, 47, 48, 49, 52, 54

Mark of Zorro, The (Johnston McCulley, #553), fc, 72

Markowitz, Barbara, xviii, 21

Marple, Miss, in Agatha Christie's mysteries, 29

Mars, map, 88

Marseilles, map, 92

Marshall, Edison: *Benjamin Blake* (#431), 11; *Castle in the Swamp* (#487), bc, 88;

Forlorn Island (#364), bc, 88; *Great Smith* (#D102), 34; *Jungle Hunting Thrills* (#468), fc, 81, bc, 87; *The Splendid Quest* (#188), bc, 92; *The Upstart* (#233, 341), 34, bc, 87; *The White Brigand* (#144), 126, bc, 96; *Yankee Pasha* (#353), 34, bc, 87

Marshall, John, in James M. Fox's mysteries, 72

Marshall, Peter, *Mr. Jones, Meet the Master*, 35

Marshall, Rosamond, *Celeste the Gold Coast Virgin* (#382), 34; bc, 91

Maryland, map, 113

Mason, Sara Elizabeth, 113; *The Crimson Feather* (#207), bc, 101, 104, 110, 113

Massage Parlor (Jennifer Sills, ed.), 51

Masterpiece in Murder (Richard Powell, #915), 135 n.3 (Chap. 2)

Masur, Harold Q., 24

Mattel, Inc., 46

Maugham, W. Somerset, *Mrs. Craddock* (#D106), 34

Maule, Harry E., ed., *The Fall Roundup*, 24-25; *Rawhiders and Renegades* (#D367), 25

Maupassant, Guy de, *Guy de Maupassant* (Francis Steegmuller, ed., #LC135), 25; World #C949, 25

Maverick, Bret, 40

Mayflower Books, Ltd., 54

Mayflower Books (Laurel-Leaf Library), 47

Medicine Hat, Utah, 113

Meier, Frank, *Men Under the Sea* (#265), bc, 87

Men and War (M. Jerome Weiss), 47

Men Under the Sea (Frank Meier, #265), bc, 87

Mercator projection, 86, 89

Meredith, Scott, 40

Merlinville-sur-mer, France, map, 92

Merril, Judith, 40

Mersand, Joseph, 48

Merton, Thomas, 38

Message from a Stranger (Marya Mannes, #515), bc, 109

Messner, Julian, 35

Metalious, George, and June O'Shea, *The Girl from "Peyton Place,"* 35-36

Metalious, Grace, 35-36; *No Adam in Eden*, 35; *Peyton Place* (#F61), xv, xix, 9, 19, 26, 27, 35-36, 130; *Return to Peyton Place* (#F91), 35, 45; *The Tight White Collar* (#S25), 35

Mets (New York), 55, 137 n.22

Mexico City, map, 92

Meyer, Helen, xvi, 4, 5, 10, 19, 27, 42, 45, 49, 54, 74, 118

Meyers, Bob, 71

Miami and Miami Beach, maps, 91

Michael Shayne's Long Chance (Brett Halliday, #112), 127

Middle East, map, 88

Midnight Sailing (Lawrence G. Blochman, #43), bc, 107

Midsummer Nightmare (Christopher Hale, #150), bc, 94-95

Millar, Kenneth, *Blue City* (#363), bc, 93

Millar, Margaret: *Fire Will Freeze* (#157), bc, 104; *The Iron Gates* (#209), bc, 96; *Wall of Eyes* (#110), 125

Miller, Arthur, *The Misfits* (#F115), 42

Miller, Helen Topping, *Desperate Angel* (#462), bc, 104

Miller, Warren, 35

"Million Year Picnic, The" (Ray Bradbury), 88, 111

Milne, A. A., 46

Miracle of the Bells, The (Russell Janney, #474), 35; bc, 88, 93

Misfits, The (Arthur Miller, #F115), 42

Misfits, The (motion picture), 42

Mitchell, Walter B. J., Jr., xviii, 19, 27, 50

Modern American Painting and Sculpture (Sam Hunter, #LY102), 20

Modern Criminal Investigation (Harry Söderman and John J. O'Connell), 83-84, 86

Modern French Painting (Sam Hunter, Dell First Edition #FE98), 20

Monarch Notes, 48

Monet, Claude, 59

Monroe, Marilyn, 42

Monsarrat, Nicholas, 79; *Leave Cancelled* (#327), fc, 79, bc, 109

Moon, map, 88

Moon's Our Home, The (Faith Baldwin, #368), 31; bc, 88

"Morning Watch, The" (James Agee), 33

Morrow, William (publisher), 11, 73

Morse, Mark M., xviii, 19, 45

Mortimer, Lee, and Jack Lait: *Chicago Confidential* (#D101), 34; *New York: Confidential!* (#400, 440, 534), 34, bc, 90; *Washington Confidential* (#D108), 34, 35

Moses, 33, 39

Moses and the Ten Commandments (Paul

Ilton and MacLennan Roberts, #B105), 33

motion pictures. See *Anna Lucasta; Bravados, The; Career; Dark Passage; Great Locomotive Chase, The; Help!; House of Numbers, The; Invasion of the Body Snatchers; King and Four Queens, The; King Solomon's Mines; Little Women; Man from Laramie, The; Misfits, The; Naked Jungle, The; Now, Voyager; Proud and Profane, The; Rope; Storm Warning; Ten Commandments, The; While the City Sleeps*

motion-picture tie-ins, 19, 22, 26, 33-34, 40, 71

Mound Avenue offices, Western Printing & Lithographing (Racine), 8

Mountain Cat Murders, The (Rex Stout, #28), 30; Century edition, 110

Mourned on Sunday (Helen Reilly, #63), 127; bc, 110

Mouron, Adolphe Jean-Marie. See Cassandre

Mr. Jones, Meet the Master (Peter Marshall), 35

Mrs. Craddock (W. Somerset Maugham, #D106), 34

Mrs. Murdock Takes a Case (George Harmon Coxe, #202), bc, 105

Murder and the Married Virgin (Brett Halliday, #128, 323), 34

Murder at the Vicarage, The (Agatha Christie, #226), 128

Murder Begins at Home (Delano Ames, #552), bc, 88

Murder for the Asking (George Harmon Coxe, #58), 125

Murder for Two (George Harmon Coxe, #276), bc, 110

"Murder Ink." mysteries, 49-50, 118

Murder in Mesopotamia (Agatha Christie), 83, 108

Murder Is a Kill-Joy (Elisabeth Sanxay Holding, #103), 124, 125; fc, 80

Murder Is My Business (Brett Halliday, #184), 127, 128

Murder on Angler's Island (Helen Reilly, #228), 128

Murder on the Links (Agatha Christie, #454), bc, 93

Murders at Scandal House (Peter Hunt, #42), bc, 85, 94

Murder Takes No Holiday (Brett Halliday,

#D379), 30

Murder That Had Everything, The (Hulbert Footner, #74), bc, 103

Murder Twice Told (Donald Hamilton, #577), 39; fc, 72; bc, 112

Murder Wears a Mummer's Mask (Brett Halliday, #78, 388), 34, 128; bc, 93

Murder Wears Mukluks (Eunice Mays Boyd, #259), 129; bc, 109

Murder within Murder (Frances and Richard Lockridge, #229), bc, 90

Murder with Pictures (George Harmon Coxe, #441), 126; fc, 72; bc, 92, 105

Murder with Southern Hospitality (Leslie Ford, #505), 27

Murdock, Kent, in George Harmon Coxe's mysteries, 30, 72, 105

Murray, Max, *The Neat Little Corpse* (#560), 124

Murray Printing, 52

Myers, David, and Richard L. Williams, *What, When, Where and How to Drink* (Dell First Edition #55), 40

My Gun Is Quick (Mickey Spillane), 140 n.1

mysteries, 8, 21, 24, 28, 29-31, 36-37, 41, 49-50, 60, 83-84, 86, 89-90, 90-92, 93, 94-95, 99, 103, 111-14, 115, 116-17, 119, 121, 124-25, 126, 127-29, 130, 135 n.2 (Chap. 2)

Mystery Writers of America, 23, 78

My True Love Lies (Lenore Glen Offord, #476), bc, 113-14

Naked Jungle, The (motion picture), 95-96

Name Your Poison (Helen Reilly, #148), fc, 80

Nash, Ogden, 29

Nast, Thomas, 115

Natchez, Miss., map, 92

Neat Little Corpse, The (Max Murray, #560), 124

Nellie's Bedfellows (Kaz, #A209), 131

Nelms, Henning, 85. See also Talbot, Hake

Nelson, Carl, xviii, 13

New American Library, 3, 9, 17, 21, 28, 74

New Centurions, The (Joseph Wambaugh), 51

New Hammond-Dell World Atlas, The (Dell First Edition #FE84), 20

New Mexico, map, 88

New Orleans, La., map, 92

Newsom, John D., *Wiped Out* (#165), 124; fc, 61, 64

newspapers. See *Detroit News, The; Economist* (London); New York *Times;* New York *World, The*

Newsstand Division, Western Printing & Lithographing, 18, 19

New Worlds of Modern Science (Leonard Engel, ed., #B102), 20

New York (state), 104; map, 89; Dutchess county, map, 89

New York: Confidential! (Jack Lait and Lee Mortimer, #400, 440, 534), 34; bc, 90

New York City, 112; Central Park, map, 96-97; city maps, 89-90, 93, 96-97, 98, 99, 106, 116; Dell offices, 58; Harlem, map, 90; Western Printing & Lithographing offices, 18-23, 25, 74, 85

New York Mets, 55, 137 n.22

New York Supreme Court, 35-36

New York *Times,* 37

New York World, The, 84

New Yorker, 20

Nice, France, map, 92, 116-17

Nielsen, Lou, xvi, 7, 8

Night and the City (Gerald Kersh, #374), bc, 92

Nightmare Town (Dashiell Hammett, #379), bc, 91

Nightwork (Irwin Shaw), 51

Nixon, Richard, 50

No Adam in Eden (Grace Metalious), 35

Noble and Noble, Publishers, 54

Noble House (James Clavell), 51

Nobody Knows My Name (James Baldwin), 49

No Highway (Nevil Shute, #516), bc, 87

No Mask for Murder (Andrew Garve, #571), bc, 111

non-fiction, 19, 20, 21, 22, 28, 32-33, 49, 50, 130

N or M? (Agatha Christie, #187), 128

North, Sterling, *So Dear to My Heart* (#291), 34

Not Quite Dead Enough and Booby Trap (Rex Stout, #267), bc, 105

Nova-Dell books, 54

Novarro Organization, 54

Now, Voyager (motion picture), 31, 62

Now, Voyager (Olive Higgins Prouty, #99), 31; fc, 62, 65; bc, 87

numbering systems, xxi, xxiii-xxiv, 27, 53

numbers on Dell magazines, 4

O'Connell, John J., and Harry Söderman, *Modern Criminal Investigation,* 83-84, 86

Octagon House (Phoebe Atwood Taylor, #171), bc, 117

Odor of Violets (Baynard Kendrick, #162), 128; fc, 62, 69; bc, 104

Oehler, Milton, 52

O'Farrell, William, *Brandy for a Hero* (#306), bc, 90

offices, Dell, 4, 5, 58

offices, maps, 106

Offord, Lenore Glen, 113; *The Glass Mask* (#198), bc, 104; *My True Love Lies* (#476), bc, 113-14; *Skeleton Key* (#96), bc, 113, 114

O'Hara, John, *Pal Joey* (10¢ series #24), 38

Old Bones (Herman Petersen, #127), 128; bc, 96

Old Gold Cigarettes, 43, 44

Olsen, D. B., *The Cat Saw Murder* (#35), bc, 106

On Becoming a Woman (Mary McGee Williams and Irene Kane, #A179, B200), 36

Once in a Lifetime (Danielle Steel), 51

Once in Vienna (Vicki Baum, #524), 120; bc, 92

One Angel Less (H. W. Roden, #247), bc, 96, 107

Onion Field, The (Joseph Wambaugh), 51

On the Road (Jack Kerouac), 9

Opening Door, The (Helen Reilly, #200), bc, 96

Operation, The (Russell Boltar, #F171), 122

Oregon Trail, map, 86

Original Novels (Australia), 25

O'Shea, June, and George Metalious, *The Girl from "Peyton Place,"* 35-36

Out of Control (Baynard Kendrick, #376), fc, 71

Outlaw on Horseback (Will Ermine, #284), bc, 86

Outsiders, The (S. E. Hinton), 47

Overholser, Wayne D., 21, 32, 50, 114-15; *Buckaroo's Code* (#372), 126, bc, 114; *Draw or Drag* (#556), bc, 114; *West of the Rimrock* (#499), bc, 114

Pacific area, map, 86

Packard, Vance O., and Dr. Clifford R. Adams, *How to Pick a Mate* (#224), 34; bc, 109

Packer, Vin, *The Girl on the Best-Seller List,* 36

Pageant Press, 21

page proofs, 12

paging of Dell paperbacks, 7
Painted for the Kill (Lucy Cores, #87), bc, 106-7
Pal, George, 96
Pal Joey (John O'Hara, 10¢ series #24), 38
Palm Springs, Calif., maps, 88, 92
Panorama (R. F. Tannenbaum, ed., #LC107), 32, 40
paperback collections, xxi-xxii, 143
paperback publishers. *See* Ace; Albatross; Anchor; Avon; Ballantine; Bantam Books; Bantam Publications; Bart House; Berkley; Century books; collection marabout; Dell; Delta Books; "Every Child's First Color and Learn Book Series"; Fawcett Publishing Company; Gold Medal; Graphic; Grove Press; Harlequin Romances; Home Activity Series; Ivy Books; Laurel Editions; Laurel-Leaf Library; Lion; Mayflower Books; Mayflower Books, Ltd.; New American Library; Nova-Dell books; Original Novels; Paper Editions Book Club; Penguin books; Phantom; Pinnacle Books; Pocket Books; Pony Weldun books; Popular Library; Presses de la Cité; Red Arrow; Regal; Special Student Editions; Spur Westerns; Star Western; Sunrise Semester Library; Tauchnitz; "Told-in-Pictures" series; "Twilight" series; Viking; Vintage; Visual Books; Warner Books; World; Yearling Books. *See also* publishers and imprints
Paper Editions Book Club, 20
Paper Money (Adam Smith), 51
Paris, France, 81
Paris Opera House, map, 106
Parker, Al, 77
Parker, Robert, *Passport to Peril* (#568), fc, 81, 92
Parone, Edward, xviii, 23, 32-33; ed., *Six Great Modern Plays* (Dell First Edition #FE100), 32; ed., *Six Great Modern Short Novels* (Dell First Edition #F35), 32, 33
Parrott, Ursula, 27; *The Tumult and the Shouting*, 27
Passport to Peril (Robert Parker, #568), fc, 81, 92
Patriotic Murders, The (Agatha Christie), 35
Patzke, Elmer, xviii, 13
Pelé (Clair and Frank Gault), 47

Penguin books: Great Britain, 3, 5, 7; United States, 13, 21
Perfect Stranger, A (Danielle Steel), 51
Perfect Victim, The (James McKimmey, #A159), 42
Perkins, D. M., *Deep Throat*, 50
Peters, Jean, "Publishers' Imprints," xxi
Petersen, Herman, *Old Bones* (#127), 128; bc, 96
Petty, George, 78
Peyton Place (Grace Metalious, #F61), xv, xix, 9, 19, 26, 27, 35-36, 130
Phantom of the Opera, The (Gaston Leroux, #24), 34; bc, 106
Phantom paperbacks (Australia), 25
Philadelphia, Pa., map, 92
Philadelphia Murder Story, The (Leslie Ford, #354), 127; bc, 92
Phillips, Barye, 77
photo covers, 71, 80
Pick Your Victim (Pat McGerr, #307), bc, 106
Pigman, The (Paul Zindel), 47
Pine Brook, N.J., distribution center, Dell Publishing Company, 52
Pines Corporation, 16
Pinkerton's Detective Agency, 119
Pinnacle Books, 51
Pioneers, The (Courtney Ryley Cooper, #290), bc, 86
Pirates of the Range (B. M. Bower, #466), fc, 72; bc, 109
Pittsburgh, Pa., map, 92
Plain, Belva, *Random Winds*, 51
Plain Murder (C. S. Forester, Dell First Edition #30), 40
Playboy, 50
Pocket Books, xix, 3, 5, 7, 13, 17, 28, 35-36, 42, 119, 124, 130, 139 n.16
Poirot, Hercule, in Agatha Christie's mysteries, 29, 72
Poker According to Maverick (#B142), 40
Pollini, Frances, *Pretty Maids All in a Row*, 51
Polsky, Thomas, *Curtains for the Editor* (#82), fc, 62; bc, 106
Pony Weldun books, 124
Popkin, Zelda: *Dead Man's Gift* (#190), 84, 127, bc, 105-6; *Death Wears a White Gardenia* (#13), fc, 62, bc, 106
Poplawski, Gerald, xviii, 85
Popular Library, 3, 16, 17, 28, 82
Porter, Katherine Anne, 33; *The Leaning*

Tower and Other Stories, 48-49
posters, 59-60
Poughkeepsie, N.Y., Western Printing &
Lithographing plant, frontis., xvi, 6, 7, 8,
12-16, 19, 25-26, 52-53, 59, 72, 73, 75,
130
Powell, Richard, 111; *Masterpiece in Murder*
(#915), 135 n.3 (Chap. 2); *Shell Game*
(#518), bc, 109, 111
Powers, Richard, 77-78
Powers, Tom, *Virgin with Butterflies* (#392),
bc, 87, 89
Practical Cogitator, The (Charles P. Curtis,
Jr., and Ferris Greenslet, eds.), 50
Presses de la Cité paperbacks (France), 25
Pretty Maids All in a Row (Frances Pollini),
51
Price, Roy, 71
prices, xxiii, 5, 27, 38, 39, 40, 49, 50, 75,
131
printers. *See* Colonial Press; Electronic
Perfect Binders; Murray Printing;
Riverside Press; West Side Printing
Company; Western Printing & Lithographing
printers of Dell paperbacks, 52-53
printing: of Dell paperbacks, 7, 13-16, 26,
52-53, 129; of Dell paperbacks' covers,
75
printing dates, 40-41
print runs, 13, 19, 22, 26, 40, 42, 51
Private Practice of Michael Shayne, The
(Brett Halliday, #23, 429), 34; bc, 91
production costs, 12, 134 n.24
Production Editorial Department, Western
Printing & Lithographing, xvi, 25-26
Promise, The (Danielle Steel), 51
Promise of Love (Mary Renault, #298), bc,
115
promotional devices, 26, 38, 52
proofreading, xviii, 7, 12
proofs, xv, 7, 12
Proud and Profane, The (motion picture), 19
Prout, George, 71
Prouty, Olive Higgins, 31; *Now, Voyager*
(#99), 31, fc, 62, 65, 99; bc, 87
"Publications for Parents," 48
publishers and imprints. *See* American
Heritage Publishing Company, The; Big
Little Books; Borzoi Books; Chapel-
Books; Cliff Notes; Delacorte Press; Dial
Press; Doubleday & Co.; Droemer;
Dutton, E. P.; Fawcett Publishing
Company; Feffer and Simmons; Feltri-
nelli; Gallimard; Globe Mini Mags;
Golden Press; Goodman Publications;
Grosset & Dunlap; Haldeman-Julius
Publications; Hamming-Whitman;
Harper & Row; Hearst Company;
Knopf, Alfred A.; Lane, Allen; Little
Blue Books; Livermore and Knight;
Macmillan; Messner, Julian; Monarch
Notes; Morrow, William; Noble and
Noble, Publishers; Novarro Organiza-
tion; Pageant Press; Pines Corporation;
"Publications for Parents"; Purse Books;
Putnam's Sons, G. P.; Radcliffe Biogra-
phy Series; Random House; Reynal and
Hitchcock; Rinehart; Ronalds Co., Ltd.;
Schuster, Max; Scribner's Sons, Charles;
Select Publications; Simon, Richard;
Simon and Schuster; Spot Notes; Toby
Press; Western Printing & Lithograph-
ing; Whitman books; Wiley, John. *See
also* list of paperback publishers
Publishers Clearing House, 55
"Publishers' Imprints" (Jean Peters), xxi
Publishers Weekly, 39, 50, 52, 54
pulps and magazines, xvii, 4, 5, 43-44, 119
Purse Books, 48
Push-Pin Studios, 68, 78
Putnam's Sons, G. P., 54
puzzle books, 119
Pyle, Howard, 115

Q as in Quicksand (Lawrence Treat, #301),
bc, 101, 115
Queen, Ellery (pseud. of Frederic Dannay),
83, 110-11; *The American Gun Mystery*
(#4), 9, bc, 106
Queen of the Flat-Tops (Stanley Johnston,
#37), 34; bc, 86
Quiet Horror (Stanley Ellin, #D325), fc, 68
Quist, Harlin, 47

Racine, Wis., Western Printing & Litho-
graphing plant, frontis., xv-xviii, 5, 6, 8,
26, 53, 57, 58, 59, 67, 85
Radcliffe Biography Series, 48
Radcliffe College, 48
Rafferty, Kathleen, *Dell Crossword Diction-
ary* (#434), 34; later edition, 51
Raft, The (Robert Trumbull, #26), 34; bc,
109
Ragtime (E. L. Doctorow), 54
Raine, William MacLeod: *The Bandit Trail*

(#424), bc, 86; *Rutledge Trails the Ace of Spades* (#383), bc, 108; ed., *Western Stories* (#282), bc, 111

Raintree County (Ross Lockridge, Jr., #F58), 19, 35

ranches, maps, 95-96, 98

Randau, Carl, and Leane Zugsmith, *The Visitor* (#132), fc, 81; bc, 108

Random House, 20, 42

Random Winds (Belva Plain), 51

Rat Began to Gnaw the Rope, The (C. W. Grafton, #180), bc, 104, 109, 112

Rawhiders and Renegades (Harry E. Maule, ed., #D367), 25

Rawson, Clayton, 29, 31, 85; *The Footprints on the Ceiling* (#121), 124, bc, 88; *The Headless Lady* (#176), bc, 96

Ray, Elizabeth, *The Washington Fringe Benefit*, 52

RCA records, 74

Reasoner, Charles, 47

Rechy, John, 52; *Sexual Overflow*, 52

Red Arrow paperbacks, 16

Red Bull, The (Rex Stout, #70), 125, 126, 127

Red Sector (Donald Hamilton), 25

Red Tassel, The (David Dodge, #565), fc, 73

Red Threads (Rex Stout, #235), bc, 106-7

Regal paperbacks, 25

Reilly, Helen, 29, 30, 89, 124; *The Dead Can Tell* (#17), bc, 96, 99, 103; *The Farmhouse* (#397), bc, 89; *Mourned on Sunday* (#63), 127, bc, 110; *Murder on Angler's Island* (#228), 128; *Name Your Poison* (#148), fc, 80; *The Opening Door* (#200), bc, 96; *The Silver Leopard* (#287), bc, 93; *Staircase 4* (#498), bc, 90

reissues: Dell First Editions in hard cover, 41-42; 4-digit, 13, 85

rejected titles, 9

Remembering Laughter (Wallace Stegner, 10¢ series #17), 38

Remington, Frederic, 50, 115

Renault, Mary, xx, 11, 31, 79, 115, 117; *Kind Are Her Answers* (#189), bc, 115; *Promise of Love* (#298), bc, 115; *Return to Night* (#394), bc, 88-89, 115

Renoir, Pierre-Auguste, 59

Report for a Corpse (Henry Kane, #330), bc, 109

Return of the Continental Op (Dashiell Hammett, #154), 128; bc, 91

Return to Night (Mary Renault, #394), bc,

88-89, 115

Return to Peyton Place (Grace Metalious, #F91), 35, 45

Reynal and Hitchcock, 20, 42, 43

Rice, Craig, 38; *Innocent Bystander* (#461), bc, 96

Rich Girl, Poor Girl (Faith Baldwin, #196), 31

Ride the Pink Horse (Dorothy B. Hughes, #210), 130; bc, 114

Riding High (T. T. Flynn, #B209), fc, 73

Ridin' Kid from Powder River, The (H. H. Knibbs, #399), 11

Rights & Royalties Division, Western Printing & Lithographing, 12

Rim of the Pit (Hake Talbot, #173), bc, 85, 100, 104

Rinehart (publisher), 25

Rinehart, Mary Roberts, 29; *The Bat* (#652), fc, 66, 75-76; *The Case of Jennie Brice* (#40), fc, 69; *The Circular Staircase*, 35; (#585), bc, 117; *The Great Mistake* (#297), bc, 110; *Haunted Lady* (#361), bc, 104; *The Man in Lower Ten* (#124), bc, 107; *The State versus Elinor Norton* (#203), 29, bc, 95, 110; *The Window at the White Cat* (#57, 506), 34

Ritzman, Ed, 58

Riverside Press, 52

Robbed Heart, The (Clifton Cuthbert, #512), fc, 72; bc, 90

Robbins, Harold, 9

Roberts, MacLennan (pseud. of Robert Terrall), and Paul Ilton, *Moses and the Ten Commandments* (#B105), 33

Robin Hill (Lida Larrimore, #119), 31; bc, 95

Robinson, Glen, xviii, 21

Robinson, Robby, xviii

Rockwell, Norman, 59, 60

Roden, H. W., 29; *One Angel Less* (#247), bc, 96, 107; *Too Busy to Die* (#185), fc, 69; *Wake for a Lady* (#345), fc, 80-81; *You Only Hang Once* (#102), bc, 106

Rogers, Ginger, 34

Rogers, Roy, 32

Rogue Queen (L. Sprague de Camp, #600), fc, 80

romances, 8, 28, 31, 47, 50, 62, 65, 69, 84, 86, 89, 90, 92, 95, 119, 121, 128

Ronalds Co., Ltd. (Toronto), 16

Roos, Audrey and William, 111

Roos, Kelley, 29, 31, 111; *The Frightened*

Stiff (#56), bc, 105; *Made up to Kill* (#106), 124; *Sailor, Take Warning!* (#255), bc, 96-97, 99

Root of Evil (Eaton K. Goldthwaite, #442), bc, 111

Root River (Racine, Wis.), 5

Rope (motion picture), 33

Rope (#262), 33

Rope Began to Hang the Butcher, The (C. W. Grafton, #232), 129; bc, 112

Rosemary's Baby (Ira Levin), 51

Rosenson, William, and Bela Schick, *The Care of Your Child* (#340), 35

Roueché, Berton, *The Last Enemy* (Dell First Edition #D90), 42; fc, 76

royalties and advances, 7, 8, 11-12, 16, 35, 40, 49, 134 n.21

royalty cards (Western Printing & Lithographing), 71, 135 n.2 (Chap. 2), 135 n.13, 143

Rozenzweig, Julius, 73

Rutledge Trails the Ace of Spades (William MacLeod Raine, #383), bc, 108

Sad Cypress (Agatha Christie, #172, 529), 34

Sagan, Françoise: *Bonjour Tristesse* (#D166), 19, 24, 26, 35; *A Certain Smile* (#D206), 19

Sailor, Take Warning! (Kelley Roos, #255), bc, 96-97, 99

St. Louis, Mo., Western Printing & Lithographing plant, 26

Salbreiter, Bernard, xvi, 57, 60, 63, 70, 74

Sale, Richard, *Benefit Performance* (#252), bc, 91

sales, 5, 16-17, 19, 20, 21, 22, 26, 34-35, 40, 42, 48, 50

Sales Department, Dell Publishing Company, 68, 74, 75, 76, 130

Salinger, J. D., 9

Salsinger, H. G., 44

San Antonio, Tex., map, 92

Sandburg, Carl, *The Fiery Trial* (#F77), fc, 79

Sandiford, Frank ("Paul Warren"), 41

San Francisco, maps, 90-91, 97

Santa Fé, N. Mex., 114; map, 92

Satin Straps (Maysie Greig, #309), bc, 92

Saturday Review of Literature, 9

Saul, John: *Comes the Blind Fury*, 51; *Cry for the Strangers*, 51

Savage, Les, Jr., *Treasure of the Brasada* (#253), 126; bc, 88

Savage Gentleman, The (Philip Wylie, #85), bc, 88

Saxon, Charles, xviii, 5

Scarecrow (Eaton K. Goldthwaite, #193), bc, 92

"Scene of the Crime" mysteries, 49-50, 118

Schick, Bela, and William Rosenson, *The Care of Your Child* (#340), 35

Schick, Frank, 120

Schmidt, Dori, xviii, 22

Schreuders, Piet, frontis., xxii

Schuster, Max, 5

science-fiction and fantasy, xix, 8, 28, 32, 39-40, 50, 84, 93, 94, 98, 131

Scotland, map, 86, 97

Scotland Yard: The Department of Queer Complaints (Carter Dickson, #65), 127; bc, 92, 97, 117

Scott, Mary Semple, *Crime Hound* (#34), bc, 85

Scribner's Sons, Charles, 39

Scudellari, Robert, xviii, 46

Seal Books, 46-47

Secret of Chimneys, The (Agatha Christie, #199), bc, 95

See You at the Morgue (Lawrence G. Blochman, #7), bc, 99, 103, 104

Select Publications, 4

Self-Made Woman (Faith Baldwin, #163), fc, 69; bc, 90

Semi-Tough (Dan Jenkins), 51

Sensual Man, The, 51

Sensuous Man, The ("M."), 51

Sensuous Woman, The ("J."), 51

Seven Deadly Sisters, The (Pat McGerr, #412), bc, 108

Seventh Avenue (Norman Bogner), 120

sex on Dell paperback covers, 27, 78, 80, 81, 120

Sexual Overflow (John Rechy), 52

Shakespeare, William, 26, 47, 48, 118, 119

Shane, Ted, ed., *Jokes, Gags and Wisecracks* (#152), fc, 61, 65

Shanghai, map, 92

Shann, Renée, *Student Nurse* (#234), bc, 92

Sharpe, Elizabeth, xviii, 4

Shaw, Irwin, 55; *Bread Upon the Waters*, 51; *Nightwork*, 51

Shayne, Michael, in Brett Halliday's mysteries, 30, 72, 79, 80, 91, 105, 108, 129

She (H. Rider Haggard, #339), fc, 80; bc, 93, 117

She Ate Her Cake (Blair Treynor, #186), fc, 60, 63; bc, 95

Sheik, The (E. M. Hull, #174), 34, 35; bc, 88

Shell Game (Richard Powell, #518), bc, 109, 111

Sherwan, Earl, xvi, 43, 59, 66, 70-71, 81, 85

Sherwan, Marguerite, 70

She Walks Alone (Helen McCloy, #430), bc, 89, 107

Shoes of the Fisherman (Morris L. West), 82

Shōgun (James Clavell), 51

Short, Luke, 21; *Bold Rider* (#A134), 120

Short Story Masterpieces (Robert Penn Warren and Albert Erskine, eds., Dell First Edition #F16), 20, 33, 42

Showdown (Errol Flynn, #351), bc, 86

Shoyer, William, 71

Shulman, Irving, *Harlow*, 51

Shute, Nevil, *No Highway* (#516), bc, 87

Sidney, Sir Philip, 43

Signal Shirt Company, 8, 59, 62

Sills, Jennifer, ed., *Massage Parlor*, 51

Silver Leopard, The (Helen Reilly, #287), bc, 93

Simon, Richard, 5

Simon and Schuster, 13, 15

Sirens of Titan, The (Kurt Vonnegut, Jr., #B138), 41-42

Six Centuries of Great Poetry (Robert Penn Warren and Albert Erskine, eds., Dell First Edition #FE69), 20, 33

Six Great Modern Plays (Dell First Edition #FE100), 32

Six Great Modern Short Novels (Dell First Edition #F35), 32, 33

sizes of Dell paperbacks, 26

Skeleton Key (Lenore Glen Offord, #96), bc, 113, 114

Skyline Riders (Francis W. Hilton, #250), 126; fc, 66, 71

Skyscraper (Faith Baldwin, #236), 124

Small, Richard, 72

Small Books Program, Information Center Service of the U.S. Information Agency, 43

Smell of Money, The (Matthew Head, #219), bc, 85, 95, 111

Smith, Adam, *Paper Money*, 51

Smith, Betty, *Tomorrow Will Be Better*, 35

Smith, Lloyd E., xvi, 6-7, 8, 9, 11, 12, 18, 32, 38, 58, 70, 83, 119, 124, 129, 130

Smith, Robin, 54-55

Smithsonian Institution, xxii

So Blue Marble, The (Dorothy B. Hughes, #100), bc, 114

So Dear to My Heart (Sterling North, #291), 34

Söderman, Harry, and John J. O'Connell, *Modern Criminal Investigation*, 83-84, 86

Soul on Ice (Eldridge Cleaver), 49

South Africa, map, 88

South America, map, 88

South Seas, map, 86

So Young, So Cold, So Fair (John Creasey, #985), fc, 78

Spade, Sam, in Dashiell Hammett's mysteries, 72

Spain, map, 89

Spanish-language Dell books, 54

Speak No Evil (Mignon G. Eberhart, #25), 30

Special Editorial Division, Western Printing & Lithographing, 12

Special Student Editions, xxiii, 43

Spencer, R. A., xviii, 5

Spillane, Mickey, 9; *My Gun Is Quick*, 140 n.1

Spill the Jackpot (A. A. Fair, #109), 34; fc, 81

spine blurbs, 120

Splendid Quest, The (Edison Marshall, #188), bc, 92

Spot Notes, 48

Spring Harrowing (Phoebe Atwood Taylor, #98), bc, 104

Spur Westerns paperbacks (Australia), 25

Stafford, Gene, ed., *Generation Rap*, 50

Staircase 4 (Helen Reilly, #498), bc, 90

Stanley, Barbara, 73

Stanley, Rhoda, 67, 72, 73

Stanley, Robert, xvi, 67, 71-73, 79, 81, 82

Stapleton, Douglas, and Helen A. Carey, *The Corpse Is Indignant*, 124

Star Western paperbacks (Australia), 25

State versus Elinor Norton, The (Mary Roberts Rinehart, #203), 29; bc, 95, 110

Steegmuller, Francis, ed., *Guy de Maupassant* (#LC135), 25; World #C949, 25

Steel, Danielle: *Once in a Lifetime*, 51; *A Perfect Stranger*, 51; *The Promise*, 51

Steel, Kurt, *Judas, Incorporated* (#244), 124; fc, 62

Steele, Wilbur Daniel, *That Girl from Memphis* (#548), 120

Steel Mirror, The (Donald Hamilton, #473), fc, 81; bc, 112

Stegner, Wallace, *Remembering Laughter* (10¢ series #17), 38

Stein, Aaron Marc, 111-12, 124; as Hampton Stone, *The Corpse in the Corner Saloon* (#464), bc, 101, 105, 111-12

Steinbeck, John, *To a God Unknown* (#358, 407), 34; bc, 95

Steinberg, S. H., xxi, 129

Stephenson, Carl, "Leiningen versus the Ants," 95-96, 98

Sterling, Stewart, 89, 106; *Dead Sure* (#420), fc, 71; *Dead Wrong* (#314), bc, 106; *Where There's Smoke* (#275), 124; bc, 90

Stern, David, *Francis* (#507), bc, 109

Stoffel, Albert, 32

Stone, Hampton (pseud. of Aaron Marc Stein), *The Corpse in the Corner Saloon* (#464), bc, 101, 105, 111-12

Stone, Russell, 59

Storch, Otto, xvi, 58, 71, 119

Stories for the Dead of Night (Don Congdon, ed., #B107), 23

Storm Warning (motion picture), 34

Stout, Rex, 29, 30; *Alphabet Hicks* (#146), 128, bc, 96, 109; *Bad for Business* (#299), 30, fc, 62, 65, bc, 110, Century edition, 110; *The Broken Vase* (#115), fc, 62; *Double for Death* (#9), bc, 94; *The Hand in the Glove* (#177), 30, bc, 95; *The Mountain Cat Murders* (#28), 30; *Not Quite Dead Enough and Booby Trap* (#267), bc, 105; *The Red Bull* (#70), 125, 126, 127; *Red Threads* (#235), bc, 107; *3 Doors to Death* (#626), 39; *Too Many Cooks* (#45, 540), 11, 34, bc, 106. Characters: Dol Bonner, 30; Nero Wolfe, 30, 105, 106

Strawstack Murders (Dorothy Cameron Disney, #62), bc, 110

Strohmer, William, xvii, xviii, 56-57, 58, 59, 61, 63, 65, 71

Student Nurse (Renée Shann, #234), bc, 92

Study in History, A (Arnold Toynbee), 50

Sturgeon, Theodore, xvii, 24

Such Good Friends (Lois Gould), 51

Suez Canal, map, 88

"Suicide Is Scandalous" (Henry Kane), 109

Summers, Richard, *Vigilante* (#471), 32

Summersby, Kay, *Eisenhower Was My Boss* (#286), 34; bc, 87

Sunnier Side, The (Charles Jackson, #504), bc, 93

Sunrise Semester Library, xviii, 43

Surdez, Georges, *The Demon Caravan* (#501), fc, 72

Suspense Stories (Alfred Hitchcock, ed., #92), bc, 95-96, 98

Sussex, England, map, 88

Sutcliff, Rosemary, 47

Swanberg, W. A., xvii, 4-5; ed., *Fact Detective Mysteries* (#332), bc, 87

Swift Hour, The (Harriett Thurman, #141), bc, 94

Tabu perfume, 81

Tai-Pan (James Clavell), 51

Taking of Pelham One Two Three, The (John Godey), 51

Talbot, Daniel, ed., *City of Love* (Dell First Edition #45), 33; ed., *Thirteen Great Stories* (Dell First Edition #D99), 33

Talbot, Hake (pseud. of Henning Nelms), *Rim of the Pit* (#173), bc, 85, 100, 104

Talent for Murder, A (Anna Mary Wells, #66), 125

Tannenbaum, R. F., ed., *Panorama* (#LC107), 32, 40

"tantalizer-pages," 119, 127

Target: Mike Shayne (Brett Halliday, #D355), 30

Tarzan and the Lost Empire (Edgar Rice Burroughs, #536), 126; bc, 93

Taste of Violence, A (Brett Halliday, #426), bc, 92

Tauchnitz paperbacks, 5

Taylor, Frank E., xvii, xviii, 6, 18, 19-20, 21, 24, 26, 27, 32, 40, 41, 42, 43, 45, 47, 74, 117-18, 120

Taylor, Phoebe Atwood, 29, 30; *Banbury Bog* (#251), 128; *Octagon House* (#171), bc, 117; *Spring Harrowing* (#98), bc, 104

Teason, William, 75, 78

10¢ series. *See* Dell 10¢ series

Ten Commandments, The (motion picture), 33

Tender Mercy (Lenard Kaufman, #444), bc, 108

Terrall, Robert, 30, 33, 80. As Brett Halliday: *Fit to Kill* (#D314), 30; *Murder Takes No Holiday* (#D379), 30; *Target: Mike Shayne* (#D355), 30. As MacLennan Roberts: *Moses and the Ten Commandments* (with Paul Ilton, #B105), 33

Tesuque, N. Mex., 114

Texas, maps, 88, 113

Texidor, Fernando, xvii, 19, 58, 69, 71, 74, 81-82

Thames, the, 92

That Girl from Memphis (Wilbur Daniel Steele, #548), 120

Their Ancient Grudge (Harry Harrison Kroll, #435), 120, 130; bc, 86

They Can't All Be Guilty (M. V. Heberden, #401), bc, 93

'' 'They've Shot Jug Murphy' '' (S. Omar Barker), 111

Thirteen Great Stories (Daniel Talbot, ed., Dell First Edition #D99), 33

This Is It, Michael Shayne (Brett Halliday, #533), bc, 108

This Time for Keeps (John MacCormac, #32), 34; bc, 109

Thompson, Sydney, *Dr. Parrish, Resident* (#215), bc, 95

Thorndike, Joseph, 24

3 Doors to Death (Rex Stout, #626), 39

3500 Names for Baby, 48

Through a Glass, Darkly (Helen McCloy, #519), bc, 104

Thurman, Harriett, *The Swift Hour* (#141), bc, 94

Tight White Collar, The (Grace Metalious, #S25), 35

Tilton, Alice, *Cold Steal* (#142), fc, 61, 65

title changes, 24-25

title-pages, 83, 119, 122, 129

To a God Unknown (John Steinbeck, #358, 407), 34; bc, 95

Tobey, Carl, xviii, 41, 54

Toby Press, 120

Tocqueville, Alexis de, 28-29

''Told-in-Pictures'' series, xxiii, 44

Tolstoy, Leo, *War and Peace* (#F53), 19, 20, 24

Tomorrow Will Be Better (Betty Smith), 35

Tompkins, Walker A.: *Manhunt West* (#551), 32; *West of Texas Law* (#310), 32

Too Busy to Die (H. W. Roden, #185), fc, 69

Too Many Bones (Ruth Sawtell Wallis, #123), 128

Too Many Cooks (Rex Stout, #45, 540), 11, 34; bc, 106

Too Near the Sun (Gordon Forbes, Dell First Edition #D56), 40

Tootsie Rolls, xix, 54

To Wake the Dead (John Dickson Carr,

#635), fc, 81

Toynbee, Arnold, *A Study in History*, 50

Tracy, Dick, 32

Trail Boss of Indian Beef (Harold Channing Wire, #97), bc, 86

Training Institute, Western Printing & Lithographing, 57

Treasure of the Brasada (Les Savage, Jr., #253), 126; bc, 88

Treat, Lawrence, 101, 115; *H as in Hunted* (#218), bc, 115; *Q as in Quicksand* (#301), bc, 101, 115

Treynor, Blair, *She Ate Her Cake* (#186), fc, 60, 63; bc, 95

Trinity College, 6

trompe l'oeil covers, 58, 61, 62, 63, 65

Trouble on Big Cat (Glenn Corbin), (Dell First Edition #25), 25; Star Western, 25; Viking #235, 25

Trumbull, Robert, *The Raft* (#26), 34; bc, 109

Tumult and the Shouting, The (Ursula Parrott), 27

Turn on the Heat (A. A. Fair, #59), bc, 105; (#59, 620), 34

Tuscaloosa, Ala., 113

20,000 Years of World Painting series, 47

''Twilight'' series, 50

Two If by Sea (Roger Bax, #634), bc, 111

Two-Shoot Gun, The (Donald Hamilton), 25

typesetting, xv, 7, 8, 12-13, 41, 129

typography, xviii, 21, 130; on covers, 74, 75

UPC codes, 75

Uncle Dynamite (P. G. Wodehouse, #469), bc, 95

Uncomplaining Corpses, The (Brett Halliday, #386), 27; fc, 72

Unicorn Murders, The (Carter Dickson, #16), bc, 85

Uninhibited Treasury of Erotic Poetry, An (Louis Untermeyer), 49

United States, maps, 86-87, 88, 89

Universe (Robert Heinlein, 10¢ series #36), 9

unnumbered Dell books, xxiii, 32

Untermeyer, Louis, *An Uninhibited Treasury of Erotic Poetry*, 49

Until You Are Dead (Henry Kane, #580), bc, 93

Upstart, The (Edison Marshall, #233, 341), 34; bc, 87

U.S. Information Agency, Information Center Service, Small Books Program, 43

Vallely, H. E., 71
Vance, Louis Joseph, *The Lone Wolf* (#10), bc, 93
Van Zwienen, John, 46, 79, 82
Vargas, Alberto, 78
Vienna, map, 92
Vigilante (Richard Summers, #471), 32
Viking paperbacks (Great Britain), 25
Vilirgas, Vera V., 46
Vineyard Books, 48
Vintage paperbacks, 49
Virginia (state), map, 88
Virgin with Butterflies (Tom Powers, #392), bc, 87, 89
Visitor, The (Carl Randau and Leane Zugsmith, #132), fc, 81; bc, 108
Visual Books, xvii, xxiii, 43
Vitek, Jack, and Judy Chavez, *Defector's Mistress*, 51
Vonnegut, Kurt, Jr., 41, 49; *Deadeye Dick*, 49; *The Sirens of Titan* (#B138), 41-42

Wadewitz, Edward H., xvii, xviii, 5, 6, 13
Wadewitz, William R., xviii, 5, 13
Wait for the Dawn (Martha Albrand, #544), bc, 109
Wake for a Lady (H. W. Roden, #345), fc, 80-81
Walker, Charles, 23, 75
Walker, Mort, xvii, xix, 5
Wallace, Irving, et al., *The Intimate Sex Lives of Famous People*, 120
Wallis, Ruth Sawtell, *Too Many Bones* (#123), 128
Wall of Eyes (Margaret Millar, #110), 125
Wambaugh, Joseph: *The New Centurions*, 51; *The Onion Field*, 51
War and Peace (Leo Tolstoy, #F53), 19, 20, 24
Ward, Don, xvii, 8, 11, 12, 24, 38, 43, 44, 78, 84; *Rope* (#262), 33
Warhorse (John Cunningham, #D177), 40
Warner Books (Warner Paperback Library), 55
Warner Bros., 5, 70
Warren, Paul (pseud. of Frank Sandiford), 41
Warren, Robert Penn, and Albert Erskine,

eds., *Short Story Masterpieces* (Dell First Edition #F16), 20, 33, 42; *Six Centuries of Great Poetry* (Dell First Edition #FE69), 20, 33
Washington, D.C., map, 92
Washington Confidential (Jack Lait and Lee Mortimer, #D108), 34, 35
Washington Fringe Benefit, The (Elizabeth Ray), 52
Waugh, Evelyn, 42, 118
Web and the Rock, The (Thomas Wolfe, #LY103), 26
Webb, Jean Francis, 33; *Anna Lucasta* (#331), 33, bc, 90; *King Solomon's Mines* (#433), 33, 34, 35, bc, 93; *Little Women* (#296), 33-34, 34-35, 124, bc, 108
Web of Evil, The (Lucille Emerick, #479), fc, 72
Wedding Journey, The (Walter D. Edmonds, 10¢ series #6), 38
Week-End Marriage (Faith Baldwin, #73), bc, 100, 109
Weiss, M. Jerome, 47; *Men and War*, 47
Welles, Orson, ed., *Invasion from Mars* (#305), 8, 32; bc, 88, 111
Wells, Anna Mary, *A Talent for Murder* (#66), 125
Wells, H. G., *The First Men in the Moon* (#201), 8, 34, fc, 71, bc, 88; *The Invisible Man* (#269), 8, bc, 88
Werewolf of Paris, The (Guy Endore), 27
West, Morris L., 41; *The Ambassador*, 51; *Kundu* (#A116), 41; *Shoes of the Fisherman*, 82
Westcott, Jan, 111; *The Border Lord* (#439), bc, 111
Westerner, The, 13, 18, 23, 52, 67, 71, 72
Western Printing & Lithographing (formerly West Side Printing Company; later Western Publishing), 5-27, 129; after 1962, 46; Art Department, 8, 22-23, 70, 74, 85, 99, 110 (*see also* Creative Department); Bantam Publications, 6; Big Little Books, 59; Cambridge, Md., plant, 26; "Catechectical Guild Society" books, 39; comic books, 46; Commercial Sales Division, 18, 21; Creative Center, 85; Creative Department, 57, 62, 63 (*see also* Art Department); Golden Press, 8, 12, 43, 46; Guild Family Readers, 39; K. K. Comics, 18; Liberty Street wing, 8, 59, 62; Los Angeles branch, 6; Mound Ave-

nue (Racine, Wis.) offices, 8; Newsstand Division, 18, 19; New York City office, 18-23, 25, 74, 85; offices and plants, frontis., xvi, 5, 6, 7, 8, 12-16, 18-23, 25-26, 52-53, 57, 58, 59, 67, 72, 73, 74, 75, 85, 130; origin, 5; Poughkeepsie, N.Y., plant, frontis., xvi, 6, 7, 8, 12-16, 19, 25-26, 52-53, 59, 72, 73, 75, 130; Production Editorial Department, xvi, 25-26; purchase by Mattel, 46; Racine, Wis., plant, frontis., xv-xviii, 5, 6, 8, 26, 53, 57, 58, 59, 67, 85; relationship with Dell Publishing Company, xxi, 3, 5-27, 39, 45, 46, 74; Rights & Royalties Division, 12; royalty cards, 71, 135 n.2 (Chap. 2), 135 n.13, 143; St. Louis, Mo., plant, 26; Special Editorial Division, 12; Training Institute, 57; Whitman books, 5, 6, 7, 8, 12, 18, 44, 46, 58

Western Printing & Lithographing employees and consultants. See Bachorz, Edwin; Barnard, Allan; Barta, J. J.; Becker, Stephen; Bell, William; Bezucha, Robert; Black, Don; Brehm, Lawrence; Brooks, Walter; Burger, Knox; Cissman, Jeanette; Di Stefano, Anne; Donovan, Arlene; Dunleavy, Peggy; Eiger, Richard; Ferrone, John; Fine, Donald I.; Fisher, Richard; Fortier, Yolande; Frederiksen, George A.; Frey, Don; Geller, John; Gere, Byron; Greene, David H.; Gregg, Gerald; Gunn, James E.; Hallam, Ben; Hawkins, James E.; Hawkins, Virginia; Heilman, Harry; Hinds, Ruby; Jaffe, Marc; Kaiser, William; Kapilow, Mildred; Kissner, Robert; Kuhn, Paul; Lamm, Joan; Lemay, Harry; Locke, June; Locke, V.; Lowe, Sam; Mabon, John Scott; MacNichol, Ralph; Margolies, Pete; Marine, Edmund; Markowitz, Barbara; Morse, Mark M.; Nelson, Carl; Nielsen, Lou; Parone, Edward; Patzke, Elmer; Poplawski, Gerald; Ritzman, Ed; Robinson, Glen; Robinson, Robby; Salsinger, H. G.; Schmidt, Dori; Small, Richard; Smith, Lloyd E.; Spencer, R. A.; Stoffel, Albert; Stone, Russell; Strohmer, William; Sturgeon, Theodore; Taylor, Frank E.; Wadewitz, Edward H.; Wadewitz, William R.; Ward, Don; Wilbur, Richard; Williams, Stella; Wright, Betty Ren; Zulli, Floyd

westerns, xvii, xviii, 8, 21, 24-25, 28, 31-32, 50, 66, 69, 71, 78, 84, 86, 87, 89, 94, 95, 114-15, 119, 121, 131
Western Stories (Gene Autry, ed., #153), fc, 69, 71
Western Stories (William MacLeod Raine, ed., #282), bc, 111
Western Writers of America, 21
West of Texas Law (Walker A. Tompkins, #310), 32
West of the Rimrock (Wayne D. Overholser, #499), bc, 114
West Side Printing Company, 5. See also Western Printing & Lithographing
West Virginia, map, 86
What, When, Where and How to Drink (Richard L. Williams and David Myers, Dell First Edition #55), 40
What a Body! (Alan Green, #483), bc, 100, 109
What Is Art? (John Canaday), 60
What Rhymes with Murder? (Jack Iams, #631), bc, 101, 116-17
Wheeler, Harvey, and Eugene Burdick, Fail-Safe, 50
When Dorinda Dances (Brett Halliday, #D359), fc, 78
Where There's Smoke (Stewart Sterling, #275), 124; bc, 90
While the City Sleeps (motion picture), 22
While the Wind Howled (Audrey Gaines, #51), bc, 96
Whisper, 119
Whistling Hangman, The (Baynard Kendrick, #113), bc, 105
Whitcomb, Jon, 77
White, E. B., 46
White, Stewart Edward, The Long Rifle (#D147), 24; fc, 78
White, Theodore H., Breach of Faith, 50
White Brigand, The (Edison Marshall, #144), 126; bc, 96
Whitman books, xviii, 5, 6, 7, 8, 12, 18, 44, 46, 58; "Pop-up" books, 70
Whitmore, Coby, 77
Who's Calling? (Helen McCloy, #151), fc, 62; bc, 110
Wickware, Francis Sill, Dangerous Ground (#248), bc, 104, 109, 110
Wilbur, Richard, xviii, 42-43
Wiley, John (publisher), 21
Wilkinson, Max, 40
Williams, Idabel, Hell Cat (#521), bc, 90

Williams, Mary McGee, and Irene Kane, *On Becoming a Woman* (#A179, B200), 36

Williams, Richard L., xviii, 40; with David Myers, *What, When, Where and How to Drink* (Dell First Edition #55), 40

Williams, Stella, xviii, 7

Window at the White Cat, The (Mary Roberts Rinehart, #57, 506), 34

Winds of War, The (Herman Wouk), 51

Winner Take All (James McKimmey, #A185), 37

Winterton, Paul, 111; as Andrew Garve, *No Mask for Murder* (#571), bc, 111; as Roger Bax, *Two If by Sea* (#634), bc, 111

Wiped Out (John D. Newsom, #165), 124; fc, 61, 64

Wire, Harold Channing, *Trail Boss of Indian Beef* (#97), bc, 86

Wisteria Cottage (Robert Coates, #371), 27

With This Ring (Mignon G. Eberhart, #83), 125; fc, 69; bc, 95, 98

Wives to Burn (Lawrence G. Blochman, #134), bc, 88

Wodehouse, P. G., 30; *The Code of the Woosters* (#393), bc, 96; *Leave It to Psmith* (#357), bc, 96, 103; *Uncle Dynamite* (#469), bc, 95

Wohl, Burton, *The Jet Set*, 49

Wolfe, Nero, in Rex Stout's mysteries, 30, 105, 106

Wolfe, Thomas, *The Web and the Rock* (#LY103), 26

Woman in Black, The (Leslie Ford, #447), 125

Woman in the Dark (Dashiell Hammett), 139 n.15

Women Must Weep (Ruth Adams Knight, #482), bc, 85

Wood, Grant, 60

Woolrich, Cornell, 29, 31; *The Black Curtain* (#208), 31. *See also* Irish, William

Woolworth, F. W., Co., Canada, 16

world, maps, 87, 89

World paperbacks (Great Britain), 25

"World's Great Novels of Detection," 84

Wouk, Herman, *The Winds of War*, 51

Wright, Betty Ren, xviii, 7

Wright, Lee, 38

Wyeth, Andrew, 59

Wylie, Philip, *The Savage Gentleman* (#85), bc, 88

Wyoming Hills, Pa., map, 88

Xaviera (Xaviera Hollander), 51

Yank, 21

Yankee Pasha (Edison Marshall, #353), 34; bc, 87

Yates, Bill, xviii

Yates, George Worthing, *If a Body* (#159), bc, 85-86, 86-87, 89

Yearling Books, 46, 120

Year of Consent (Kendell Foster Crossen, Dell First Edition #32), fc, 40

Yerby, Frank, *The Girl from Storyville*, 50

Yore, Clem, *Age of Consent* (#622), 9; fc, 72; reissue (1965), 9

Young, Chic, *Blondie and Dagwood's Footlight Folly*, 32

Young Claudia (Rose Franken, #528), fc, 81

Young Doctor Kildare (Max Brand, #329), bc, 110

"Young Love" series, 47

You Only Hang Once (H. W. Roden, #102), bc, 106

Yours Ever (Maysie Greig, #446), bc, 88

Zane Grey's Western Magazine, xvii, 8, 43

Zane Grey Western Award Stories (#523), bc, 87

Zindel, Paul, *The Pigman*, 47

Zola, Emile, *The Human Beast* (#608), 34

Zorro, 72

Zugsmith, Leane, and Carl Randau, *The Visitor* (#132), fc, 81; bc, 108

Zulli, Floyd, xviii, 43

About the Author

WILLIAM H. LYLES teaches in the Writing Program at the University of Massachusetts, Amherst. He has just completed work on *Dell Paperbacks, 1942 to Mid-1962: A Catalog-Index* published by Greenwood Press (1983). He wrote *Mary Shelley: An Annotated Bibliography*, and articles that have appeared in *Biographical Memoirs, Modern Language Notes*, and *Paperback Quarterly*.

Recent Titles in
Contributions to the Study of Popular Culture

Tarzan and Tradition: Classical Myth in Popular Literature
Erling B. Holtsmark

Common Culture and the Great Tradition: The Case for Renewal
Marshall W. Fishwick

Concise Histories of American Popular Culture
M. Thomas Inge, editor

Ban Johnson: Czar of Baseball
Eugene C. Murdock